SYNTACTIC CHANGE
A CUPAN (UTO-AZTECAN) CASE STUDY

SYNTACTIC CHANGE

A Cupan (Uto-Aztecan) Case Study

BY

RODERICK A. JACOBS

UNIVERSITY OF CALIFORNIA PRESS

BERKELEY • LOS ANGELES • LONDON

UNIVERSITY OF CALIFORNIA PUBLICATIONS IN Linguistics

Volume 79

Approved for publication September 21, 1973

Issued August 15, 1975

UNIVERSITY OF CALIFORNIA PRESS
BERKELEY and LOS ANGELES
CALIFORNIA
•
UNIVERSITY OF CALIFORNIA PRESS, LTD.
LONDON, ENGLAND

ISBN: 0-520-09511-1
LIBRARY OF CONGRESS CATALOG CARD NUMBER: 73-620215

CONTENTS

ABBREVIATIONS

ABS	=	absolutive
ACC	=	accusative
BEN	=	benefactive
CAUS	=	causative
COMP	=	complementizer
COND	=	conditional
D	=	distributive
D.Ca	=	Desert Cahuilla
DES	=	desiderative
DUB	=	dubitative
DUR	=	durative
EMPH	=	emphatic
EXP	=	expective
FUT	=	future
HAB	=	habitual
IMP	=	imperative
IN	=	active thematic affix
INCEPT	=	inceptive
INDEF	=	indefinite
INTR	=	intransitive
LJ Lu	=	La Jolla Luiseño
M.Ca	=	Mountain Cahuilla
N	=	noun
NOM	=	nominalizing affix
NP	=	noun phrase
OBJ	=	object
PC	=	Proto-Cupan
PCC	=	Proto-Cahuilla-Cupeño
PL	=	plural
POT	=	potentive
PRES	=	present
QUOT	=	quotative
[+R]	=	realized aspect

[-R]	=	unrealized aspect
RD	=	relative-demonstrative particle
REL	=	relative suffix
S. Lu	=	Soboba Luiseño
SUB	=	subordinator
SUBJ	=	subject enclitic
TR	=	transitive
USIT	=	usitative
V	=	verb
W. Ca	=	Wanikik Cahuilla
W. Cu	=	Wilaqalpa Cupeño
YAX	=	stative thematic affix

Underlined items in the literal glosses of sentences are Indian elements for which no literal translation is available.

ACKNOWLEDGMENTS

I wish to thank my Indian teachers and consultants both for their linguistic work and their friendship. Mrs. Florence Barrett (Baron Long Diegueño), Mr. Ted Couro (Mesa Grande Diegueño), Mrs. Christina Hutchinson (Mesa Grande Diegueñò), and Mrs. Mary Paipa Lechappa (Iñaja Diegueño) were my first teachers. My major consultants for Takic were Mrs. Villiana Hyde (Rincon Luiseño), Mr. Ben Amago (La Jolla Luiseño), Mrs. Roscinda Nolasquez (Kupa Cupeño), the late Mr. Cyrillo Welmas (Wilaqalpa Cupeño), Mrs. Katharine Saubel (Los Coyotes Cahuilla), Mrs. Rosanda Lugo (Cahuilla Cahuilla), Mrs. Alice Lopez (Desert Cahuilla), Mr. David Quatti (Wanikik Cahuilla), and Mrs. Sarah Martin (Morongo Serrano). There were, however, numerous others who assisted.

Professor Margaret Langdon has been unfailingly helpful in my long searches for consultants. The present study shows the influence of her advice and teaching, and indirectly that of her own teacher at Berkeley, Professor Mary Haas, herself a student of Sapir's. I am especially grateful to Professor Ronald Langacker, for his patient and perceptive criticism and to my first teacher of linguistics, Professor Noam Chomsky, who has continued to be helpful in any way he can. His seminal ideas of language underlie the present study, as they do so much other linguistic work today.

Mrs. Margaret Blakey and Ms. Jane Walsh provided useful assistance for my research at the Smithsonian Institution. I have gained much from discussions with Peter Benson, Ross Clark, Donald Crook, Larry Gorbet, Pamela Munro, and Susan Steele.

Field work for this study was supported in part by Grant GS-27732 from the National Science Foundation, and by the Department of Linguistics at the University of California, San Diego. I am grateful for this assistance.

PREFACE

This book, written originally in 1972, is a case study in diachronic syntax, one involving the reconstruction of significant parts of the grammars of earlier stages of the particular Amerindian languages investigated. The method I use is basically the classic method of internal reconstruction except that here it has been applied to the domain of syntax. The goal is not merely to reconstruct earlier stages but to determine significant directions of syntactic change. What I found particularly interesting was the close resemblance of the diachronic reconstructions to the kind of abstract, semantically-based generative syntax used in synchronic analyses.

For example, the various tense and aspectual affixes on verbs are reconstructible for earlier stages as higher predicates. There is clear morphological evidence not only for the original verbness of these affixes, but also for the nounness of the sentences embedded beneath the predicates. Moreover the transformations needed to generate strings with such structures are also required for the modern languages.

I found that in all three languages, but most clearly in Luiseño, fairly complex tense systems have evolved from a relatively simple aspectual system. This is not to claim that there may not have been an earlier tense system but just that evidence from the modern languages does not appear to justify positing any such system. Moreover, not only do certain constructions in all three languages retain this older system but also one dialect of Cahuilla, as Fuchs (1970) has shown, preserves this system in full.

The kinds of syntactic change I observed—for example the adaptation of motion and location predicates as aspectual or temporal markers—are observable in many language families. Goal-directed verbs representing unrealized events frequently become future markers, as did aller in French. Location verbs such as qal "be there, live" in Cupan, like its equivalent in Mandarin, zài "be there," come to be used as durative or progressive aspect "auxiliaries." In Cupan the form yax, occurring as a verb root, verb suffix, or, rarely, as a separate auxiliary verb, is translatable variously as "do," "occur," "happen," "become," "behave like" and even as -ed, the English past tense suffix. The semantic differences

xi

correspond in part to the kinds of semantic entities these verbs predicate.
Some are embedded sentences, others animate or inanimate nouns.

My subsequent work in Austronesian languages indicates that there is
a range of meanings from CAUSE, DO, ACT LIKE to BECOME and
HAPPEN which may be represented by copular-like verbs covering part or
all of this range, the particular parts of the range covered varying somewhat among languages but never covering both ends of the scale without
including what lies in between. A form having a causative meaning may
also occur with an ordinary action or as a transitivizer. But I have found
no instances of forms representing both CAUSE and OCCUR which do not
also signify in the appropriate syntactic contexts ACT or DO. In English,
of course, do is an action verb, but it can also be used to represent,
usually anaphorically, OCCUR or HAPPEN, as in "It will rain tomorrow,
just as it did yesterday," and "What's doing?" And at earlier stages of
English we find do as a causative verb, as in Doþ þat þas men sitton,
"Make the men sit down." Similar kinds of semantic overlapping are to
be found in Polynesian, and Indonesian languages and in Thai.

This semantic range might be characterized as embodying some very
general notion of interruption or replacement of a state by an event, happening or occurrence. Predicated of a single animate entity, the notion
DO or ACT is represented, predicated of a sentence entity, HAPPEN or
OCCUR. If the predicate relates two such sentential entities, the notion
CAUSE is represented. This suggests that some part of the semantic
interpretation of a sentence arises from the number and type of "argument"
nominals co-occurring with a particular predicate.

If these differences are to be represented on the level of underlying
structure, then semantic grammarians may have to reconsider their
imposition of a single meaning on each underlying predicate after the manner of first order predicate calculus. Since the goals of logic and linguistics are quite distinct, the need for such a reconsideration should not be
too surprising. Or alternatively, the semantic shifts might be ascribed
to the operation of transformational processes like raising, which seem to
have a topicalizing function. The present static models of generative
grammar are not equipped to deal with such phenomena.

Related to this is another significant phenomenon. In Cupan, as in
other language families, there is a hierarchy of linguistic constructions
from main sentences to clauses and quasi-clauses to morphemes, presumably involving differing degrees of assertiveness and presupposition.
Some languages such as Diegueño manifest through morphological mark-
ings a high degree of embedding in sentences which correspond

For example, Edward Klima's diachronic study of relative pronouns
and personal pronouns (1965) provided more than an account of the specific
changes in the forms and uses of these pronouns. It also provided a
hypothesis that syntactic change takes place through such processes as the
addition, reformulation, or dropping of syntactic transformations, and the
re-ordering of sets of transformations. R. Lakoff's 1968 study, Abstract
Syntax and Latin Complementation, is written within the same general
transformational tradition but is based upon a later modification of transformational theory. In this newer version, transformations operate on a
much more abstract deep structure containing abstract verbs which might
not be realized as verbs in surface structure. Lakoff points out (213) that
traditional grammarians had assumed that certain grammatical rules
depend on meaning classes. She defines a meaning class as a set of
semantic markers functioning in syntactic rules, and an abstract verb as
a verb whose semantic markers are all syntactically relevant. This postu-
lation captures the intuitive notion that a verbal concept can be expressed
without the presence of a verb in surface structure. "A suffix, or a
marker of mood, can carry verbal meaning" (167). Moreover, it allowed
Lakoff to express important generalizations about Latin syntax that earlier
transformational models could only have captured with a considerable
amount of ad hoc machinery. Now, for example, the fact that ut in ut
venias behaves like the ut in volo ut venias need not be described as
almost coincidental. In both cases the ut and its independent subjunctive
are complementizers determined by verbs of the same meaning class,
one of them being abstract.

Within this framework the changes in complement structures result
not from changes in the transformational component, as Klima had proposed, but in "redundancy rules governing the application of these
[transformational] rules in specific meaning-classes of verbs" (234).
Thus Lakoff is able to claim that the deep structures of Latin, English,
and Spanish complement structures are the same, and so are the transformational rules applying to them. The differences reside in the scope
of application of these transformations, and the language-specific morphology. However, if it were not for an obviously unrelated morphology,
we could claim that Cupeño might also be related to these other languages
since it should be possible to postulate a common base for all four languages, and the Cupeño complement transformations are very much like
those needed for the other languages.

For historical study, this framework places a heavy burden on a separate morphological component. Moreover, determining meaning classes for a semantically interpreted deep structure is not as straightforward as it appears in Lakoff's analysis. Lakoff has to allow these abstract verbs idiosyncratic features, just like real surface verbs, a useful but overly powerful device.

From this kind of framework, a newer one has been developed in which transformations start to operate on a semantic rather than syntactic base. With such a base, meaning classes can be treated as primes. Unfortunately, the notion of a universal base which this framework appears to imply has been shown by Peters and Ritchie (forthcoming) to be vacuous, since, given any number of proposed universal bases, transformations can be formulated to generate the appropriate surface forms from any one of them. This does not invalidate the particular procedures and results described by Lakoff since, regardless of the arbitrariness of the base and the transformations, it seems likely that if these are held constant when describing different stages of a language, the degree and, in part, the nature of the change should be the same for different models. Changes in transformations and changes in the domain of application of transformations may in some models turn out not to be materially different. At present it appears that both kinds of change have to be postulated for language.

Moreover, in that transformational framework now referred to as "generative semantics" (see, for example, McCawley 1971) morphology is not so abruptly separated from syntax. The future endings in the Romance languages, for example, are related historically to independent verbs meaning "have." For an earlier stage of these languages, when the ending was an independent verb, we might reasonably posit syntactic structures in which the "have" verb is a higher predicate and the other verb is part of an embedded sentence. Such a structure might also be feasible for the modern languages as an underlying structure for sentences with future tense main verbs. Such structures fit quite neatly into a "generative semantic" higher verb framework. However, once elements that were formerly separate words are incorporated into a single word, new and quite idiosyncratic meaning shifts may occur. As the present study will show, some physical motion and location verbs took on more abstract modal and temporal functions once they were incorporated as suffixes into verbs formerly embedded beneath them. This kind of phenomenon has not yet been dealt with adequately within a generative semantic framework. A similar phenomenon also presenting some problems for this theoretical

approach is the occasional reversal of emphasis: Cupan sentences that
originally may have meant "He went along singing" now mean "He sang as
he was going along." This change accompanies an assumed incorporation
of the "go" verb as a suffix on the other verb. It is quite possible that a
different approach, perhaps the lexicalist framework described in
Jackendoff 1969, might better handle this kind of data.

What all this suggests is that while recent formulations of generative
theory have proven useful in suggesting models for linguistic change, there
is presently no theoretical model rich enough, yet restricted enough, to
account for the variety of syntactic change observable in human language.
Each model captures certain valuable insights about language which would
need to be incorporated within a single, more adequate model.

We have therefore decided in the present study to avoid any doctrin-
aire commitment to a theoretical viewpoint. However, because, in these
languages, morphology is more closely related to syntax than it is, say,
in English, it seems to us that a very loosely formulated semantically
based framework will reflect more easily and adequately both the morphological and syntactic characteristics of the Cupan languages. As our
fourth, fifth, and sixth chapters will indicate, the nominalization processes
and the kind of verb incorporation characteristic of Cupan are remarkably
close to the kinds of syntactic operation suggested by a theoretical model
such as that of McCawley 1971. Cupan retains morphological signs of
processes which, in English, are much less obvious because lexicalization of semantic units in English leaves far fewer morphological traces.
The fact that some suffixes that we treat as higher verbs are morphologically close—and sometimes almost identical—to surface structure higher
verbs provides support for our deliberately pragmatic choice.

1.3 The Position of Cupan in Uto-Aztecan

The three Cupan languages resemble each other more or less as
Spanish, Portuguese, and Italian resemble each other. Luiseño, which
corresponds to Italian in the Romance analogy, is significantly different
from the other two languages. Cahuilla and Cupeño are almost, but not
quite, mutually comprehensible. Cahuilla appears more accessible to
Cupeño speakers than Cupeño is to Cahuilla speakers.

These languages are more distantly related to several other southern
Californian languages, only one of which, Serrano, still survives.
Serrano is spoken on Morongo reservation, near Banning. There may be

other speakers further north. Kitanemuk, for which some information is
available (mainly from the field notes of J. P. Harrington), appears almost
close enough to Serrano to be considered a related dialect. Harrington's
very limited material on Gabrielino and Fernandeño suggests that they are
too much alike to be considered as separate languages. Although
Gabrielino, once spoken around Los Angeles and (with minor dialectal
variations) on some nearby islands, has to be grouped separately from
both Cupan and Serrano-Kitanemuk; it bears some interesting resemblances
to Luiseño. Possibly Serrano-Kitanemuk and Alliklik and Vanyume (about
which we know nothing) became separated from some common source earlier than Cupan and Gabrielino-Fernandeño. This whole family of languages, known as <u>Takic</u> (Miller 1967) after the word for "person" in these
languages, is a major branch of Uto-Aztecan. There is, however, a possibility that Hopi, which is presently treated as a separate branch of Uto-
Aztecan, may be more closely related to Takic than to other major
groupings of Uto-Aztecan such as Numic (Southern Paiute, Chemehuevi,
Comanche, Shoshone, etc.). We hope to examine this possibility in a
subsequent study.

The following diagram shows the relationships we have discussed. A
broken line is used where a relationship has not been adequately
established.

1.

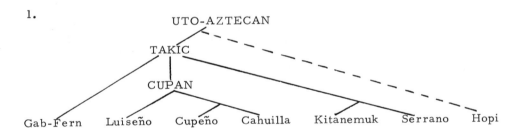

1.4 Dialects of the Cupan Languages

Dialect divisions are found in all three Cupan languages, the sharpest
divisions being in Cahuilla and the least obvious in Luiseño.

In Cahuilla there are three major dialects, the differences being manifested by differences in negative words, aspectual suffixes, some lexical
items, stress assignment and a number of other phonological processes.
The differences sometimes hinder but do not prevent mutual intelligibility.
Our description and discussion in this study refers to the Mountain dialect
except where otherwise stated. We have incorporated Desert Cahuilla

material where we found this useful, drawing from our own fieldwork,
from the publications of Seiler and Fuchs, and from J. P. Harrington's
field notes in the Smithsonian. Our experience with the third dialect, the
almost extinct Wanikik, has been very limited.

Cupeño consists of two major dialects: the speech of Kupa (Warner's
Springs), the largest Cupeño village; and that of the two smaller settlements of Wiláqalpa and Paloqla, nearby. The smaller settlements have
disappeared since the Cupeños were evicted from Kupa in 1903. The dialects differ a little in lexicon, in stress, and in some minor syntactic features such as pronominal copying. The death in 1971 of the singer
Cyrillo Welmas, apparently the last speaker of the Wiláqalpa dialect, cut
short our own work on this dialect, and here again our data are limited.
Unfortunately, the Kupa dialect may soon be extinct also. Our Cupeño
material is from the Kupa dialect unless described otherwise. We have
drawn mainly from our own field notes, but have also consulted J. Hill's
dissertation and some field notes she kindly made available to us—all on
the Kupa dialect. An additional source of material was Faye's field notes
in the Lowie Museum archive in Berkeley. Faye, like J. Hill, was
unaware of the existence of the Wiláqalpa dialect. But we found in his
notes some paradigms with Wiláqalpa characteristics and then noted that
one of his native-speaker consultants was a C. Welmas, a female relative
of our own Wiláqalpa consultant.

Luiseño appears to be more uniform in character and the minor differences noted do not group together consistently to suggest any clear dialect
separation. Speakers on the more northerly reservations—Soboba,
Pichanga, and, to a lesser extent, La Jolla—are more likely to retain
older forms of some verb suffices and drop some of the enclitics, while
speakers from Pauma and Rincon are more likely to use shortened forms
of some verb suffixes and retain enclitics. Our Luiseño material is drawn
from our fieldwork, from the Kroeber-Grace revision of Sparkman's
grammar, and from Harrington's field notes and texts in the Smithsonian
(all of which were taken from Adan Castillo, from Soboba). Unless otherwise identified, all Luiseño material is from the Rincon dialect.

1.5 Previous Work on Cupan Syntax

Of the three languages, Luiseño has received the most attention. The
first known grammar was written by a Luiseño, Pablo Tac (1822-1841).
Kroeber and Grace (1960:221) describe it as essentially an outline grammar
entitled La Lingua degli Indi Luiseños. However, it was not published

until 1926. It appears to be a very Latin-like grammar, using the five
Latin noun cases, although three of them have identical forms in Luiseño
and the other two are normally the same. Sparkman was certainly
unaware of Tac's grammar when he wrote his own very useful Sketch of
the Grammar of the Luiseño Language of California in 1905. Kroeber's
few grammatical notes in his 1907 Shoshonean Dialects of California added
nothing of value for the student of syntax or morphology. His 1909
follow-up, Notes on Shoshonean Dialects, gave a vocabulary for "Juaneño."
An examination of this, of other details given by J. P. Harrington in his
annotations to the 1933 reprint of Boscana's Chinigchinich, and of a tape
of a text fragment kindly provided by a Juaneño, all suggested that, as
Kroeber claimed, Juaneño "is a subdivision or dialect of Luiseño." The
differences between it and Rincon Luiseño seem of much less significance
than those between Desert and Mountain Cahuilla, and, according to some
of my older Luiseño consultants, it was perfectly comprehensible to any
Luiseño speaker. Syntactically we could detect no differences though, of
course, we had very little running text in Juaneño. Despite a careful
search, we were unable to find any fluent speakers of this dialect.

Kroeber and Grace's revision of Sparkman's grammar in 1960 provided a rich, if sometimes untidy, source of insights and information on
Luiseño. Some of the editors' additions are clearly inadequate. For
example, an appendix on the place of Luiseño in Uto-Aztecan fails to mention a single other Takic language although Kroeber had himself published
almost twenty pages on Cahuilla, Agua Caliente (Cupeño), Gabrielino, and
Serrano, with a reference to a "general Luiseño-Cahuilla group," in his
1909 paper referred to above.

J. P. Harrington, who did extensive fieldwork in Luiseño, never published anything more than his rather sketchy annotations to Chinigchinich,
referred to above. Some interesting field notes and a few texts are held
by the Smithsonian. The bulk of his Luiseño field notes appear to be
missing.

Malécot, who had earlier written a very severe review of the
Kroeber-Grace work (Malécot:1961), himself wrote four articles on the
language in 1963 and 1964. We found that they add only a little to the
Kroeber-Grace account. The text material provided, taken from a
La Jolla speaker, is very useful. Further comments on this work appear
later in the present study in our discussion of specific grammatical topics,
such as the Luiseño past tenses in the fifth chapter.

Finally, Bright, who had previously written on Luiseño phonemics in
a 1965 article, produced an invaluable Luiseño dictionary in 1968, while

V. Hyde's <u>An Introduction to the Luiseño Language</u> (1971), to which the present author contributed, is a teaching grammar intended for Indian use. However, it fills in a number of major gaps in previous work in Luiseño and served as a take-off point for much of our own work in the language.

Before the 1960's, little work had been done on Cupeño, apart from the word lists and very brief comments in Kroeber (1909). The Lowie Museum archive in Berkeley has extensive field notes based on fieldwork around 1920 by L. Faye. Faye also collected some excellent texts which, we believe, are currently being prepared for publication by J. Hill. Faye's grasp of Cupeño is often insecure and his anecdotal conclusions are frequently wrong, but these are only field notes and they are well worth examining for the student of Cupeño.

J. Hill's 1965 dissertation on Cupeño grammar is a very useful one despite its somewhat overformalized early transformational framework. Our own investigations, primarily with Hill's own informant, confirm her general outline of the tense and enclitic systems, although we have made some necessary revisions in our analysis. For example, we were unable to find any trace of the object enclitics she reported, nor of a special recent past tense. Her account of the dubitative enclitic makes no mention of its role in yes-no questions. Finally, we have dealt with areas of complementation and relativization that were not considered in her study since she was concentrating primarily on morphology. A few more detailed comments of ours appear in our grammatical discussions. Bright and J. Hill's 1967 paper on Cupeño linguistic history deals with phonology and lexicon. Their conclusions agree with ours as to the interrelationships of the three Cupan languages. An interesting article by J. Hill, "Volitional and Non-Volitional Verbs in Cupeño" (1969), is a revision of material in her dissertation. In a later paper (1972), she discusses the puzzling relationships between lexicalization and meaning. From our own checking it appears that she will need to re-examine her data, although her conclusions are very reasonable.

In addition to Kroeber's 1909 discussion of Cahuilla, a very rudimentary one; there are voluminous field notes and several aborted grammars, some in English, some Spanish, among the J. P. Harrington papers at the Smithsonian. As with Faye, although his knowledge of the language was limited, his comments were very insightful. His Indian consultant, Adan Castillo, who was fluent in both Luiseño and Cahuilla, not only gave Harrington lengthy texts in both languages but also remarked frequently on parallels between the two languages.

More recent work on Desert Cahuilla has been done by H. Seiler, and by A. Fuchs. In addition to Seiler's 1957 paper on vowel phonemes, interesting material relevant to syntax and morphology appears in articles of his published in 1958, 1965, and 1967. The last of these, "Structure and Reconstruction in some Uto-Aztecan Languages, " is especially interesting and, despite some errors in his references to Cupeño, it deserves far more credit than it received from Hill and Hill (1968). Fuchs' Morphologie des Verbs im Cahuilla (1970), which we have reviewed in some detail elsewhere, contains some very interesting though occasionally confusing discussion of aspect in Desert Cahuilla. Despite some omissions and a somewhat rigid theoretical approach, this work is a very careful and accurate presentation of the verb morphology. Much of its linguistic data is drawn from Seiler's 1970 collection of Desert Cahuilla texts. One of Seiler's former students, Hioki, has written both master's and doctor's dissertations on Cahuilla enclitics. The doctoral dissertation, Die Klitika im Cahuilla (1972), which came into our hands rather late in the writing of the present study, is primarily a revision of the master's dissertation, Zur Beschreibung des Systems der Klitika im Cahuilla (1970) with no substantive changes relevant to our study, as far as we can determine. These works present carefully detailed accounts of various kinds of particles in Desert Cahuilla within Seiler's structuralist framework.

Other relevant studies are K. Hill's Serrano dissertation (1967), which unfortunately does not cover many of the topics discussed here, and Steele's 1972 paper "Futurity, Intention and Possibility, " a very interesting exercise in semantic reconstruction in Uto-Aztecan.
R. W. Langacker's "Predicate Raising: Some Uto-Aztecan Evidence" (forthcoming) is a careful consideration of Uto-Aztecan evidence (including Cupeño) relevant to the theory of generative semantics. The most complete ethnographic study is still Strong's 1929 Aboriginal Society in Southern California, recently reissued (1972).

II. VERBS AND CUPAN SYNTAX

2.1 Preliminary Remarks

In this chapter is provided an outline of the verb systems of Cahuilla, Cupeño, and Luiseño,[1] and of other areas of Cupan syntax relevant to this inquiry. The purpose of this is two-fold:

i. to supply a broader syntactic perspective for the grammatical analysis and reconstructions described in subsequent chapters;

ii. to provide in one place the bulk of the linguistic data upon which later chapters will draw and expand.

---

[1]Indian forms are given in approximately their systematic phonemic shape. Word-internal morpheme boundaries relevant to the discussion are marked by hyphens. Word stress in Cupan is normally on the first syllable of a root. It will therefore not be indicated unless either the stress is divergent or the stress position is particularly relevant to the discussion. Stress is represented by an acute accent, ´. If it is necessary to indicate secondary stress, it will be represented by a grave accent, `. Long vowels are shown as geminates, palatalization by means of a tilde, ˷, and the glottal stop by an apostrophe, ʼ. In all three languages, c is realized as [č] before vowels, and [š] elsewhere. But a qualification to this generalization is necessary for Cahuilla, where a late vowel-dropping rule reduces, for example, the accusative nouns [náxaniči], "man," to [náxanič] in certain positions in a sentence. There is thus a surface contrast in the final consonant between the nominative form [naxaniš] and the accusative form [naxanič].

Luiseño and Cupeño ș is a voiceless retroflex sibilant. The Cupeño form is less retroflexed than the Luiseño one, and is sometimes hardly distinguishable from [s]. The labialized consonants [qʷ] and [kʷ] are shown as qw and kw respectively. And [ŋ] is shown as ng.

The following phonological processes are worth noting here.

i. In Cupeño, and sometimes in Cahuilla, m becomes ʼ before another m.

ii. Before q,

    q is often deleted, in all three languages;

    k either becomes q or is deleted, in all three languages;

    q is usually deleted, except in very careful speech, in all three languages;

    n is deleted in Cupeño, if it is in an unstressed syllable.

iii. Cupeño l in an unstressed syllable is deleted before n.

iv. Mountain Cahuilla e and Cupeño ə optionally become a at the end of a word.

v. In unstressed position, the contrast between Luiseño o and u, and that between Luiseño e and i is neutralized.

In our literal glosses of Cupan sentences and related forms, we endeavor to place the gloss for each morpheme under the morpheme, or as close as practicable. To do this, we make use of a number of abbreviations, such as DUR for "durative," and USIT for "usitative." A list of these abbreviations, together with the terms they represent, appears after our Table of Contents. Where the Indian words contain epenthetic vowels, or thematic affixes not so susceptible to translation, our literal glosses repeat the Indian forms in order to preserve the item by item sequence. In such cases, these forms are underlined, to distinguish them more clearly. Wherever possible, we have used our consultants' glosses, despite their often highly colloquial nature. Examples taken from other studies are given with their original glosses, although we may provide a morphemic breakdown where this would be relevant to our discussion.

A summary in table form of the major details of Cupan verb forms is to be found in Appendix C. We suggest that readers who wish to follow the arguments of this study without going into the fuller details of Cupan syntax consult this appendix and either omit this chapter or reserve it for later reading.

The mode of presentation here is primarily taxonomic, since we wish this description to be a compact one which does not anticipate the work of later chapters. In general, analytical and theoretical discussion and argumentation will be reserved for later chapters. Much of the data presented in this chapter is new. Some of the data have been reported only as fragmentary items found in unpublished field notes collected by Harrington or Faye. In neither case is much discussion required. But some explanation is necessary where our data conflict in non-trivial ways with data or interpretations of data provided by previous investigators.

Certain terms employed in this outline require some prior clarification or definition.

The term verb root will be used for the core part of the verb, that part remaining when derivational, inflectional, and syntactic affixes are stripped from a verb.[2] The term verb stem will be used for a verb stripped of all but derivational affixes. The term verb form will be used for the verb root plus affixes, of whatever kind they may be.

The distinction between inflectional and derivational affixes is generally a clear one in Cupan. But there are verb affixes which are not so clearly one or the other. Inflectional affixes in Cupan are, in all but one special Cupeño case, further from the verb root than are any derivational affixes. Only a few syntactic affixes like the Cahuilla complementizer pic-can occur further from the verb root. The position of these inflectional affixes is invariant in the sense that when more than one occurs in a verb

---

[2] This informal definition owes much to Hockett (1958:32-38).

form, they are always in the same positions relative to each other as well
as to the verb root and other affixes. On the other hand, where more than
one derivational affix appears on a verb root, these may be arranged in
different orderings in relation to each other, and, indeed, a particular
derivational affix may occur more than once within a verb form. With the
exception of the Cupeño case referred to above (where an inflectional element, a person marker, is infixed on the stem directly after the verb
root), derivational affixes are always closer to the verb root than inflectional markers.

Inflectional affixes are the affixes traditionally presented in verb
paradigms. They mark tense, number, person, subjects and/or objects,
realized or unrealized aspects, durative or non-durative aspects, and
such "moods" or "voices" as conditional, potential, and imperative.
Derivational affixes on Cupan verb forms express such varied notions as
causative, benefactive, desiderative ("want to ... "), as well as physical
motion accompanying or preceding the "action" denoted by the verb root.
They are more restricted as to the verb roots on which they may occur,
the restrictions being primarily, but not completely, semantic. We differ
from Fuchs in treating durative suffixes as inflectional rather than derivational. These suffixes have a wider distribution than derivational suffixes
and meet the other criteria mentioned above. This, together with the fact
that they also mark tense in all but Desert and Wanikik Cahuilla, outweighs
for us the fact that a small group of inherently durative verbs in Cahuilla
cannot have these durative suffixes.[3]

The Cahuilla verb form 'axpenke'ngenacne, "I will be going around
biting it, " may be broken down in the following way.

---

[3]These stems, qal "be, be there," wen "be, be there," nem "go around," and
neken "come" are further discussed in Fuchs (25, 65-66). This group of verbs, all of
which are irregular in a number of other, often idiosyncratic ways, provides an interesting case of a more complete lexicalization in the root of material which, in other verbs,
appears in an affix. These verbs share with verbs having durative affixes a number of
grammatical properties. For example, they take the suffix -ve rather than -nuk, and
allow certain localization affixes (Fuchs:66-67). The conditioning factor thus appears to
be semantic—an interesting problem for lexicalist-interpretivist theorists.

2.

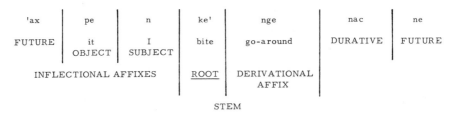

2.2 Word Order in Cupan

Word order in these highly inflected languages is considerably more free than in English. Sentences commonly begin with a sentence intro-ducer such as Cahuilla pe' and Luiseño pi', and Cupeño mə, all signifying something like "well" or "and then." In Cupeño, an enclitic usually fol-lows, suffixed to the introducer. In Luiseño, the introducer apparently does not "count" as the first word, since the enclitics are attached to the following word if pi' opens the sentence. Then subject and object noun phrases, verbs, temporal and locative phrases, and various other ele-ments follow, in almost any order. However, certain tendencies are prev-alent. Subject noun phrases are likely to precede verbs. The reverse order occurs mainly when the verb is intransitive or when the subject is a pronoun.

The relative ordering of verbs and object noun phrases depends on whether the object is pronominal. Pronominal objects normally precede verbs while other kinds of object usually follow verbs. This suggests a more basic OV ordering with "heavier" noun phrases being shifted to the right. This kind of optional process is already needed to account for the separation of long relative constructions from their head when the noun phrase containing them is the subject, and also a similar extraposition of noun phrase complement structures. Moreover, where an object noun phrase is júst a single noun, it quite often precedes the verb. The Cupan languages have postpositions rather than prepositions, and inflected aux-iliaries follow main verbs. Greenberg (1963:110-111) has pointed out such characteristics as typical of languages whose dominant order is SOV. Lehmann (1972:273), commenting on the Bantu languages, where a similar situation obtains, argues that this kind of a situation reflects an earlier,

more general OV ordering, with the pronominal object position indicating
a syntactic position that has been replaced.

2.3 Sentence Enclitics in Cupan

Sentence enclitics are stressless affixes normally suffixed to the first
word of a sentence or clause, no matter what the class or function of that
first word. As Kroeber and Grace point out for Luiseño, the primary
relation of an enclitic is to the sentence or clause as a whole, rather than
to the particular word to which it is attached. They describe the role of
the characteristic cluster of enclitics in Luiseño sentences as one of

> indicating person, number, tense, mode, and voice or aspect of
> subject and predicate—usually as a preliminary outline duplica-
> tion of the fuller indication of these factors in noun and verb ... .
> (p. 60)

There are, in all three languages, independent particles having regular word stress which appear to have either very similar functions to
those of enclitics, or even the same functions, and these will be treated
under the same headings. Quite often, these particles bear a close morphological resemblance to particular enclitics in the same language or in
a related one. For example, Luiseño has a word wúɫkapi, meaning
"I wonder"; it is probably related to Gabrielino woɫaʼax "I wonder," But
although the Luiseño wúɫkapi apparently cannot be broken into smaller
parts, there is a clearly related Cupeño form wə-ɫ-qwə-pə "I wonder
if ... ," where wə is a sentence introducer corresponding approximately
to English whether, ɫ(ə) is a dubitative/interrogative enclitic, qwə is the
unreality enclitic, and pə is the unrealized action enclitic. Mountain
Cahuilla ʼesána ـʼesáne ـʼesáxne "I guess" is obviously related to the
Mountain Cahuilla enclitic realized variously as -san, -sane, -sana and,
according to J. P. Harrington's notes, -saxa.[4] It is likely that all these
forms are related to the Luiseño dubitative enclitic -ɫan -ɫun. Many of
these independent but enclitic-like words were probably enclitics originally, although there is the possibility that some enclitics may have
developed from other elements, for example, the -san/-sax forms are
not unlike the Cahuilla verb root sunax "I wonder," which has cognates
in Cupeño and Luiseño.

---

[4]Our own consultants would not accept the form given by Harrington, although one
speaker from Cahuilla, our oldest consultant for Cahuilla, recalled hearing "the old folks
saying it."

2.4 Nouns in Cupan

Cupan nouns are almost all marked as either <u>possessed</u> or <u>absolute</u>, i.e. non-possessed. Possessed nouns have a possessive pronoun prefix denoting the possessor.[5] Absolute nouns have no such prefix. But they do have suffixes, known as <u>absolutive</u> suffixes, which appear to be just formal elements without special meaning.[6] As our fourth chapter will show, these absolutive suffixes turn out to be significant for the analysis of certain verb forms. The <u>absolutive endings</u> are as follows:

3.   <u>Cahuilla</u>   <u>Cupeño</u>   <u>Luiseño</u>

      c   c   c , ca

      t   t   t , ta

      l   l   l , la

The first set, the -<u>c</u> or -<u>ca</u> suffixes, normally occur after <u>i</u>. The second set occur after any other vowel but <u>i</u>, while the distribution of the third set, the -<u>l</u> or -<u>la</u> suffixes, does not appear to be conditioned by the preceding vowel. In Cupeño and even more commonly in Cahuilla, the -<u>l</u> ending is faintly palatalized, usually after an <u>i</u>. The syllabic <u>absolutives</u> -<u>ca</u> and -<u>ta</u> in Luiseño occur most often on monosyllabic noun stems.

In plural nouns, the <u>plural suffix</u> <u>follows</u> the <u>absolutive</u> ending, if there is one. The plural suffix is <u>m</u> if the noun ends in a vowel. Otherwise, it is as given below:

4.   <u>Cahuilla</u>   <u>Cupeño</u>   <u>Luiseño</u>

   em , am   im , am   um/om , am

The -<u>am</u> variants appear most often where there has been vowel apocope in the stem. Thus Cupeno 'ísil "coyote" becomes 'íslam in the plural, and sú'ul "star" has two plural forms: sú'ulim and sú'lam.

Except where ambiguity might arise, <u>accusative marking</u> is optional. The accusative suffix is -<u>i</u> and it follows any other suffixes. Except for

---

[5] Strictly speaking this is not quite correct, since the third person singular possessive prefix in Cahuilla, <u>he</u>-, does not appear unless it is stressed. In general, stress is not shifted to prefixes unless the stem is monosyllabic.

[6] The <u>absolutive endings</u> on deverbalized nominals do appear to have special meanings associated with them. These meanings are discussed in some detail in later chapters of this study.

the a that appears in the plural suffix after vowel syncope in the stem, the
vowel of a plural suffix is usually dropped when an accusative suffix follows the m, perhaps in order to avoid a three consonant cluster. Thus the
plural accusative form of Luiseñó 'awáal "dog" is 'awáalmi, although
'awáalumi occurs also. The plural accusative form of Cupeño 'ísil
"coyote" is 'íslami. In Luiseño, the accusative -i is not used for absolute
nouns if they denote inanimate entities.[7] Where the absolutive suffix is
syllabic, the vowel is dropped for the accusative form and, if no vowel
precedes the absolutive suffix -l (reduced from -la) in such cases, and i
is inserted before it. Thus the accusative form of 'éng-la "salt" is
'éng-i-l.

2.5 Postpositions and Cupan Nouns

Postpositional suffixes appear on pronouns as well as on inanimate
nouns. When nouns are animate, postpositions almost always appear on
a pronominal copy of the noun immediately following the noun. In Luiseño
absolute nouns lose their absolutive and plural endings when a postposition
is suffixed. For example, the Luiseño postposition meaning "to" or
"towards" is -ik, realized as -yk after vowels and, much more rarely,
as -yuk after some consonants. The inanimate noun too-ta "rock" becomes
too-yk "to the rock." But the animate noun ya'ác cannot have the postposition suffixed to it. Instead it must be suffixed to a pronoun copy following it, po "he." So, "to the man" is, in Luiseño, ya'ác po-yk.
Cahuilla and Cupeño nouns are just like Luiseño nouns with regard to postpositions except in two respects: they sometimes retain their absolutive
suffixes when postpositions are attached, and they sometimes have accusative marking when the "to" postposition is attached to a pronominal copy.
Most of the cases of absolutive retention seem to occur when loss of this
suffix would make the noun homophonous with another noun having a postposition, or when different meanings are associated with the forms.
Cupeño təmá-l means both "land" and "soil." But təmá-l-nga means "on
the land" while təmá-nga means "in the soil."

We shall not concern ourselves further with postpositions on pronouns
since only the noun forms are relevant to this study. Although Kroeber
and Grace follow Pablo Tac in giving nouns with postpositions case labels,
they recognize that these "cases" differ from the accusative case both

---

[7]There is some variation in this regard. Kroeber and Grace report slightly different
practices (88-91), but the differences are slight.

formally (they normally require absolute suffixes to be dropped, and can appear on pronouns) and functionally (the accusative is a non-concrete, purely relational, syntactic case, while these other "cases" are non-syntactic or concrete).[8] For convenience of reference, we give the Kroeber and Grace case labels with the accompanying list of noun postpositions below. We omit their "partitive" case since these endings (Cahuilla and Cupeño -ngaxwic and Luiseño -ngawic, "those belonging to ... ") result from a special nominalization of an ablative or locative noun form.

5.	CASE AND MEANING	CAHUILLA	CUPEÑO	LUISEÑO
	Locative "at, in, on"	-nga, -pa	-nga, -'aw	-nga
	Ablative "from, since, because of"	-ngax, -pax	-nga	-ngay, -ngax[9]
	Terminalis/ Dative "to, toward, behind"	-yka, -ika	-yka, -ika ONLY WITH MOTION VERBS	-ik, -yk, -yuk
	Comitative "with, along with, in company with"	-man		-man
	Instrumental "by means of, with	-pic	-ci (RARE WITH NOUN STEMS)	-tal (-cal after i)

The Cahuilla forms with p are at first puzzling. The -pa, for example, appears to be the same element as the -pa in mipa, which means "when?" in both Cahuilla and Cupeño, as well as the -pa suffix on

---

[8]See especially pages 88 and 91.

[9]In fact, the final x of these postpositions should probably be considered as a separate postposition. In Cahuilla, nga is also a word meaning "edge." In this language, -a also appears to be used as a postposition, as in n-a "on me," and m-a "on them." This is argued by Hioki (1972:50). There is at least one piece of Luiseño data which might support Hioki's claim. The Cahuilla simultaneous time suffix on embedded verbs is -pa, which in other environments means "at it," "on it," or "at that place/time." The Luiseño equivalent is simply -a. On the other hand, in yet other environments, pa appears to be synonymous in Cahuilla with pe-nga "there, then," and may well be a contracted variant of it. In the present study we have found it simpler to consider these monosyllabic forms as contractions.

non-finite verb forms, meaning "while, " as in the Cahuilla ne-hívin-qal-
i-pa "while I was collecting them, " as well as the pa-prefix on Cahuilla
verbs, meaning "where, " as in

6.   pa - pe -n- yáw - ici - ve

        where-it-I-hold-going-[+R]

        "where I carried it"

There are several indications that the p in all these forms was originally
a third person singular pronoun. First, the absolutive suffix is always
retained when the -pa or -pax suffixes are used on absolute nouns. When
-nga or -ngax is used, the absolutive suffixes are dropped. Secondly,
when the notions "there" and "from where/there" are expressed as independent words, the forms pe-nga and pe-ngax respectively are used. We
assume that pa and pax are contractions of these independent forms.
Thirdly, as Hioki (1972:50) has pointed out, there are forms with person
markers other than the third person singular where the contracted form
is in free variation with the fuller form:

7. $\left\{ \begin{matrix} \text{n-ax} \\ \\ \text{ne-ngax} \end{matrix} \right\}$ hem-hic-'i

        me-from-they-go-PAST

        "They went away from me. "

The instrumental suffix in Cahuilla, -pic, merits special attention
because it appears to be basically the same as a syntactic prefix pic-
which serves as a complementizer for sentences embedded as noun phrase
complements. A detailed discussion of these complement structures
appears in a later chapter. Like the -pa and -pax forms considered above,
the instrumental -pic was almost certainly an independent form containing
a third person object pronoun. It too occurs after absolutive endings.
Hioki (1972:42-47), in a fuller discussion of this element, identifies it
with an independent pic meaning "about it, him, because of it/him, around
some particular time or place, " with all the ambiguities of the English
words given here as the meaning. There are also forms without p, such
as n-ic "about me, " and m-ic "about them" However, like Fuchs,[10] Hioki

---

[10]See, for example, Fuchs, page 34, fn. 62.

explicitly differentiates this pic from the complementizer pic which he
calls a "Konjunction, "

> die sich nicht weiter analysieren lasst und auch ganz andere
> Distributionseigenschaften besitzt.
>
> (p. 32)

It is likely that all of these pic forms go back to an independent form
*pe-ci "him/it-with/about, " i. e. "with him/her, " "about it, " etc.   The
form *pe-ci may have become *pi-ci by the pervasive Cupan vowel harmony processes, and then, like many other Cahuilla forms, it lost its
final vowel and became pic.   It is significant that the independent pronominal form in Cupeño which serves as the instrumental is pə́-ci, which
also means "about it. "   There are Cupeño forms like nə́-ci "about me, "
as well as a very few forms like nə-ma-ci "with my hand. "   But this pə́-ci
has another function—like pic- in Cahuilla, pə́-ci serves as a complementizer for sentences embedded as noun phrases, the same kinds of embedded
sentences, in fact, as those following pic- in Cahuilla.   However, while
pic- is obligatory for such sentences, except when they are embedded
sentence-initially, pə́-ci is optional.   Indeed it rarely occurs in the speech
of our major Cupeño consultant.

Even if this Cahuilla-Cupeño correlation is not considered, the com-
bined force of formal and semantic considerations seems strong enough to
justify treating the various manifestations of pic as deriving from a single
underlying form.   The various distributional differences referred to by
Hioki arise naturally from the varying syntactic environments and from
the nature of the entities to which the pronominal part of pic refers.   So
pic as a complementizer does not vary in form because its function
requires that it serve as anaphor for its complement sentence.   Hioki's
claim that it cannot be further analyzed arises from an unnecessarily
restrictive structuralist framework which has, in this case, obscured the
underlying unity of the various pic forms.

The same kind of complementizer apparently does not appear in
Luiseño, although the Luiseño instrumental is like the others in allowing
an extra pronominal element, also a pi, as in 'óno-pi-cal "by means of
that. "

2.6 Cahuilla: Sentence Enclitics and Verb Forms

2.6.1 Sentence Enclitics

In contrast to their major role in Cupeño and Luiseño, sentence enclitics play a minor and infrequent role in Cahuilla syntax. There are two that can be considered sentence enclitics in all three dialects of Cahuilla, or perhaps three enclitics if a differently inflected form of one of the two is treated separately. The forms are -saxne, dubitative, -saxalu, which appears to be the same sax root with a potentive suffix -alu rather than the future suffix -ne, and another dubitative, -hema. In addition, there is an enclitic variant in the Desert dialect for the quotative particle yal, one realized either as -el or -l.

As might be expected, quotative particles or enclitics are common in traditional narratives, although their frequency appears to be lower in Cahuilla than in the other Cupan languages. The other enclitics appear so infrequently that we were unaware of their existence after twelve hours of elicitation. Verb suffixes, special verb forms, or other independent elements, separately or in combination, carry out functions performed by enclitics in the other two languages. For example, the English sentence

8.   I might eat the jackrabbit.

has Cupeño and Luiseño versions each containing a "potentive" enclitic and a future or "unrealized" enclitic. They are -qwə and -pə respectively in Cupeño, and -kwa and -po in Luiseño.

9.   Cu   nə'-qwə-n-pə   su'ic-i   qwa'

                I-POT-I-[-R]   rabbit-ACC   eat

10.   Lu   noo-nu-po-kwa   śu'íc-i   hilá'i-n

                I-I-[-R]-POT   rabbit-ACC   eat-FUTURE

But there are no enclitics in the following Wanikik Cahuilla version:

11.   W.Ca   qa-miyaxwen-i-pa   su'ic-i   pe-n-qwa-nem

                INDEF-be-i-while   rabbit-ACC   it-I-eat-FUTURE

The Cahuilla sentence contains a construction rather like a participial
construction and this construction carries out the role of the potentive and
unrealized enclitics in the other languages. The construction is very
similar to the Latin quae cum ita sint, "which things being thus"
construction.

The dubitative enclitic root sax communicates the speaker's belief
that his utterance represents a probable rather than merely possible situation. Cahuilla speakers use phrases like I suppose or I guess as English
translations. In contrast, -hema indicates possibility, without any commitment as to probability or improbability. English expressions like
I wonder whether (or not) and I'm not sure are used as translations.

In all three dialects, the sax enclitic is realized as -san. In
Mountain Cahuilla it is also realized as -sane, -sana, and -saxne. There
are also the free forms 'esáxne, 'esáne, 'esána, and 'esán. In the Desert
dialect, the enclitic forms -sanem and -saxnem and the free forms 'esán,
'esánem, and 'esáxnem are variants. Our Wanikik consultant used the
same forms as for the Desert dialect and also sáxnem as a free form in
sentence-initial position. However, he had a tendency to drop the final m
from the -nem suffix when it occured on a stem having more than two
syllables.

It is likely that all these forms contain the future suffix that is realized on verbs as -ne in Mountain Cahuilla, as -nem in the Desert dialect,
and as either -nem or -ne in Wanikik. This seems all the more likely
since another verb suffix, the potentive -alu, also appears on sax. Unlike
the other Cahuilla enclitic forms, which may occur either on the first
word in a sentence or on the last, -saxalu often occurs on a word in the
middle of a sentence. Also, unlike the other sax enclitics, and unlike
-hema, -saxalu can appear on words other than the first or last one in a
sentence. It may also have secondary stress on one of its vowels. We
have been unable to determine the conditioning factors for the occurrence
and placement of this stress. This enclitic, which might be labeled
"potentive dubitative," is usually translated as "be supposed to" or "ought
to" or "should," as in

12.   'á'cay-sax-alù   pic-'e-miyaxwen-ap

       good-DUBIT-POT   COMPL-you-be-UNREALIZED
                             (that)

       "You should be good."

In addition to the dubitative enclitic -hema, there is a stressed free form héma "maybe or maybe not" or sometimes "whether" which precedes an embedded yes-no question and its complementizer (if any); it occasionally is used also as an introductory word meaning "maybe, perhaps." Once again, it seems unnecessary and counter-intuitive to treat this free form, as Hioki does (1972:81), as quite unrelated to the enclitic form, when both the shape and the semantic interpretation are so close.

The dubitative enclitics and free forms discussed above appear in the following sentences:

13.   kikit-am-sana   'ax-pe-m-saamsa-ni   wayikiwenet-i

        child-PL-DUBIT   FUT-it-they-buy-FUT   food-ACC

        "I guess the kids will buy food, won't they?"

14   kúktac-qa-'-sax-ne   man ceqe pe-kina-ngi-qa-'a

        talk-DUR-PAST-DUBIT-FUT and just her-marry-go-DUR-PAST

        "She must have talked him into going and marrying her."

15.   'ípa-hema hí-yi   tax-qayin-qa-'

        here-DUBIT her-mother self-wash-DUR-PAST

        "Perhaps her mother washed herself here."

16.   W.Ca   sáx-nem   pe-mekan-nem

                 DUBIT-FUT him-kill-FUT

                 "Maybe he'll kill him."

17.   M.Ca pe-n-'ayaw-qa   pe-n-'e'nan-ka' héma   pe-qwa-qa

              it-I-want-DUR   it-I-know-INCEPT   whether it-eat-DUR
                     PRES   PRES

        wiwic-i

        acorn mush-ACC

        "I want to know whether he eats acorn mush."

The quotative particle yal is hardly translatable. Perhaps "it is told" comes closest to it. Unlike the other enclitic or enclitic-like elements

discussed so far, it can appear many times in a sentence. It indicates
that the discourse in which it occurs is a traditional narrative. In Desert
Cahuilla, yal is sometimes realized as an enclitic -el or -l. Harrington
records the free form as yaal and remarks on a possible connection with
the Luiseño "realized" enclitic -il, a connection suggested by his consultant, who spoke both languages. A historical connection is not unlikely,
since yal is probably related to the verb yax, "speak, tell" and the final l
may well be a reflex of an older "realized" enclitic, perhaps *-el. And
the Desert Cahuilla -el or -l quotative looks like the Luiseño -il in its
positions of occurrence, as the sentences below show. Many of our
Desert Cahuilla examples are taken from Seiler (1970), henceforth
referred to as Texts.

18.   D. Ca   pé-l   'ay   kile   pa-'ayaw-qal ....

                  and-QUOT   then   not   him-want-DUR

                  "The man didn't like him ..."

                                                        (Texts:101)

19.   D. Ca   qawa'l-i-l   pe-waway-qal

                  woodrat-ACC-QUOT   her-marry-DUR

                  "He married the rat."

                                                        (Texts:101)

20.   Lu   qawla-y-il   po-y   to'ma-qus

                  woodrat-ACC-[+R]   she-ACC   marry-DUR

                  "He married the rat."

        In his Zur Beschreibung des Systems der Klitika im Cahuilla, Hioki,
whose definition of "Klitika" is considerably broader than our definition of
"sentence enclitic," suggests that the word wam, translated by our consultants variously "already," "now," "I guess," and "really," is the
counterpart of yal. He claims (1970:53-54) that wam never appears in
traditional narratives, except in dialogue, and that it signifies "this is my
own experience" rather than "this is the way I have heard it." He includes
among his "Klitika" a number of other free forms that are clearly not like
the free-form variants of sentence enclitics discussed so far, elements

like the emphatic ta', mu "still, " ca "just, " tu (tum in Mountain Cahuilla,
Cupeño and Luiseño) "any, " and the negative kile "not. "

2.6.2 Cahuilla Verb Forms

There are eight positions for the constituents that may occur in a verb
form. Of course, it is not necessary that each position be filled for every
verb form. Object prefixes, for example, are required only for transitive verbs. Furthermore, there are certain interdependencies, for
example, the 'ax- future prefix can occur only if the verb form as a -ne
or -nem future suffix.

It should be noted that this description primarily concerns Mountain
Cahuilla and that parts of it will be considerably revised in subsequent
chapters, especially our account of durative and present tense forms.

The eight positions referred to are as follows:

21.	I	II	III	IV	V	VI	VII	VIII
	mainly temporal and locative anaphors	object pre-fixes	subject pre-fixes	pe	ROOT	deriva-tional affixes	future dura-tive affixes	tense suffixes

Details of the particular constituents that can appear in each position will
be given below in a separate section for each position.

POSITION I

'ax- is an optional future prefix for verbs with the future suffix -ne
(or -nem in the Desert dialect and Wanikik). Seiler (1967:143) has suggested that 'ax- represents in Desert Cahuilla a semantic constituent
ABSOLUTE which "stresses the perspective of the speaker-addressee
relation and dissociates it from the action as such. " He speculates that
this 'ax- may be connected etymologically with 'ax, a shortened form of
'engax "away from thee, " and that the "thee" in this case denotes the
addressee. We were unable to confirm or refute this account in our work
with Desert and Wanikik consultants. There is, however, good evidence
in Wanikik and in Desert Cahuilla for a general absolute/non-absolute distinction of the kind Seiler posits, especially for verb forms referring to
past or ongoing events. Those of our consultants who attempted to translate 'ax- said something like "he may do it, he will do it. "

pa-   is a shortened form of pe-nga "there."

pax- is a shortened form of pe-ngax "from there, thence."

pic- is an instrumental suffix, "with it," which also means "about it, her, him." Where the reference of the "it" is an embedded sentence, the pic- may be regarded as a complementizer.

piyk- or piyik signifies "to that place, thither."

POSITION II

The object prefix forms are as follows:

22.   SG   PL

    ne-, "me"   ceme- , "us"

    'e- , "you"   'eme- , "you"

    pe- , "him, it, her"   me- , "them"

We have also elicited in this position piyk- "to him, her, it," and tax- "each other," "self," "one another."

POSITION III

These are the subject prefixes:

23.   SG   PL

    ne- , "I"   cem- , "we"

    'e- , "you"   'em- , "you"

    he- , "he, she, it"   hem- , "they"

Note that when these affixes are preceded by object affixes, those subject affixes consisting only of a consonant (including the glottal stop ') plus a vowel always lose the vowel. The sequence he is deleted if it is unstressed. Thus the "him-they" object-subject combination, pe-hem-, becomes pem-. However, in Wanikik and Desert Cahuilla, he deletion in medial position is optional, and sometimes only the h is deleted, allowing the two vowels to become a single long vowel. Thus there are forms like pehem- and peem-.

POSITION IV

pe- is a locative or temporal adverbial anaphor that may occur in verb forms having non-future, durative suffixes. There has to be, elsewhere in the sentence, an adverbial element referring to a point in time or space, that is, to a fairly limited period of time (tuku "yesterday, " but not tu-háye-manic "always") or to a fairly restricted and definite location (Pala-nga "in Pala, " but not mivá'-sana "somewhere").

POSITION VI

Quite a number of derivational affixes occur in this position and several can occur together, the relative order being determined mainly by semantic factors. An exception to this is -vaneke "come V-ing, " which occurs only as the last derivational affix. The affixes which occur in this position are given below with their most common translations. The meanings vary considerably, since they depend in part upon the verb root's meaning and, to a minor extent, on other verb affixes. The V abbreviation used here refers to the verb root plus any other derivational affixes preceding the affix described.

24.

-'ayaw	"try to V, almost V"
-ikaw, -kaw	"be here and there V-ing, be V-ing intermittently"
-ici	"V while going"
-lew, -law	"go there to V"
-max	"V for someone, V on someone's behalf, " known as BENEFACTIVE
-ni	"cause to V, " known as CAUSATIVE
-ngi, -nga	"go away V-ing, go around V-ing, start V-ing while going"
-puli	"come here and V, come here to V"
-vicu	"want to V, start to V, try to V, " DESIDERATIVE (not used in Desert or Wanikik dialects)

| -va-neke | "come V-ing;" future form: <u>va-max</u>; Desert and Wanikik (non-future: <u>va-neken</u>) |
| -xa | "make someone V" |

The following Mountain Cahuilla examples illustrate not only some possible combinations but also the variety of orderings possible. The longer and more complex verb forms given below would almost certainly never occur in texts or in conversation. We constructed many of them ourselves, asked the native speaker what they meant, and then asked if they were "good Indian." Only those that the speaker could translate and would accept as "good Indian" are shown below. The reason for this procedure is that although native speakers avoid such utterances because they are so difficult to process, they can distinguish consistently between the well-formed and ill-formed strings. The very long forms illustrate normal Cahuilla processes carried to extremes. The length enables us to illustrate economically a variety of possible orderings.

25.   pe-n-kus-qa

        it-I-get-DUR
                PRES

        "I'm getting it."

26.   pe-n-kus-max-qa

        him-I-get-BEN-DUR
                    PRES

        "I'm getting it for him."

27.   pe-n-kus-ici-qa

        get-going-DUR
                PRES

        "I'm going along getting him/it."

28.   pe-n-kus-max-vicu-qa

        get-BEN-want-DUR

        "I want to get it for him"

29.   pe-n-kus-ici-max-vicu-qa

      get-going-BEN-want-DUR
                         PRES

      "I want to go along for him getting it."

30.   pe-n-kus-lew-max-vicu-ngi-ni-qa

      get-go-BEN-want-go-CAUS-DUR
                   around   PRES

      "I made him go around wanting to go for him and get it."

So far, no variation of ordering has been shown. The affix _max_ has always preceded _vicu_, _lew_ has preceded both _max_ and _vicu_. This is not the case in the next two examples:

31.   pe-n-kus-vicu-ni-max-lew-qa

      get-want-CAUS-BEN-go-DUR
                       PRES

      "I'm going on his behalf to make her want to get it."

32.   pe-n-kus-ni-vicu-ngi-max-'ayaw-qa

      get-CAUS-want-go-BEN-try-DUR
               around   PRES

      "For his sake, I'm trying to go around wanting him to make her get it."

The last two examples show an affix occurring more than once within a complex verb stem:

33.   pe-n-kus-lew-ici-vicu-max-lew-qa

      get-go-going-want-BEN-go-DUR
                       PRES

      "I'm going over there wanting, for his sake, to go along going to get it."

34.   pe-n-kus-vicu-ni-lew-vicu-qa

      get-want-CAUS-go-want-DUR

      "I want to go and make him want to get it."

POSITION VII

nac is the singular future durative affix. It may be followed either by the future suffix -ne (-nem in the other dialects) or (in all dialects) by the inceptive suffix and the potentive suffixes.

wen is the plural durative affix. It may be followed by -ne (-nem), or the plural inceptive -katem.

POSITION VIII

-qa is the present durative singular suffix.

-we is the present durative plural suffix.

-qa' or -qa'a is the past durative singular suffix.

-we' or -we'e is the past durative plural suffix.

-'i is the past non-durative suffix for both singular and plural subjects. However, when the verb is negated with the particle kiĺe, the -'i suffix is dropped.

The Wanikik and Desert Cahuilla forms are slightly different, and they are sometimes used a little differently. The Wanikik present durative singular and plural suffixes are -qal and -wen respectively, the same forms as the Desert Cahuilla ones. But Wanikik differs from the Desert dialect in allowing deletion of the final consonant of each suffix, the deletion apparently being conditioned by stress. Our Wanikik data are unfortunately too limited and inconsistent for precise determination of the environment for deletion. The Wanikik and Desert past durative suffixes are -qal'e or -qa'le for the singular, and -wen'e or -we'ne for the plural. The past non-durative suffix for these dialects is -'i, as in the Mountain dialect. Here again, this suffix is dropped when the verb is negated. The Desert negative particle is kiĺe, and the Wanikik form is qawa.

However, the terms "present" and "past" are less appropriate for Wanikik and Desert Cahuilla than they are for the Mountain dialect—or for the other two Cupan languages. The so-called present tense forms are often used for past time reference, as a kind of unmarked past. The presence of a distant time adverb like yewi "long ago, " requires that the verb be marked for past. There are a few cases in which "past" durative forms have been recorded by Seiler for ongoing events—we exclude from consideration here traditional narratives because they present some special problems. But all the examples appear to denote activities or events which have gone on for some time and are portrayed as still going on by a speaker describing some stickman drawings. The two examples

following are characteristic of the six sentences we have showing this
phenomenon. As for our other examples for Seiler's texts, the morphemic
breakdown and the accompanying literal "translation" are ours, the more
idiomatic translation is Seiler's.

35.   D. Ca   hax-ami 'ax-ne-tetiyamax-nem yax-'i yal 'et

         someone FUT-me-tell-FUT   say-PAST QUOT he

         man hiw-we'ne pe-teew-qa'l

         and stand-DUR   it-look-DUR
                 PAST   PAST

         "'... someone will tell me,' he says, and he
         stands and looks."

                                                  (Texts:193)

36.   D. Ca   'i' pe' pe ne-na' wes'ah, man hiw-we'neh

         this that it my-father (his-) planting and stand-DUR
                                                         PAST

         "This is my father's crop that grows here."

                                                  (Texts:193)

Examples like these are far from convincing, since drawings can just as
well be described as representing past events as present ones. This is
especially true here since the father that the consultant mentions had been
dead for many years. Fuchs uses Seiler's examples as evidence for her
claim that the forms with -qal'e, -wen'e, and -'i show events that the
speaker sees to be immediately relevant for the speaker and/or listener.[11]
We have not been able to elicit any instances of this in our own investigations of Desert Cahuilla and Wanikik, although we too have found that the
unmarked durative forms are often neutral as to the present/past
distinction.

     -pu' is the potentive suffix. It may be translated as "may," "might,"
"can," "may have," "might have," "could have," "would have," "would,"
with almost all the varied meanings associated with these English auxiliaries. Indeed, potentive verb forms are also used for "would that ..."
expressions. There is a variant form, -alu which occurs when the preceding segment is consonantal—although there are enough exceptions to

[11]Personal communication, June 5, 1972.

suggest that morphological and lexical factors might be involved. A few verbs, such as teew "see, " allow either. The Desert Cahuilla forms are -pulu and -alu; the only Wanikik form that we have is -pil̃, and it is often followed in our data by the Wanikik auxiliary yaax, which is described later in this chapter. The other dialects sometimes have the corresponding auxiliary yaya, sometimes the copula miyaxwe(n), but most often no such verb at all. Except in Wanikik, the potentive never co-occurs with the negative particle: the regular -ne or -nem future suffix is usually used instead. The potentive forms allow either past, present, or future time reference. Thus, the Mountain Cahuilla sentence:

37.   ne' pen-n-namq-alu   man pen-n-pepáqin-pu'

        I   him-I-meet-POT   and him I-hit-POT

can mean either

        "If I had ever met him, then I would have hit him"

or

        "If I ever meet him, I'll hit him. "[12]

The following sentences illustrate some of the other uses of the potentitive. The examples are taken from our work in the other dialects:

38.   W.Ca pe'em tuku   qawa   hem-hici-pil̃ pi-yka   yaax

              they yesterday not they-go-POT it-to   do

              "They wished they hadn't gone yesterday. "

39.   W.Ca 'e'e   'e-cengen-pil̃   tuku

              you   you-dance-POT   yesterday

              "You should have danced yesterday. "

40.   D.Ca men-n-nanal-pulu

              them-I-ask-POT

              "I want to ask them. "

---

[12]Fuchs, especially on page 30, gives the impression that Desert Cahuilla -pulu and -alu cannot occur on forms with past time reference. However, we have found the same time reference ambiguities in all three dialects.

41.   D. Ca   pe-'-mex-alu

        it-you-do-POT

        "Do it, please."

-ka' is the inceptive singular suffix. The plural suffix is -katem. On
some verbs, many of which have a consonant immediately preceding the
inceptive suffix, this suffix is realized as -ik, with the plural form -iktem.
Inceptive verbs can be translated as "will V," but far more common are
"be going to V" and "be about to V." The time reference is usually near
future. However, complex tenses are possible if the appropriately
inflected copular verb miyaxwe(n) is added, resulting in forms meaning
"I was going to V" and "I might have been about to V." With intransitive
inceptive verbs, a special pronominal prefix paradigm is used, one
occurring only with inceptives and certain other nominal-like constructions. These forms are shown below with the verb hici "go":

42.   hen-hici-ka'   "I'm going to go."

        'et-hici-ka'   "You (sg) are going to go."

        hici-ka'   "He's going to go."

        hec-hici-katem   "We're going to go."

        'em-hici-katem   "You all are going to go."

        hici-katem   "They're going to go."

Here, for comparison, is the present durative paradigm:

43.   SG   PL

        ne' ne-hici-qa   cem   cem-hici-we

        'e' 'e-hici-qa   'emem   'em-hici-we

        pe'(e) hici-qa   pe'em   hem-hici-we

The pronominal prefixes for the inceptive forms of transitive verbs are
not so different from those for other finite paradigms. In the following
examples, a third person singular object pronoun form is used; the verb
illustrated is teew "see."

44.   INCEPTIVE   PRESENT

     ne'   pe-n-teew-ik   ne'   pe-n-teew-qa

     'e'   pe-'-teew-ik   'e'   pe-'-teew-qa

     pe'(e)   pe-Ø-teew-ik   pe'(e)   pe-Ø-teew-qa

     cem   pi-c-teew-iktem   cem   pi-cem-teew-we

     'emem   pe-'em-teew-iktem   'emem   pe-'em-teew-we

     pe'em   pe-Ø-teew-iktem   pe'em   pe-m-teew-we

An alternative pronominal prefix can replace both subject and object prefixes. It is the accusative form, which happens to be pe'iy or pey in this
case. This accusative prefix, which appears to be limited to nominalized
forms such as the inceptive, occurs more often than the object-subject
pronominal combination in the second and third person inceptive verbs.
But it has not been found in the first person inceptive forms.

    As in all the Cupan languages, inceptive forms in embedded sentences
are used with the meaning "in order to V." The inceptive also occurs in
another construction which has not been verified for Wanikik and Desert
Cahuilla. The suffix -'a can be added to the inceptive form to change the
time reference to past time:

45.   M. Ca   'ne pe-n-walin-ka-'a

                 I   it-I-dig-INCEPT-PAST

                 "I was going to dig (it)."

46.   M. Ca   'et-em pe-walin-kat-em'a

                 that-PL it-dig-INCEPT-PL-PAST

                 "They were going to dig (it) but...."

    The inceptive occurs with the particle hani, which means approxi-
mately "I wish that ..." or "if only," as in

47.   M. Ca   hani pe-n-kwa'-ik

                 if only it-I-eat-INCEPT

                 "I wish I had eaten."

48.   M. Ca   hani pi-c-kwa'-ikt-em

                    if only it-we-eat-INCEPT-PL

                    "We should have eaten."

Finally, inceptive suffixes appear in constructions like the following:

49.   D. Ca   man pe'em kiĩ pey-'ac-kat-em

                    and they   not it-domestic-INCEPT-PL
                                          animal

                    "But he didn't belong to them."

                                        (Texts:187)

which means something more like

         "They were not in the role of owning him."

or even, less colloquially,

         "They were not in the way of being pet-owning to it."

where the role is seen as a kind of direction that one might take.

The Wanikik and Desert Cahuilla sentences below illustrate for these
dialects some of the characteristics not already illustrated.

50.   W. Ca   pa-'ayáw-qal-i-pa   'et-ngiy-ka- ne'   'e-n-numu-nem

                    it-want-DUR-i-ing   you-go-INCEP I   you-I-take-FUT

                    "If you want to go, I'll take you."

51.   D. Ca   pe-kus-ngiy-qal   hici-ka   yal   'i-ka   luupiy

                    it-get-go-DUR   go-INCEPT QUOT this-to   Lupi
                            away

                    pi-yik   piy-mamayw-e-law-ik

                    him-to   him-help-e-go-INCEPT

                    "He's taking it to Lupi, whom he's going to help."

-ne is a future suffix for both singular and plural verbs. The Wanikik
and Desert Cahuilla form is -nem. It serves as a less definite future
inflection than the inceptive, and is often better translated as "will
probably," or "may." It may co-occur with the future prefix 'ax-

described earlier, but the 'ax- cannot occur without -ne. As the first
example sentence below shows, -ne may also have an imperative meaning:

52. W. Ca qawa me-'-tetiyax-nem   taxlist-em-i   pic-'e-hici-ve

         not   them-you-tell-FUT person-PL-ACC that-you-go-[+R]

    tamit   he-ki-yka

    sun   his-house-to

    "Don't tell the people that you went to the sun's home."

53. M. Ca taxliswet-em   'i-pa   'angapa' 'ax-he'-meteq-ne   hem-

      Indian-PL   this-at again   FUT-they-increase-FUT their-

      hawawa'ñi-y   'ax-pe-m-'e'nan-ne   'angapa'

      language-ACC FUT-it-they-know-FUT   again

      "Indians will again increase here and they will know their
language again."

54. D. Ca tiwma miyaxwen-e-pa' 'ax-cem-hici-nem 'esán qawic-pi-yk

      warm be-e-ing   FUT-we-go-FUT DUBIT mountain-it-to

      "If it's warm, we'll go up into the mountains."

    2.6.3 Other Cahuilla Forms

    This section is concerned with forms which do not fit quite so neatly
into the eight position framework used just above, perhaps because they
are non-finite verb forms, perhaps because they are auxiliary forms
appearing separately from the main verb form. As will be seen in subsequent chapters, some of the forms to be considered here would be grouped
with forms already described if our taxonomy were based on more sophis-
ticated criteria than the mere labelling of forms on a somewhat superficial level. In chapters IV, V, and VI, we shall consider more
fundamental linguistic processes within a considerably more abstract
theoretical framework. The presentation there, however, takes for
granted much of the data presented here. As before, the account here is
a description of affixes and their relation to the function of the verb form.

    -'e is the most common singular imperative suffix for verb stems
ending in a consonant. The plural suffix is -am, but the singular suffix is

often used for the plural too. Verb stems ending in a vowel usually take a
glottal stop for the imperative singular and either -am or -yam for the
plural. We encountered considerable variation among speakers as to the
plural imperative forms, and also some inconsistencies on the part of
individual speakers. However, if the stem ended in i, the plural imperative ending was always -yam. Where stems ended in a glottal stop, there
was either no change for the imperative, or the vowel preceding the glottal
stop was repeated after the glottal stop for the imperative singular. For
the plural ending, the glottal stop was commonly dropped and -am added if
the preceding vowel was a; if not, then -yam was added to the stem and the
glottal stop was retained. Quite frequently the -'e suffix is realized as a
discontinuous affix with the glottal stop infixed before the final consonant.
The -e was often realized as -a.

Imperative forms have no subect or object prefixes if the subject is
second person singular or plural and the object is third person singular.
First person plural subjects are the only other subjects possible ("Let's
V"), but these have to be marked with the prefix cem-. In such cases,
the object must also be represented by a prefix. When an object prefix
occurs, a subject prefix also occurs—with the single exception of the
reflexive object pronoun tax-, as in tax-wayni-yam "call each other" (or
"call yourselves").

The Desert Cahuilla imperative forms appear to be much the same as
the Mountain Cahuilla forms.[13] We have only a little data on Wanikik
imperatives, but this also reveals no significant differences.

The examples following are all taken from Mountain Cahuilla:

55.	SG	PL
	ne-'-naqma-'	ne-'em-naqma-'am
	me-you-listen-IMP	me-you-listen-IMP
	"Listen to me. "	
	ku'p-e (< kup)	kup-am
	"Sleep!"	
	tav-e/tav-'e	tav-am
	"Put it...."	

[13]For a more detailed description of the Desert forms, see Fuchs (18, 31-34).

SG	PL
paxa-ni' 'e-'ac	paxa-ni-'am 'em-'ac-m-i
enter-CAUS-IMP your-horse	enter-CAUS-IMP your-horse-PL-ACC
"Stable your horse."	"Stable your horses."
wayi-'	wayi-'yam
"Swim!"	
way-ni-∅	way-ni-yam
"Call him!"	
	pi-cem-qwa-'a pi-cem-qwa-am
	it-we-eat-IMP
	"Let's eat it!"
mu'aqi-'	mu'aqi-yam
"Pile it up!"	

-na is the exhortative suffix. Since there is no negative imperative, the exhortative suffix is used instead. The semantic difference between the imperative and an affirmative -na appears to be primarily one of degree. The exhortative is somehow felt to be more polite and less threatening than the rather abrupt imperative. However, Fuchs, in her monograph on the Desert dialect (32), has grouped the imperative and the -na forms together under the rubric "Injunktiv" and has differentiated them by means of the "absolut"/"nich-absolut" contrast referred to earlier. Though both are requests, she says, the -na forms represent the situation from the viewpoint of the participant, while imperatives, presumably, represent the action through the perspective of the speaker or listener. Fuchs' distinction is far from clear for these forms, and her discussion of these examples provides little clarification:

56. D. Ca neken takuc pe-cem-wati 'et, ... 'ay 'esan kwas'i

    "Came Takwish, 'Let's take him out (of oven), already
    I'm sure he's done.'"

57. D. Ca   'et pi-hiw-qal menro·y 'enga hem-yax-wen, havun

pi-cem-pangalin-nah pic-cem-kus-na hem-yax-wen

"Indeed he's sitting there Menroy, they say,

first let's lassoe him, let's tease him."

For convenience we shall translate Fuchs' discussion of these sentences:

> In the first example, with the imperative form pecemwáti, the
> performance of the request is relevant mainly in its result: it is
> important that the food is ready for Takwish. In the second
> example, the act of lassoing is more the point, and the teasing
> itself, rather than catching him with the lassoe or making him
> angry; therefore the action is seen from the viewpoint of the
> participant.
>
> (pp. 31-32)

This kind of explanation, while it may be suitable for the analysis of
narrative, does not provide a very clear or consistent basis for character-
izing ordinary spoken usage. One characteristic difference seen in both
Fuchs' examples and our own Mountain and Wanikik forms is that imperatives referred only to immediate action whereas exhortatives could refer to
action further in the future, as for example in the following example, also
from Fuchs:

58. D. Ca   'enga pax-e 'enga tavt-em- me'-mua'-na

"There go in, there the rabbits them you shoot."

or, more idiomatically,

"Go in there and you can shoot the rabbits there."

The exhortative, -na suffix has a variant -an whose occurrence seems
to be governed by the same conditions as those for the -alu variant of the
potentive -pulu or -pu', and the -ap(i) variant of the unrealized affix -pi.

-ve and -pi denote realized and unrealized events respectively. They
are suffixed to verbs which are, most characteristically, in embedded
sentences. Both suffixes occur in five constructions which appear, on the
surface level at least, to be quite distinct.

First, they are suffixed onto verb forms to which pic-, the subordinating or "complementizing" prefix, has been attached.

59. M. Ca   pi-cem-'e'nan-we'   pic-pe-qwa-qal-i-ve

           it-we-know-DUR   that-it-eat-DUR-i-[+R]
                 PAST

           "We knew that he had been eating it. "

60. M. Ca   pe-m-'e'nan-we'   pic-pe-'-qua'-ap

           it-they-knew-DUR   THAT-it-you-eat- [-R]
                 PAST

           "They knew that you would eat it. "

61. W. Ca   tamyat   'ekwacmal   pi-yik   yax-qal   qawa

           sun   boy   him-to   tell-DUR   not

           pic-hici-pi   tewalavel pi-yik

           THAT-go-[-R]devil   him-to

           "The Sun told the boy not to go the Devil. "

Note that -pi is realized as -ap (and, rarely, as -api) after certain stems with final consonants.

    Secondly, both -ve and -pi occur on verbs which form part of what Fuchs calls festen Wendungen "fixed expressions, " with the copular verb miyaxwen. With -ve, this construction means "have V-ed, " and with -pi, the meaning is "have to V" or "must V":

62. ne-pacxam-ve   miyaxwe

    I-wash-[+R]   be

    "I've done some washing. "

63. D. Ca   ne-hici-pi   miyax-wen'e   'ayax

           I-go-[-R]   be-DUR   then
                   PAST

           "I had to go, then. "

    Relative clauses are the third type of construction in which these affixes appear. The affix -ve occurs on verbs in past relative construc-tions where the subject of the relative is not coreferential with the head noun phrase in the matrix sentence. The relative constructions in which

-pi occurs are of the same type except that the relative construction is a
future one. However, when durative markers also occur in -ve forms,
the forms can appear in constructions where the lower subject is the
coreferential noun phrase. And -pi is used a little more often for relative
constructions with coreferential lower subjects than is -ve.

64. M.Ca naxanic pe' Luupi mamayaw-ve

      man   that   Lupi help-[+R]

      "The man that Lupi helped...."

65. M.Ca naxanic pe' ne-mamayaw-pi

      man   that   I-help-[-R]

      "The man that I will help...."

The realized affix -ve and, somewhat more rarely, the unrealized
affix -pi also occur on verbs containing the location prefixes listed earlier
for position one. Such forms, unlike the relative forms just described,
never occur with a plural noun suffix:

66. M.Ca pa-hem-hici-ve

      where-they-go[+R]

      "...where they went."

67. M.Ca pi-yk-ne-hici-pi

      it-to-I-go-[-R]

      "...to where I will go."

However, these forms can take postpositions, as the following example
shows:

68. W.Ca ngiy-law-qal   tamyat nac-qal-i-vi-yka

      return-to-DUR sun   sit-DUR-i-[-R]-to

      "He was coming back to where the sun set."

Finally, both -ve and -pi appear on verb forms which have no subject
prefix either present or, as with the third person singular, understood.

In such cases, the realized and unrealized suffixes have an extra consonant, l and c respectively. The suffixes are thus -vel and -pic. In a
sense, such verb forms are understood as having a subject, but the subject
is unspecified in about the same way as it is unspecified in the English
sentence

69. The fortress was attacked yesterday.

The following Mountain Cahuilla examples are not atypical:

70. M. Ca 'aya   nanvanek   qua'-ap(i)c

        now   ready   eat-[-R]

        "They (the beans) are ready to eat."

71. M. Ca kikit-am qwa'-i-vel-em

        child-PL eat-i-[+R]-PL

        "The children have been eaten."

72. M. Ca pi-cem-teew-'i   wa'ic   qwa'-apic-i

        it-we-see-PAST meat   eat-[-R]-ACC

        "We saw the meat to be eaten."

The suffix -ve occurs on verb forms in one other kind of construction,
one rather like the English gerundive form, snarling, in

73. The lion leapt at me snarling.

where the subject understood for snarling is the lion, not me. The time
reference of this Cahuilla "gerundive" is, as in English, either simultaneous with that of the higher verb or included within the time span for the
higher verb. The subjects of the higher and lower verbs are coreferential,
and the -ve suffix always follows immediately after a durative suffix, -qal
for singular subjects and -wen for plural subjects.

74. M. Ca 'e-menvax-ne   pa-'-'ayáw-qal-i-ve

        you-come-FUT   it-you-want-DUR-i-[+R]

        "You can come if you want."

75. M. Ca   pi-'-sicúmin-qa   pic-pe-'-temin-pi

    it-you-remember-DUR   THAT-it-you-shut-[-R]

    'e-hici-qal-i-v

    you-go-DUR-i-[+R]

    "Do you remember to close the door as you go out? "

It should be noted that verb forms like these are identical in form to those of past durative verbs in relative constructions where the lower subject is not coreferential with the head noun phrase in the higher sentence. This can lead to ambiguity, as in sentences like the following:

76. M. Ca   naxac   pe-haal-qal-<u>i</u>-ve   taatwal-lew-qa

    man   him-look-DUR-<u>i</u>-[+R]   blind-go-DUR
             for

which can mean either

    "The man is going blind looking for him. "

or

    "The man he was looking for is going blind. "

-<u>nuk</u> appears on non-durative verbs without subject prefixes. Its understood subject is always coreferential with the subject of the sentence in which it is embedded. The time reference of -<u>nuk</u> verb forms is to a time previous to the time reference of the verb form in its higher sentence.

77. M. Ca   pe-'áyw-alu'u   taxmu'at-i   pe-'-naqma-nuk

    it-you-like-POT   song-ACC   it-you-hear-after

    "You might like the song, having heard it. "

78. M. Ca   me-n-kwapi-ni-nuk   me-n-wayiki-ni-qa'

    them-I-wake-CAUS-after   them-I-eat-CAUS-DUR
                                                       PAST

    "After awakening them, I fed them. "

-<u>nax</u> is an infrequent nominalizing suffix meaning "be supposed to V. " Its accusative form is -<u>naxti,</u> or sometimes -<u>naxati,</u> which suggests

*-naxat as the underlying nominative form. The plural subject and object forms are -naxtem and -naxtemi respectively. Occasionally the suffixes -wetem and -wetmi are used instead. We shall call this suffix the EXPECTIVE suffix (EXP).

79. M. Ca me-n-teew-'i   pe'   pe-walin-wen-naxt-em-i

    them-I-see-PAST which it-dig-DUR-EXP-PL-I

    "I saw those who were/are to dig (it)."

80. M. Ca ne'e-y new-wayiki-n-nax   pic-ik

    I-ACC   me-eat-CAUS-EXP arrive-INCEPT

    "The one who's going to feed me is coming."

These constructions are something like relative clauses without a lexical head noun phrase. When there is a lexical head, the inceptive suffix -ka' is optionally added after -nax. So the nominative and accusative singular endings are -nax-ka' and -nax-kat-i respectively, and the plural endings, -nax-kat-em and -nax-kat-(e)m-i. These occur in relative constructions with future time reference. The lexical head is always coreferential with the subject of the lower verb:

81. M.Ca nicil̃   pe' pe   ney-yaw-ici-nax-ka'   hí-yi   'ayax-we

   woman that which me-hold-go-EXP-INCEPT her-mother be-DUR
                     like PRES

   "The woman who is going to carry me is like her mother."

 -ic and -et are nominalizing suffixes used in present and past relative constructions in which the head noun phrase is coreferential with the lower subject. -et, which must be preceded by the durative qal in such constructions, appears in present relative constructions, while -ic, which never occurs after a durative affix, appears in past relative constructions.

82. W. Ca 'ekwacmal-em pi' tew-ic-em   'awal-i   'i-pa   hém-qa

    boy-PL   who find-REL-PL dog-ACC this-at they-be
            PAST

   "The boys who found the dog are here."

83. M.Ca pe-'-e'nan-qa   nawicmal-i pe' taxmu-qal-et-i

    her-you-know-DUR   girl-ACC   that sing-DUR-REL-ACC
         PRES   PRES

    "Do you know the girl who is singing?"

-pa is a syntactic suffix attached to verbs. When suffixed to a verb
form, it marks the subordination of that form as an adverbial modifier of
time, reason, or condition to some higher clause. The verb form is
always a realized form.

84. M.Ca pal   muy-vaneke-pa

    water   fill-come-as

    "As the water rose...."

85. W.Ca 'angapa tamyat ngiy-lew-qal-i-pa   'ekwacmal-i

    again   sun   return-go-DUR-i-as boy-ACC

    pe-teteya-qal taxliswet-em me-teew-qal-i-ve   tema-yka

    him-tell-DUR person-PL   them-see-DUR-i-[+R] earth-to

    "The Sun having returned again, he told the boy that he had
    seen people on the earth."

86. W.Ca qawa 'em-yax-i-pa huyta pal   tax-'em-vukmeni-nem qawal

    not   you-say-i-as   huyta water self-you-turn-FUT   rock

    "If you (plural) don't say 'huyta,' the water will turn you into
    rock."

-'a is a nominalizing suffix on non-durative verb forms, converting
them into forms having either nominal or adjectival function. Although the
action or event represented by the verb form is understood as having been
realized, these forms seem to represent a resulting state rather than a
completed activity. So this affix might well be called a "realized state"
affix. The verb form, which always (except for the third person singular)
has a subject prefix, takes the usual accusative and plural noun inflections.

88. M.Ca   hem-cung'ic-lew-'a   ne-heñew-ni-'i

             they-lie-go-[+R]   me-anger-CAUS-PAST

             "Their lying angered me."

One other process, one which is now no longer productive, is reduplication. It will not be dealt with in detail here since it is complex, often
dependent on quite idiosyncratic lexical properties, and only marginally
related to the focuses of the present study. There is a useful but incomplete description in Fuchs (69-73) of some reduplication phenomena in
Desert Cahuilla, and our own work on the other two dialects suggests that
they differ only in relatively trivial detail from the Desert dialect, in this
respect at least.

As in many other languages, the reduplication of part or all of a verb
stem is most often associated with past or perfective forms on the one hand,
and distributive forms on the other. The latter is a particularly common
phenomenon in Cahuilla. The notion distributive is notoriously hard to
define. It includes the representation of actions or events as repeated
simultaneously by more than one "performer," or occurring at several
different times or locations, or, being performed on more than one object,
or, especially in the case of a single event, happening in an especially
intense way.

The most common form of distributive reduplication is the repetition
of the initial consonant and vowel of a root. Thus the verb root nac "be
somewhere," "sit," "live, inhabit" has a reduplicated version ná-nac
"dwell for a long time or permanently." Fuchs has pointed out (54) that
reduplicated distributives are almost all intransitive, while the apparently
equivalent transitive distributive forms are usually unreduplicated but have
an -an suffix (realized sometimes as -n), -i or -e, and, with certain roots
and derivational affixes, -m or -ay. Our own observations suggest a
correlation of -m and -ay with the affix -ngi "go around V-ing," but the
evidence for this is scanty.

One example of the often unpredictable alternations are the various
distributive forms corresponding to the non-distributive stem pangálin
"lassoe," used in our example 57. Fuchs gives pangálamn, pangánglami
and pangálayn as alternative distributive stems. Our own investigations
suggested that each of these has very slightly different interpretations but
we are unable to pin down precisely what the differences were. One of our
consultants several times substituted pangáli-ngi for pangálayn, translat-
ing both as "going around lassoing everyone."

There are two special verb stems serving functions like those of such English auxiliary verbs as do. The two Cahuilla forms are almost certainly historically related, one as a reduplicated version of the other. Both normally follow another verb, a verb which carries most of the semantic content.

The form yáya (in Mountain and Desert Cahuilla) or yaax (in Wanikik Cahuilla) sometimes has a subject prefix, sometimes not. It takes no other kind of inflection. It is usually translated as "try to V" when it has a subject prefix, and "for sure" when there is none.

89. M. Ca   pi-cem-kukul-ne   yaya

            it-we-do-FUT   try

            "Let's go and do it!"

90. M. Ca   ne-cengen-'i   yaya

            I-dance-[+R]   begin

            "I began to dance."

91. M. Ca   cem-yayax   pe-cem-yaw-'i

            we-try   it-grasp-PAST

            "We tried to grab hold of it."

The verb yax, which also occurs normally after another verb, is, in most cases, translated as "V a little," but occasionally it appears to have no isolable semantic interpretation at all. Unlike the yaya/yaax forms, this yax can take the regular verg inflections, and even the derivational affixes. The verb preceding it is uninflected, but may have derivational affixes such as -ici.

92. D. Ca   pe-l   pe-nga naxaac ca   pax-a-lu yax-'i   wilal

            then-QUOT it-at   man   just   enter-go do-PAST Ferret

            "Then Ferret slipped in."

                                              (Texts:61)

The effect of yax can most easily be gauged by a comparison of the left- and right-hand columns of table 93 below. The sentences are all in Mountain Cahuilla.

93.	I.	pe-teew-'i	teew pi-yax-'i
		"He saw it."	"He glanced at it."
	II.	pi-hivin-qa'a	hiv pi-ya-qa'a
		"He was taking it."	"He was taking a little."
	III.	'ax-hem-taxmu-ne	taxmu 'ax-hem- ya-ne
		"They will sing."	"They will sing a little."

2.7 Cupeño: Sentence Enclitics and Verb Forms

2.7.1 Sentence Enclitics

As noted earlier in this chapter, sentence enclitics are normally suffixed to the first word of a sentence. In Cupeño, they only occasionally appear in smaller units within a sentence. The first word, which can be almost any word with any function, is quite often me, which can serve either as a sentence introducer or a conjunction meaning "and." There is an interesting possibility of a link with the plural noun suffix and with the plural subject enclitic, both of them having -me as a likely underlying form. Such a link would be relevant not only to an historical framework but also to a synchronic abstract syntactic framework.

Except for the quotative enclitic, which is really a free form since it has word stress in most of its occurrences and occurs almost anywhere in a sentence, Cupeño enclitics are strictly ordered relative to each other. Although they are almost never all filled, there are four possible positions in an enclitic complex. In the first position the dubitative -še may appear. In the second, either the potentive -qwe or a -t may occur. This -t, identified by J. Hill as an emphatic enclitic, frequently occurs in contexts where an emphatic interpretation would seem inappropriate, and is easily confused with the second person singular subject enclitic -t; its existence as a separate enclitic can only be considered questionable. In the third position are the subject enclitics, and in the fourth either the realization enclitic or a plural subject enclitic. But this account is only partially adequate since it fails to take into consideration the rather complex co-occurrence restrictions, most—but not all—of which appear to be semantic.

These cannot all be described here for they would make up a separate study in themselves. However, a few will be described here since they are relevant to matters discussed in subsequent chapters of this study. First, when the first word in a sentence is a subject pronoun, subject enclitics occur immediately after it only with present tense verbs or with predicate nominals where a present tense copular verb has clearly been deleted. Such sentences are almost always declarative. When ordinary declarative sentences have past or future tense verbs, then one of the two realization enclitics is used instead. However, when a dubitative and/or potentive enclitic intervenes, it is followed by the [+REALIZED] enclitic -əp if the verb is a past form or has past time reference; it is followed by the subject enclitic if the time reference is present; by both the subject enclitic and the [-REALIZED] enclitic -pə if the time reference is future or where a "should have" or "should" meaning is represented.

The following paradigm for the present tense of the intransitive verb stem yəkwín- "be scared" and the transitive verb stem náqma "hear" shows the subject enclitics used after pronoun subjects:

94.

nə'ə-n yəkwín-qa	nə'-nə naqma-qa
"I'm scared."	"I hear."
'ə-'ət yəkwín-qa	'ə-'ə-(pə) naqma-qa
"You (sg) are scared."	"You hear."
pə'-pə yəkwín-qa	pə-pə' naqma-qa
"He's scared."	"He hears."
cəm-ə-c yəkwin-wə	cəm-cəmə naqma-wə
"We're scared."	"We hear."
'əm-ə-m-əl yəkwín-wə	'əm-ə-m-əl naqma-wə
"You (pl) are scared."	"You (pl) hear."
pəm-ə-m-əl yəkwín-wə	pəm-əm-əl naqma-wə
"They are scared."	"They hear."

Any of the subject markers for the intransitive verb, except for the second person singular -t may optionally be used for the transitive verb, but the reverse is not the case. The various schwa forms within hyphens may be epenthetic vowels or, possibly, part of the adjacent morpheme. Where more than one subject enclitic is found, either one may be omitted.

Enclitics are often omitted from the second and third person singular forms. An alternative third person singular subject enclitic is -əm, and another alternative, -ə, which is quite common for the third singular, may really be nominative singular enclitic for both second and third person singular subjects, thus accounting for the additional -ə in the second singular, and providing a singular counterpart for the nominative plural -əl.

The same subject enclitics, with the transitive/intransitive differences, are used when a word other than a subject noun phrase begins a sentence. However, -nə, which was described earlier as occurring with transitive verbs, occasionally appears as the first person subject enclitic even when the verb is intransitive. In all such cases, the word to which it is suffixed ends in a consonant, but the exact details of the environment conditioning this CV realization are unclear. In most cases when a consonant precedes the -n enclitic, an epenthetic schwa is inserted, as in sentence example (96) below. All three sentences following show the subject enclitics for present tense verb forms only. Subject enclitics for future tense verb forms differ in some respects, as our discussion will soon show.

95. hawin-wən-m-əl   'aya

    sing-DUR-PL-SUBJ now

    "They're singing now."

96. qwa-qal-ə-n   nə-pəyi-ki-'a

    eat-DUR-ə-I my-pinole-POS-POS

    "I'm eating my pinole."

97. 'axwác-əm   kulawət-i   'itú-qa

    that-SUBJ   wood-ACC   steal-DUR

    "That one is stealing wood."

According to J. Hill's study (1966:10), Cupeño has also two object enclitics. They are given a -i for second person singular objects and -mə for third singular or plural objects. Despite considerable work with the same Cupeño consultant that Hill worked with earlier, we were unable to find any trace of these, nor do they occur in texts. Now the differences between the subject enclitics for transitive and intransitive verbs are probably relics of old object enclitics, but their form does not appear to be determined in any way by the person and number of the object, just by the subject person and number. Unfortunately, Hill gives only two example of utterances with object enclitics, the first of which is rejected by all of our consultants, including the one used by Hill, and the second obviously involves a misinterpretation of the data. We show both examples below, with Hill's literal morpheme-by-morpheme gloss and our own more collo-quial gloss based upon Hill's interpretation:

98. tukumáy   mə́-m-pə   suqəti   pati

    tomorrow and-it-FOLLOWING   deer   (he)-will
                  TIME   shoot

    "Tomorrow he will shoot the deer (sg)."

                                  (Hill, 1966:13)

99. múluk-n-i   'i-qəqəl   'ə'əy

    first-I-you   you(-I-)-was   you
                 biting

    "First I was biting you (sg)."

                                  (Hill, 1966:80)

Our Cupeño consultants only accepted 98 after adding a final <u>n</u> to the last word, making it <u>patin</u>, and then only with the interpretation

    "Tomorrow <u>they</u> will shoot the deer (sg)."

    The time reference of the sentence 98 is future, and we have not yet shown the relevant subject enclitics. They are shown here for the verb ha𝟊ax "go" (which is probably related to the Cahuilla verb with the same meaning, <u>hici</u>).

100. tukumáy-nə-pə	ha𝟊ax	"Tomorrow I'll go."
tomorrow-I-[-R]	go	
tukumáy-'ə-pə	ha𝟊ax	"Tomorrow you (sg) will go."
tomorrow-you-[-R]	go	

tukumáy-pə	ha¢ax	"Tomorrow he'll go. "
tomorrow-[-R]	go	
tukumáy-cə-pə	ha¢ax	"Tomorrow we'll go. "
tomorrow-we[-R]	go	
tukumáy-əm-pə	ha¢ax	"Tomorrow you (pl) will go. "
tomorrow-you-[-R]	go	
tukumáy-məm-pə	ha¢ax	"Tomorrow they'll go. "
tomorrow-they-[-R]	go	

The third person plural form in 100, like 98, has an enclitic məm. But in 100 the verb is clearly intransitive; there is no need to break down this enclitic form into some other element plus an object enclitic. Furthermore, since the Hill translation is incorrect, we shall have to re-analyze Hill's mə as the third person plural subject enclitic, if the Hill analysis is to be maintained, since there is no other candidate. However, since the enclitic remains the same for intransitive verbs, there seems not to be any point in positing an object enclitic.

Hill's other example, 99, is equally unconvincing. The sentence is good Cupeño and our more colloquial gloss is correct. Now if the sentence had no object enclitic, it would be:

101. múluk-nə   'i-qə-qəl   'ə'ˌəy

   first-I   you-bite-DUR   you
              OBJ

"First I was biting you. "

By an optional but very common vowel harmony process which operates across word boundaries as well as within them, the unstressed vowel of -nə would become i, and 101 would be homophonous with 99, as well as synonymous. So 99 provides no real support for the Hill analysis. In fact it can be demonstrated that it provides no support at all. If another word, such as tuku "yesterday, " is inserted between the first word and the verb, then -ni is rejected by native speakers, and only -ne is accepted. This clearly indicates that the vowel quality of the enclitic in 99 is the result of vowel harmony, and that there is no object enclitic in this sentence. It seems likely then that Cupeño is like its sister languages, Cahuilla and Luiseño, in having no object enclitics. In this respect, all three languages differ from Serrano.

We shall treat the other enclitics in the order in which they occur within the enclitic complex.

-ǰə is the DUBITATIVE enclitic. It is used when the speaker is disclaiming any definite knowledge of the truth of what he is saying, although it is often used in contexts where it is very likely that the statement is true.

102. 'iví-'aw-ǰə-m-pə   yəwaywən

    this-at-DUB-PL-[-R]   talk

    "Here is where they'll talk."

103. cəm-ǰə-t-pə   qay   pi-nanvəx-cə'-ma-n

    we-DUB-(?)-[-R]   not   it-ready-we-PL-VERB
    THEME

    "We must not have got it ready."

104. 'awál-i-ǰə-mə   məqin-wə

    dog-ACC-DUB-PL   kill-DUR
    PRES

    "They are killing the dog."

The dubitative enclitic is also used for embedded question sentences, and the less direct kind of question that in English begins with "I wonder if/whether."

105. (nə'-nə qay hiwcu-qa)   hámə-ǰə-c-pə   cəm   cəm-púy-wən

    (I-I   not know-DUR) whether-DUB-we[-R] we   we-eat-DUR
    PRES   PAST

    "I really don't know whether we ate or not."

106. wə́-ǰə   hí-ya-qal-ət

    whether-DUB   what?-be-DUR-NOM

    "I wonder what it is."

Ordinary yes/no questions differ from the Cupeño equivalent of WH questions both in having steeply rising intonation on the last syllable and in being marked, although optionally, by the dubitative enclitic. Indeed, in rapid conversation, the rising intonation is sometimes dispensed with, the questioning function being signalled by the dubitative alone. However, both markings appear in careful speech. Thus, the declarative sentence

107. 'axwác-im-əl   kikit-am   nanavə-wə

    that-PL-SUBJ boy-PL   fight-DUR
          PL   PRES

    "Those boys are fighting."

corresponds to the following question sentence (where ⟋ indicates rising intonation):

108. 'axwác-im-ɟə-l kikit-am nanavə-ẃə

    "Are those boys fighting?"

-qwə is the potentive enclitic. It is variously translated as "can" "could," "may," "might," "would," "must have," and, if the verb is in the usitative mode, "usually." However the conditional mode of the verb is more common with this enclitic. After <u>cinga</u> "whenever, if," -<u>qwə</u> may occur with the verb in either mode, and there appears to be very little difference in meaning, the conditional here suggesting a lesser degree of reality than does the usitative. A combination of -<u>qwə</u> with the unrealized enclitic -pə and the word <u>hani</u> is used to mean either that the speaker wishes that <u>S</u> (the other content of the sentence) had been the case, or that whoever the sentence subject represents wishes that, etc. There is sometimes ambiguity in this respect. However the first interpretation is far more common, and it is usually translated with the English <u>should have</u> or <u>ought to have</u>. It is just possible that the second meaning is really something more elaborate, such as "the speaker wishes that <u>X</u> had wished to V." We mét with exactly the same problem in Cahuilla with <u>hani</u>.

109. ɟa'a'aw-qwə-l   'ayəw-wən-t-im

    make bread-POT-SUBJ   want-DUR-NOM-PL
    CONDITIONAL   PL

    "They could make bread if they wanted bread."

110. qay-qwə-p   mi'a'aw   mə-qwə-n-pə   'a'a'aɟ

    not-POT-[-R]   arrive   and-POT-I-[-R| bathe
          CONDITIONAL   CONDITIONAL

    "If he hadn't come, I'd have taken a bath. "

111. hani-qwə-n-pə   'isil̃-i   mamayəw

    if only-POT-I-[-R] coyote-ACC   help

    "I wish I could help Coyote. "

112. nə'-qwə-n   haɟa'a

    <u>I</u>-POT-I   go
              CONDITIONAL

    "I can go. "

113. nə'-qwə-n   haɟana

                go
            USITATIVE

    "I usually go. "

    -əp and -pə are the realized and unrealized enclitics respectively. They are most often used to refer to past and future time; in narrative they are used to mark off preceding and subsequent events or actions, regardless of the speaker's perspective. But, as the previous section showed, -pə is used for past or preceding time if the action or event did not really occur. We shall not provide any example sentences here since so many, of every kind, occur in the rest of this study.

    ku'ut is the quotative. Used mainly in traditional narrative, the quotative is an enclitic-like element used when a speaker wishes to indicate that what he is saying is based on hearsay rather than on his own experience. Occasionally, the quotative appears as -<u>kut</u>, without word stress, and suffixed to any word anywhere in a sentence. Both the enclitic and the enclitic-like element can appear several times in a sentence, and in fact, in a Wiláqalpa story text, the sequence <u>kút-kut ku-ku-ku-kút</u> occurs as the teller tries to remember what happens next. When a quotative immediately follows the sentence introducer <u>mə</u>, it is always an unstressed suffix, and it converts the preceding vowel into <u>u</u> (through vowel harmony). The surface form, then, is <u>mú-kut</u>. However, in the Wiláqalpa dialect, the form is <u>məxwút</u>.

2.7.2 Cupeño Verb Forms

There are three quite distinct classes of verbs in Cupeño. The differences appear most obviously in conditional and past tense forms. Two of
the verb classes have special thematic affixes, -in and -yax (or -ax), after
the verb root. We shall refer to these verbs as IN verbs and YAX verbs.
The other verbs will be called simple verbs.

In the following chart, the three verb classes are conflated. Hence
not all the positions shown are possible for all three classes of verbs. To
give an obvious example, the object prefix position is never filled for
intransitive verbs. The subject prefix position is only filled for past
tense simple verbs, since subject markers are *infixed* in past tense IN
and YAX verb forms. Finally, it should be understood that this is an
interim analysis which will be revised later in the light of other data.

114.	I	II	III	IV	V	VI	VII	VIII
	Object Prefix	Subject Prefix (for past tense forms of SIMPLE verbs)	ROOT	Subject Affix (for past tense forms of IN and YAX verbs only)	Plural Affix (for past tense forms of IN verbs)	Theme (for IN and YAX verbs)	Deriva- tional Affixes (Order of affixes varies according to meaning.)	Tense- Aspect Suffix

POSITION I

Object prefixes are usually found where the object is plural, but
singular prefixes sometimes appear, especially where a sentence would
otherwise be ambiguous. In singular imperative constructions, the same
elements are suffixed instead of prefixed. Plural imperatives have no
object markers. The object prefixes are as follows:

115.   SG   PL

    1. ni "me"   cimi "us"

    2. 'i "you"   'imi "you"

    3. pi "him, her, it" mi   "them"

POSITION II

Subject markers, which have the same form as possessives, appear
on past tense forms and are prefixed to simple verbs. Occasionally they
are omitted, especially in long narrative passages, but this omission,
contrary to Hill's claim (1966:27-28), does not distinguish recent past
forms from past forms. We have found no trace of any recent past durative tense. Consultants, when questioned about the omission, almost
inevitably "corrected" it by supplying the missing element. They denied
that there was any time difference when the marker was omitted, although
the same consultants could explain quite clearly the difference between
past duratives and past non-duratives, and even the rather subtle difference between the realized action meaning of the suffix -və and the realized
state meaning of the verb suffix -'a, both of which will be discussed later.
Since subject markers are not omitted from IN or YAX verbs, and consequently past cannot be formally differentiated from recent past for these
two verb classes, the evidence for a recent past tense seems quite
inadequate.

Note that the past non-durative form of a simple verb differs from a
future non-durative only in having a subject prefix, although the presence
of a realized rather than unrealized enclitic is a further indication of
pastness. The following sentences show durative and nondurative past
forms of simple verbs. Future forms are included for comparison.

116. nə'-əp   mi-nə-puyni-qal

      I-[+R]   them-I-feed-DUR
                              PAST

      "I was feeding them"

117. nə'-əp   mi-n -puynin

      I-[+R]   them-I-feed

      "I fed them. "

118. nə'-nə-pə   mi-puynin   tukumáy

      I-I-[-R]   them-feed   tomorrow

      "I will feed them tomorrow. "

119.   nə'-nə-pə   mi-puynin-nac   'ivi-'aw

    I-I-[-R]   them-feed-DUR   this-at
                     FUT

    "I'll be feeding them here. "

    The full set of subject prefixes is given below. Note that the same
forms are also used in position IV for IN and YAX verbs. The plural
forms for IN verbs, however, have their final m replaced by a glottal
stop (!), under the regular phonological rule which is triggered by the
occurrence of an m immediately before another m. The same process
occurs, of course, whenever plural subject markers precede simple verbs
beginning with m:

120.   cəm-əp   cə'-mamayəw

    we-[+R]   we-help

    "We helped. "

121.   SUBJECT MARKERS

	SG		PL	
1.	nə-	"I"	cəm-	"we"
2.	'ə-	"you"	'əm-	"you"
3.	pə-	"he, she, it"	pəm-	"they"

    Positions III and IV require no further discussion since they have
already been covered in this description.

POSITION V

    A plural affix having an underlying form -mə is attached after plural
subject markers on IN verbs only. It combines with the -in theme following to become man. The following examples show the contrast between
singular forms, which lack the affix, and plural forms:

122.   haw-pə-n-əp   Kupa-'aw

    sing-he-IN-[+R]   Cupa-at

    "He sang at Cupa. "

123. haw-pə'-ma-n-əp   tuku

     sing-they-PL-IN-[+R]   yesterday

     "They sang yesterday."

Surprisingly, the same plural affix is infixed between one postposition and its pronominal base. The postposition is -yka "toward, behind (where motion is involved)." The Cupeño for "toward him" is pə́-yka, but for "toward them" it is pə́'-m-yka. Quite possibly this reflects an older motion verb, perhaps one also related to the inceptive "going to" suffix, realized as -qat in Cupeño, -ka' in Cahuilla, and the plural form -kutum in Luiseño.

POSITION VI

Although there are related thematic affixes in Luiseño, and traces of IN, at least, in Cahuilla, Cupeño is unique among the Takic languages in allowing subject marker infixation. J. Hill has, in a very interesting discussion (1969:348-356), claimed that IN verbs indicate volitional activity:

> The actor performs the action "on purpose," choosing from a
> universe of actions that might be possible in a given situation.
> > (p. 348)

With YAX verbs, on the other hand,

> The actor performs an action, or assumes a state, because it was
> imposed on him either by accident or by the action of some other
> actor.
> > (p. 348)

The simple verbs represent "natural" actions:

> The actor performs the action because it is culturally, psycho-
> logically, or physiologically required of him, or is completely
> natural and expected in a given situation.
> > (p. 348)

Historically, as will be further discussed in a later chapter, the -in affix is probably descended from a Proto-Uto-Aztecan causative, recon- structible as *-ina. What is probably a later reflex of this PUA causative is the Cupan causative -ni, which appears to have come in later. The -ni still appears to be productive. The -yax affix is related to a verb "be" in all three languages. As so often happens with affixes, their functions and meanings have changed in quite idiosyncratic ways so that the older causa- tive and stative meanings have not always been preserved to the same

degree with different verb roots. Hill's account appears to work for the
examples given in the paper, but an examination of dozens of other verbs
reveals them to be less amenable to such an analysis. We took almost
seventy-five verb roots and invented simple, IN and YAX variants without
checking in advance as to whether these variants existed. The basis for
our choice was alphabetical order. Below is part of our list of verbs beginning with <u>c</u>. Only those roots associated with at least two verb classes are
included. The meanings are those given by our major Kupa Cupeño
consultant.

124. ROOT	SIMPLE MEANING	<u>IN</u> MEANING	<u>YAX</u> MEANING	-<u>nin</u> CAUSATIVE
cal-	husk	Ø	be shelled	make X husk
caməl-	Ø	polish	sparkle	Ø
caqw-	Ø	catch	be caught	Ø
cangnəw-	be angry.	Ø	Ø	make X angry
ca$-	Ø	shine something	be shining	Ø
ca$pəl-	quilt	Ø	be patched	Ø
cawəl-	shake (clothes)	shake (clothes)	be shaken	Ø
caway-	Ø	make X climb	climb	Ø
cayəw-	Ø	do woman's dance	stand up	Ø
ca'ay-	Ø	raise	be risen (of Christ)	Ø
cəq-	Ø	make X lean	be leaning	Ø
cəl-	Ø	cut (tr.)	be cut	Ø
cəm-	Ø	make X be quiet	be quiet	Ø
cənen	Ø	make X roll	roll (intr.)	Ø
cəngən-	Ø	kick	be kicked	Ø
cəx-	winnow	make X clean	be clean	Ø
cilil-	Ø	jingle turtle rattle	rattle (of snake)	Ø
cipil-	Ø	make X break	be broken	Ø
civ-	taste bitter	pick (greens)	pluck (hairs) be plucked (grass)	Ø
cul-	be deep	make X deep	be deep	Ø
culup-	Ø	put in	go in	Ø
cumum-	Ø	suck out (venom)	be sucked	Ø
cung-	Ø	kiss	be kissed	Ø
cu'p-	Ø	close eyes	be closed	Ø
cuqəm-	Ø	save (food)	remain	Ø
cus	Ø	fry bread	be fried (of bread)	melt down
cux-	melt (intr.)	spit	be spat out	Ø

Our list suffers from several defects. First, we have not included
forms with other derivational affixes, some of which may fill in part of

a semantic paradigm. Secondly, the absence of causative forms does not reflect their non-existence, since our elicitation unfortunately was incomplete in this respect. Thirdly, we have not factored out probably homophonous roots, as, for example, civ-, for which the simple verb form has a meaning too different from those of the IN and YAX forms to be considered as belonging to the same root.

Nevertheless, the list suggests that, despite the idiosyncratic meaning variations and specializations, IN has some causative force, and YAX is primarily stative. Some IN/YAX contrasts look like active versus passive contrasts, others like action versus resulting state. This is not the place for a deeper analysis, for which, in any case, more data are needed. But it is interesting that where a simple verb is intransitive, there is, in our data, rarely a YAX form and the IN form has a causative meaning. Where a simple verb is lacking, it is almost always the case that there are both IN and YAX forms, and that the relation is either as active to passive or as cause to effect. It is hardly surprising that simple verbs would represent "natural" actions—these are the oldest verbs. The small number of simple transitive verbs in our list reflects the fact that these forms only infrequently have IN and YAX forms. The volitional character of IN verbs with human subjects is predictable from the fact that human causation so often involves conscious intention. The Hill characterization of YAX forms, quoted above, reflects the stative/passive character of the -yax affix. Our analysis here started with verb forms. Although we have not undertaken such an analysis, it seems likely that an analysis starting with semantic notions would be productive. For example, where more "basic" meanings such as "go" are represented by YAX verbs,[14] the IN forms are almost always causatives. Where the "basic" meanings are represented by IN verbs, the YAX forms are likely to be passive or to represent "resulting state." Thus, to go outside our list above, if haǰax "go," a YAX verb, is converted into an IN verb, haǰin, the meaning is "make go" or "make walk;" likewise, kwatax "awake" (intr.) corresponds to the IN form kwatin "cause to be awake." On the other hand, ngəpəpin "drag" and ngisin "scratch" correspond to ngəpəpyax "be dragged," and ngisax "be scratched," respectively.

---

[14]Here "basic" is used in a very informal, intuitive sense. We are, of course, making no theoretical claims as to the semantic base of a generative-semantic grammar.

POSITION VII

The affixes allowed in this position appear alone or in combination with each other, the ordering being determined primarily by semantic factors. The meanings given below for the affixes are the most common ones. In fact, the meanings can be modified considerably by particular verb roots, and also by other derivational affixes preceding the affix in question.

125. -ləw   "go somewhere else and V," "go there to V"

    -max   "V on behalf of someone," BENEFACTIVE

    -mi'aw   "arrive V-ing," "come and then V"

    -nəq and -vənəq "come along V-ing." These forms sometimes appear to be in free variation; sometimes one of the forms is required by a particular root, e.g. yawnəq "come carrying," rather than yawvənəq, although this latter form is not rejected outright. For plural subjects, the suppletive -vəmax is used. Another suppletive form may optionally replace -vənəq and -vəmax in future verb forms. This form is -mənmax.

    -nin CAUSATIVE, "make X V." This appears to be a combination of -ni and the IN theme. However, -nin occurs only on simple verb forms.

    -ngi "go away V-ing," also "go back V-ing."

    -vicu DESIDERATIVE, "wish/want to V."

The following sentences show various combinations and orderings of these affixes:

126. iví-y-nə   pa'-vicu-qa

    this-ACC-I   drink-want-DUR
                                  PRES

    "I want to drink this."

127. iví-y-nə   pa'-ni-qa

                drink-CAUS-DUR
                      PRES

I'm making him drink this," or "I'm making this one drink it."[15]

128. iví-y-nə   pa'nin-vicú-qa

    this-ACC-I   drink-CAUS-want-DUR
                          PRES

"I want to make him drink this."

129. 'iví-y-nə   pa'-vicú-ni-qa

                drink-want-CAUS-DUR
                           PRES

"I'm making him want to drink."
                  thirsty

130. 'iví-y-nə   pa'-nin-vicu-ni-qa

                drink-CAUS-want-CAUS-DUR
                               PRES

"I'm making him want to make her drink this."

131. 'iví-y-nə   'i-pa'-nin-vicu-ni-ləw-max-qat

                you-drink-CAUS-want-CAUS-go-BEN-INCEPT
                OBJ

"I'm gonna go over there for you to make him want to make
her drink."

132. 'iví-y-nə   pa'-ləw-nin-vicu-ngi-qat

                drink-go-CAUS-want-go-INCEPT
                      away

"I'm gonna go off wanting to make him go there and drink."

---

  [15]Because it is not necessary to represent third person singular objects in a sentence, and because, in the more complex structures, extralinguistic factors serve to indicate reference or to disambiguate, many of our examples here will be ambiguous, sometimes multiply ambiguous. Our glosses represent particular translations given by consultants in connection with specific situations.

Normally, of course, the longer sequences of affixes are avoided, since they involve comprehension problems. Instead, separate verbs are used:

133. nə'-ən   'a-yka   ha$ax-qat   pi-yax-í-qat   pə-pa'-pi

      I-I   that-to   go-INCEPT   him-tell-i-INCEPT   he-drink-[-R]

      "I'm gonna go there to tell him to drink."

POSITION VIII

-qa and -wə are the present durative suffixes, singular and plural respectively. However, in a few verbs, the contrast between them is not one of singular versus plural number but of active versus stative, for example,

134. mukíkmal   'aya   ngaq-ya-qa   nə́-ma-nga

      bird   now   perch-YAX-DUR   my-hand-on
                                  PRES

      "The bird is now (in the act of) perching on my hand."

135. mukíkmal   'aya   ngaq-yax-wə   nə́-ma-nga

      bird   now   perch-YAX-DUR   my-hand-on
                                  PRES

      "The bird is now perched on my hand."

-qal and -wən are the past durative suffixes, singular and plural respectively. They too represent an active-stative contrast in some verbs. The past non-durative has the same form as the past durative except that it lacks the final -qal or -wən. Other elements, such as the -əp enclitic and the subject marker affixed to the verb, indicate that the verb refers to past time.

-qat and -qatim are the inceptive suffixes, singular and plural respectively. They are usually translated as "be going to V" or "be about to V." But, embedded after another verb, as in (121), they mean "in order to V." Despite their apparent future time reference, they do not co-occur with the [-REALIZED] enclitic -pə, but have the same enclitic forms as the present durative. The plural suffix is -qtam on the small class of stressless verbs such as təw "see," which has the inceptive plural form təwiqtam.

-nac and -wənə are the future singular and future plural durative suffixes respectively. The corresponding non-durative future forms lack these
suffixes of course. This lack, the presence of the [-REALIZED] enclitic
-pə, and the lack of a subject affix, indicate that future time reference is
intended. One other future form, which occurs so infrequently that it was
apparently not noticed by J. Hill (1966), is the suffix combination -nacqat,
a durative inceptive whose presumed plural forms, *-nacqatim and
*-wənəqatim are rejected by our major consultant. We might well, on the
basis of this rare combination, have posited nine rather than eight positions
in the verb form. The eighth position would then have allowed only -nac,
while all the other inflectional suffixes would have been assigned to the
ninth position.

-na and -wənə are the singular and plural usitative suffixes, meaning
approximately "usually V" or "can V." The potentive enclitic -qwə normally accompanies these suffixes, as in sentence (101) above. The usitative forms are also used in conditional sentences in the "if" clause,
sometimes in both clauses, where they appear to be almost synonymous
with the corresponding conditional verb forms. The usitative suffixes,
without an enclitic, are also used as exhortative:

136. yəwáywən-wənə-c   (or yəwáywən-wəna-c)

    talk-USIT-we
        PL

    "Let's talk."

We have not been able to find forms used as exhortatives with any but first
person plural subjects. J. Hill (1966:32) has grouped this exhortative form
together with the hani construction discussed earlier as a separate
"volitive" mode, treating it as quite unconnected with the usitatives just
described. Since the hani construction has the ordinary present durative
suffix on its verb, it seems as if Hill's grouping is on purely semantic
grounds, without any consideration of the major formal differences. Within
a semantically based grammar we would hope to be able to justify such a
grouping, but a descriptively adequate justification would be expected to
include some more explicit explanation of the interrelation of the semantic
and formal characteristics. Apparently the word hani "let's" carries the
whole modal function, whereas, in these sentences with -wən, the modality
arises from the verb suffix. A deeper analysis would perhaps start with
such observations and perhaps conclude with a linking of not only these

forms, but also the usitative modal suffixes whose formal likeness to the other forms is presently little more than coincidental. The whole matter will be discussed in more detail in the sixth chapter, where a somewhat different segmentation of the verb forms is proposed.

Imperative verbs vary in form according to the verb class. IN and YAX verbs form the imperative singular by dropping their final consonant and adding a glottal stop. The imperative singular of the IN verb hawin "sing," is hawi' "Sing!" and that of the YAX verb haɬax "go" is haɬa' "Go!" The final consonant is retained for plural imperatives, and an -am suffix is added. Thus, the imperative plural forms for hawin and haɬax are hawinam and haɬaxam respectively. Verbs with the -nin causative are like IN verbs in their imperative forms.

Simple verbs ending in consonants, such as kup "sleep," and 'aɬ "bathe," have a glottal stop inserted before the final consonant, and a schwa (often realized as a) after the final consonant. Thus the imperative singular forms are ku'p "Sleep!" and 'a'ɬa "Bathe!" The plural forms have no glottal stops inserted and end in -am: kupam "Sleep!" and 'aɬam "Bathe!" Simple verbs such as qwa "eat," and huu "break wind, fart," which end in vowels, just take on a final glottal stop: qwa' "Eat!" and huu' "Fart!" Quite commonly, if the final vowel is unrounded, it is repeated after the glottal stop: qwa'a "eat." The imperative plural ending is again -am, as in qwaam "Eat!" Note that when the final vowel is not a, a w glide links the two vowels, as in huuwam "Fart!" This glide is purely phonetic phenomenon.

Conditional verb forms also vary according to the class of the verb. For IN and YAX verbs, the conditional form, whether the subject be singular or plural, is the same as the imperative singular. Simple verbs ending in a vowel also have the imperative singular form. But the rule for forming conditionals from simple verbs with a final consonant is a complex one. J. Hill (1970) describes it well when she writes that these conditional forms

> must have two syllables following the stressed vowel of the base,
> if the base ends in a consonant.
>
> (p. 538) .

So, if the stem does not already have two syllables after the stressed one, the final vowel of the stem is reduplicated until the verb form has two syllables after the stress. The vowels are separated from each other by glottal stops. Thus cúx "melt," has the conditional form cú'u'ux; hímay "give goods at a funeral" has the conditional híma'ay; while pinə'wəx "sing songs about enemies" remains unchanged for the conditional mode since it already has two syllables after the stressed one.

The following sentences illustrate some uses of verbs in the conditional mode. A conditional sentence without such a verb in the "if" clause is included for comparison.

137. cinga-qwə-n   qay   pu'u'uy   mə-qwə-n   qa'a'aw

      if-POT-I   not   eat   and-POT-I   die
                               CONDIT   CONDIT

      "If I don't eat, I'll die."

138. hani-qwə-n-pə   tuku   mi-naməq-i   'iví-ta

      if-only-POT-I-[-R]   yesterday   them-meet-IN   this-on
                                       CONDIT

      "I should have met them here yesterday."

139. nə'-qwə-n   həlaq-ya'(a)

      <u>I</u>-POT-I   drown-YAX
                       CONDIT

      "I could/might drown."

140. 'ə'ə-qwə-'ət   hamá'a'an   Loola'a-y   pi'itú-qal-i-y

      you-POT-you   ashamed   Lola-ACC   she-steal-DUR-SUB-ACC
              CONDIT

      kuláwət-i

      wood-ACC

      "You would be ashamed of Lola if she stole wood."

-<u>və</u> and -<u>pi</u> denote realized and unrealized events respectively, and they function almost exactly as do Cahuilla -<u>ve</u> and -<u>pi</u>, and Luiseño -<u>vo</u> and -<u>pi</u>. There are some minor differences, most of which are discussed in our later chapter on complementation and relativization. Both -<u>və</u> and -<u>pi</u> are suffixed to verb stems which occur most characteristically in embedded sentences.

First, they are suffixed onto verb forms in complement sentences, usually as either the subject or object of a higher verb. As objects, these complement verb forms may have <u>pə-ci</u> preceding them as a kind of

subordinating element.　The most common meanings for pə-ci in other
syntactic contexts are "about it" and "by means of it. "

141.　'axwác-pə　nawìkat　qay　'i-yukic-i-qa　　　　　pə-'ac-i

　　　　that-she　　woman　　not　　you-believe-IN-DUR　her-dog-ACC

　　　'ə-tawáŧ-ngi-və(-y)

　　　you-lose-go-[+R]-(ACC)

　　　"That woman doesn't believe that you lost her dog. "

142.　cəm-cəmə　qay　　yikic-in-wən-t-im　　　　nicḷa'vəl-i

　　　　we-we　　　not　　think-IN-DUR-NOM-PL　old-ACC
　　　　　　　　　　　　　　　　　　　　　　　　　　woman

　　　pə-ngiy-pi-y　　　　　ki-ngax

　　　she-leav-[-R]-ACC　　house-from

　　　"We didn't think that the old woman would leave the house. "

143.　nawìcmal　pə-ngiy-və　　　　ni-cangnu-ni-qa

　　　　girl　　　　she-leave-[+R]　me-angry-CAUS-DUR
　　　　　　　　　　　　　　　　　　　　　　　　　　PRES

　　　"The girl's having left makes me angry. "

144.　'atáx-am-əp　　pəm-hiwcu-wən pə-ci　　pə-mi'aw-qal-i-və-y

　　　person-PL-[+R] they-know-DUR it-about he-arrive-DUR-i-[+R]-ACC
　　　　　　　　　　　　PAST

　　　"The Indians knew that he had arrived. "

　　　Secondly, both -və and -pi occur on verbs which are part of a compound verb construction with the copular verb miyax.　With -və, the construction means "have V-ed, " and with -pi, the construction means "have
to V. "　The verb stem to which -və or -pi is affixed has a subject affix
which is prefixed to simple verb stems and, usually, infixed to IN and
YAX stems.

145. cəmə cə'-məq-pi   pə-miyax-wən   suqat-i

      we   we-kill-[-R]   it-be-DUR   deer-ACC
                                 PAST

      "We had to kill a deer."

146. haɬi-pə-yax-və   miyax-wə

      go-he-YAX-[+R]   be-DUR
                        PRES

      "He has gone."

A third construction in which these suffixes occur is the relative construction. Both occur on verbs whose subject is <u>not</u> coreferential with the head noun phrase of the relative construction. But -və appears on past relatives, while -pi appears on future relatives. And -pi, but not -və, sometimes occurs on verbs whose subject is coreferential with the head noun phrase of the construction, though this occurrence is not common.

147. nə'-əp   nə-naqma   'axwác-i   tukumáy   haw-pə-n-pi-y

      I-[+R]   I-hear   that-ACC   tomorrow   sing-he-IN-[-R]-ACC

      "I heard the song that he will sing tomorrow."
                 what

148. naxánic pə̃'   cəm-təw-í-və 'ə́-ki-y   hum-i-qat

      man   that   we-see-<u>i</u>-[+R] your-house paint-IN-INCEPT

      "The man that we saw is going to paint your house."

Finally, both -<u>və</u> and -<u>pi</u> can occur on verbs without subject markers. In such cases they become -<u>vəl</u> and -<u>pic</u> respectively. These occur almost always in passive relative constructions.

149. tukut   pə'   hal-vəl   pí-qi-pə   mi'aw

      wildcat that look-[+R]   he-self-[-R] come
                 for

      "The wildcat that was looked for will come along."

150. 'axwác-im-məm-pə qwa'   maysi-   wəl-in-pic-i

      that-PL-they-[-R]   eat   corn-ACC   trow-IN-[-R]-ACC

      "They will eat the corn that will be grown. "

      -i is a subordinating suffix which follows a durative affix, -qal for
singular subject verbs and -wən for plural subject verbs. Like the
-qalive/-wenive construction in Cahuilla, this "gerundive" has a time
reference simultaneous with that of its higher verb or included within that
time span. However, unlike the Cahuilla construction, the subject of this
construction need not be coreferential with the subject of the higher verb.
In this respect, the construction more closely resembles Cahuilla forms
with the -pa suffix.

151. nə'-əp   nə́-təw   'axwác-i   pə-naaci-qal-i-y

      I-[+R]   I-see   that-ACC   he-pass-DUR-SUB-ACC

      "I saw him passing by. "

152. nə-naaci-qal-i   nə-əp   nə́-təw   'ət-i

      I-pass-DUR-SUB   I-[+R]   I-see   that-ACC

      "As I was passing by, I saw him. "

      -nuk occurs on non-derivative verb stems. Unlike the Cahuilla -nuk,
it does not occur on forms with subject affixes, but like the Cahuilla suffix,
its subject must be coreferential with that of the next higher construction.
Its time reference is to a period prior to that to which the higher verb
refers. It is commonly translated "having V-ed" or "after V-ing. "

153. nə'-nə-pə   cangnu-nuk   ə'əĺlic   miyax-wənə

      I-I-[-R]   angry-after   bad   be-DUR
                                                   FUT

      "When I get mad, I'll be bad. "

154. Ramóna-p   hiwen-pə-yax   haw-in-nuk   'aya cəx-pə-yax-va-nga

      Ramona-[+R]   stop-she-YAX   sing-IN-after   then   light-it-YAX

      "Ramona stopped singing when it was dawn. " OR

      "Ramona, having sung, stopped when it was dawn. "

-ic and -ət are nominalizing suffixes on verbs in past and present relative constructions respectively. They occur in these constructions where
the head noun is coreferential with the lower subject. The durative affixes
-qal and -wən always precede -ət in present relatives. However, duratives
cannot appear with -ic in past relatives. Subject markers do not occur
with either suffix.

155. pə' naxánic pə' tuku   kwiw-yax-ic   kavá'mal-i

   the   man   that yesterday whistle-YAX-REL   olla-ACC
                                         PAST

   cipíl-pə-n

   break-he-IN

   "The man that whistled yesterday broke the olla."

156. 'iví-ta nawíkat mi'aw-qa   pə' wa'ic-i   samsa-vicu-qal-ət

   this-on woman arrive-DUR that meat-ACC buy-want-DUR-REL
                        PRES   PRES

   "A woman is coming here who wants to buy meat."

An -ət suffix also occurs on non-durative forms whose time reference
may be either past or present:

157. 'ət-im-əl   'ə-yik   max-ət-im (or max-at-im)

   it-PL-SUBJ   you-to   give-NOM-PL
      PL

   "They were given to you."

Many -ət forms are indistinguishable from ordinary nouns. Indeed,
"given" in the translation of (157) could be replaced by "gifts." Such a
substitution is less obvious in cases like the following:

158 kiimal caqw-in-ət   'aya ngang-qa

   boy   catch-IN-REL   now   cry-DUR

   "The boy that was captured is crying now."

-'a is a suffix occurring on verb forms whose time reference is
neutral between past and present. We call suffixes "realized" suffixes,

([+R]). On relative verbs, this suffix indicates that the verb's subject is
not coreferential with the head noun phrase of the construction. Verb forms
with this suffix always have a subject marker.

159. kic   hum-nə-n-'a   nə́-yə   pə́-ki

      house   paint-I-IN-[+R] my-mother   her-house

      "The house I painted is my mother's house. "

160. nə'   nə-hiwcu-'a   'ivi ́-y

      I   I-know-[+R]   this-ACC

      "I learned this. "

   -va'ac is a nominalizing suffix noted by J. Hill (1966:111) as forming
animate agentives. She claims that it consists of -və, a "customary affix"
and a suffix -'acə. We would prefer not to label -və as "customary, " since
this -və appears to be the realized suffix referred to earlier, and the
"customary" meaning does not appear to be characteristic of the suffix,
except in the -va'ac forms. The 'ac may be the relative suffix -ic referred
to above. What is interesting about -va'ac is that it is a not uncommon
relativizing suffix, as one of J. Hill's examples indicates:

161. 'ət   nawi ́kat   'atáx-m-i   mi-max-i ́-va'ac

      that   woman   person-PL-ACC   them-give-i-AGT

      "That's the woman who gives things to people. "

                                                   (1966:112)

   As in Cahuilla, reduplication is a minor process dependent quite often
on idiosyncratic lexical properties of some verb roots. The stem is sometimes repeated when repetitive actions are represented: pùcaq-púcaq-pə-
ya-qal "he was going along jumping. " Sometimes, the first consonant and
vowel is reduplicated, as in cə́-cə-l-wə "they are cutting, snipping, " from
cəl-in "cut, " and kú-ku-p-qa "he's sleepy" compared with kup-qa "he's
asleep. " Other kinds of reduplication, which are not relevant to the present study, are described by J. Hill (1966:162-163, 226-230). Some of
these, which she describes as "possibly a residue of [an aspectual] system, " involve only a few verbs and cannot be related systematically to any

meaning differentiation. Several also have a special suffix -aan, of
indeterminate meaning, which may be related to the Cahuilla distributive
-an referred to earlier.

Two specialized verb stems, which might in fact be treated as separate
manifestations of a single stem, occur in combination with other verb
forms and function rather like English auxiliary verbs. They are yáyax,
sometimes translated as "for sure, " sometimes "try, " and yax "do" or
"do a little, " which is used only in Wiláqalpa Cupeño. The yayax form,
unlike yax, never takes verb suffixes.

162. nə'-nə-pə   tan-in   pə-yayax

     I-I-[-R]   dance-in   it-do

     "I'll certainly dance. "

163. cəm-yayax-cə-pə hunwut-i   caqw-in

     we-do-we-[-R]   bear-ACC   catch-IN

     "We'll try to catch the bear. "

164. W. Cu   'amay-nə   pə-yá-qal   pa'-qa

              today-I   it-do-DUR   drink-DUR
                                        PRES

     "I'm drinking a little today. "

Our literal translation gives "do" for both yayax and yax, but this is
merely a convenient abbreviation for the various meanings that these forms
have in different contexts. The meaning of these forms depends to a major
extent upon the other verb occurring with them. Quite often "be" would be
at least as appropriate. Although in Kupa Cupeño, yax is not used as in
164, it does occur with a "be" meaning if the Spanish loanword kúmu "like"
is used. Otherwise, in the Kupa dialect, yax is interpreted as "say,
speak, tell. " However, there are two copular verbs in both dialects,
miyax "be" and 'iyax "be like, " and both of these appear to contain the yax
root. Sentences (165) and (166) below are synonymous. But the second
one contains kumu and yax instead of the single stem 'iyax:

165. mə-ʃə-'ət   Felísita'-i   pi-'íyax-wən

     and-DUB-she   Felicita-ACC   she-resemble-DUR
                                      PAST
     "Was she like Felicita? "

166. mə-ȼə-'ət   kumu Felísita'-i   pə́-yax-wən

     and-DUB-she   like Felicita-ACC   she-be-DUR
                                            PAST

    "Was she like Felicita?

One interesting characteristic of the Kupa dialect is that for a few simple verbs without corresponding IN and YAX forms, there are equivalents to the "V a little" constructions in Cahuilla and in Wiláqalpa Cupeño. These equivalents are IN and YAX versions of the simple verbs. Thus, qwa "eat, " təw "see, " and pa' "drink" correspond to forms like the following:

167. qwa'-cə'-ma-n-wən

    eat-we-PL-in-DUR
                 PAST

    "We ate a little. "

168. təw-pə-∅-qal

    see-he-IN-DUR
            PAST

    "We glanced at it. "

169. cəm-cə-pə   pa'-yax

    we-we-[-R]   drink-YAX

    "We'll drink a little. "

2.8 Luiseño: Sentence Enclitics and Verb Forms

2.8.1 Sentence Enclitics

As in Cupeño, there are four possible positions in an enclitic complex. In the first, the dubitative enclitics -ȼu and -ȼan/-sun, and the desiderative enclitic -xu can occur. In the second position we find a subject enclitic. In the third position one of the realized, [+R], or unrealized, [-R], enclitics may appear. Finally, in fourth position the conditional enclitic -kwa or -ku appears.

-ȼu is a dubitative enclitic, sometimes meaning "perhaps, " sometimes functioning as an interrogative marker. In the non-interrogative sense, it often co-occurs with the unrealized enclitic -po.

170.   ya'áyc-um-ȼu-m   heela-an

    man-PL-DUB-they   sing-DUR
                      PRES

    "Are the men singing? "

171.   Maríya-ȼu   ya-qá   'awáal-ȼu-kun   wa'i-q

    Maria-DUB   say-DUR   dog-DUB-QUOT   bark-DUR
                PRES   PRES

    "Does Maria say whether the dog is barking? "

172.   wunáal-ȼu-po   paal   paa'i-k

    that-DUB-[-R]   water   drink-HAB
                       PAST

    "Apparently he used to drink water. "

This -ȼu (which is also found as -su, -ȼ, and -s), differs from the Cupeño
dubitative in appearing in the Indian equivalents of WH questions:

173.   hax-ȼu   hunwut-i   'aamo-q

    who-DUB   bear-ACC   hunt-DUR
                        PRES

    "Who is hunting the bear? "

   -ȼan or -ȼun is a dubitative enclitic meaning approximately "I
wonder. " It is used also as an interrogative marker and has been
described as a "less direct interrogative" (Kroeber and Grace:61). It is
possible that the final n is a first person singular subject enclitic, meaning "I, " and that the indirectness of questions containing it arises from the
fact that the questioner appears to be asking himself the question although
he really expects to be answered by someone else.

174.   'om-ȼan

    you-DUB

    "How about you? "
    (part of the appropriate response to the question "How are you? ")

175. wunáal-ǿun-po   po-ǿuun   loovi-q

      that-DUB-[-R]   his-heart   fine-DUR
                                     PRES

      "I wonder if he's happy. "

-xu is the desiderative (DES) enclitic. Its most common translations are "I wish that ... ," " "should, " "ought to, " "would. " It is normally followed by the unrealized enclitic -po. If the conditional enclitic -kwa or -ku follows the -po the time reference is usually past, meaning "should have V-ed, " if the usitative -ma suffix is on the verb.

176. noo-xu-n-po   naacaxan   pi' yawa-q   sinaval

      I-DES-I-[-R]   eat   but lack-DUR   money
                                    PRES

      "I'd eat, but I have no money. "

177. Toni-xu-p-ko   'aamo-ma   waxáam

      Tony-DES-[-R]-COND   hunt-USIT   yesterday

      "Tony should have been hunting yesterday. "

178. wunáal-xu-po   po-y   wati

      that-DES-[-R]   he-ACC   hit

      "He should hit him. "

Subject Enclitics, which occur in second position in the enclitic complex, are optional, although they are quite common in Luiseño. In our table of subject enclitics below, the first form is always the form that follows a vowel, while the second is the form following a consonant. However, if the subject enclitic is followed by an enclitic beginning with a consonant, such as the unrealized ([-R]) enclitic -po, then the second form is used.

179.

SUBJECT	I	II
"I"	-n	-nu
"you" (SG)	-p	-up (becomes Ø before -po)

SUBJECT	I	II
THIRD PERSON SINGULAR	-p	-up
"we"	-c	-ca
"you" (PL)	-m	-um (takes -mo instead of -po as [-R] enclitic)
THIRD PERSON PLURAL	-m	-pum[16] (becomes Ø before [-R] enclitic)

The following sentences illustrate some typical occurrences of the subject enclitics:

180. noo-n   'o-y   qwaavicu-q

     I-I   you-ACC   look-DUR
                SG   after PRES

     "I'm looking after you."

181. naxánmal-up   neexic   cipilipi-q

     old man-he   gourd   break-DUR
                            PRES

     "The old man is breaking the gourd."

182. Toni   Xwaan-weh-xu-m-po-ko   'aamomo-ma

     Tony   Juan-both-DES-PL-[-R]-COND   hunt-USIT

     "Tony and Juan should have been hunting."

Note that after -xu and -ʃu the [-R] enclitic is -po rather than -mo, and the -m subject enclitic is retained.

183. yax-wun-pum   pu-ʃuun-ʃu-kum   loovi-q

     say-DUR-they   his-heart-DUB-QUOT   fine-DUR
        PRES   PRES

     "It's said that he's happy."

---

[16]This form has been found preceding -xu, as in:
    wunaalum-pum-xu heelaan
    "They should sing."
But this ordering is rare, and appears to be confined to rapid speech.

184. 'exngay-ca-po   sinaval   laaci-maan

      tomorrow-we-[-R]   money   ask-DUR
                                              for FUT

      "Tomorrow we'll be asking for money."

-il and -po are the realized and unrealized enclitics respectively. The
[+R] enclitic is used mainly with the past tense forms of verbs. With
plural subjects, it may take the form -mil, which presumably contains a
plural subject enclitic -m.

185. wunáal-up-il   lovi-'ax

      that-he-[+R]   make-PAST

      "he made it."

186. po-xila-vuta-muk-p-il

      its-rain-POT-PAST-it-[+R]
                         REC

      "It might have rained."

187. noo-ƚ-il   teetillax-lut   'exngay

      I-DUB-[+R]   talk-INCEPT   tomorrow

      "I might talk tomorrow."

The [-R] enclitic -po, which may be replaced by -mo for second and third
person subjects, is used to indicate future time reference, together with
future tense verbs, but also occurs with other verb forms, generally indicating the speaker's awareness that he is referring to an unrealized event.
There is a probably related -pi enclitic used in command sentences having
a future tense verb form.

188. noo-nu-po   hati'a-an   'o-éec

      I-I-[-R]   go-FUT   you-with

      "I'll go with you."

189. tee-nu-po no-ma'max miyx-maan palvun-nga no-'aw-ic-i

      if-I-[-R]   my-liking   be-DUR   valley-in   my-live-NOM-ACC

                                FUT

      "I don't know if Id like living in a valley. "

190. mikinga-mo   heela-an

      sometime-[-R]   sing-FUT

      "They will sing sometime. "

191. noo-pi   tilá'-an

      I-[-R]   speak-FUT

      "I <u>will</u> speak! "

Further examples are to be found in the preceding discussion of enclitics
in the first position, as well as in subsequent chapters.

    -<u>kwa</u>, sometimes realized as -<u>ka</u>, -<u>ku</u>, or -<u>ko</u>, is the conditional
enclitic (COND). Often used in counterfactual conditionals, this enclitic
indicates possibility with reference to present or future time, and unreality
with reference to present or past time.

192. man-xu-p-ko   waxáam   ngey-ma

      or(?)-DES-[-R]-COND   yesterday   leave-USIT

      "Maybe he should have left yesterday. "

193. tee-s-po-kwa   wam' miy-qa   yax wunáal-i ʃungáal-i

      if-DUB-[-R]-COND now   be-DUR   tell that-ACC girl-ACC

                              PRES

      ne-yk-po   wu'ánila-an   kwiil

      me-to-[-R]   bring-FUT   acorns

      "If they are ready, tell the woman to bring me some acorns. "

194. caam-xu-c-po-ko   cam-sinava-ki   wan'-ma   pi   caam neci

      we-DES-we-[-R]-COND our-money-POS have-USIT then we   pay

      "If we had the money, we would pay. "

195. yax-ko   pomóom-i tee-si-po   'o-neci-vuta-q

      tell-COND   they-ACC if-DUB-[-R]   you-pay-POT-DUR
                                                        PRES

      "Tell them if you can pay. "

This enclitic never co-occurs in an enclitic complex with the realized
enclitic -il.

     ta', for which Feliz Calac, Kroeber and Grace's informant, gave -taq
(61), is an emphatic element which, as in Cahuilla, does not really appear
to be a sentence enclitic since, in our investigations at least, it occurs as
a free form in almost any position in a sentence, after the sentence constituent the speaker wishes to highlight. But, according to Kroeber and
Grace, it can appear as the final element of an enclitic complex. Unfortunately, we have been unable to find any examples of this enclitic in the
Kroeber and Grace work. In our own examples, ta' appears to have an
adversative function, as the English however also does:

196. Giyérmo   huu'uni-kat   qay   ta'   Xwaan

      Bill   teach-AGT   not   EMPH   Juan

      "Bill is a teacher, but not Juan. "

     kun is a quotative often appearing as an independent element. It can
appear as kon(o'), kunu, kuna. Some of these forms may contain an
enclitic we have not encountered, though it is reported by Kroeber and
Grace (61). This enclitic is a distant past indefinite form a(') or o', which
appears as -nila' in one of their examples of enclitic combinations with the
first person -n- and the [+R] enclitic -il- (63). The quotative is used to
indicate hearsay, especially, but not exclusively, in traditional narratives.
Where the subject of a sentence is plural, a plural ending often occurs, as
in -kunum.

197. pe'-koná'   Taakwic   ngeśngeś-yax   po-yuu-yi   kuláaw-tal

      and-QUOT   Takwish   almost-PAST   her-head-ACC   stick-with
                            pierce

      "Then, it is said, Takwish almost pierced her head with the
      stick. "

2.8.2 Luiseño Verb Forms

Unlike the corresponding forms in the other two languages, Luiseño
verb forms have no subject markers affixed except for verb forms having
the potentive suffixes -vota or -lota, a few highly idiosyncratic verbs of
emotion which (in all three languages) are normally nominalized—they
include, in Luiseño, ma'max "like, love, " and he'ax "dislike, hate"—and
most verbs in embedded sentences. In all these cases, the subject markers
have the same form as the possessive prefixes for nouns. They are shown
below with the present potentive forms of the verb wayax "swim":

198. noo-p no-wayax-vuta-q(a)

     I-it   I-swim-POT-DUR
                       PRES

     "I can swim. "

     'om-up   'o-wayax-vuta-q(a)

     "You (sg)   can swim. "

     wunáal-up po-wayax-vuta-q(a)

     "He can swim. "

     caam-up   cam-wayax-vuta-wun

     we-it   we-swim-POT-DUR
                            PRES

     "We can swim. "

     'omóm-up   'om-wayax-vuta-wun

     "You (pl)   can swim. "

     wináal-um-up pom-wayax-vuta-wun

     "They can swim. "

However, no often occurs as nu-, po- as pu-, and cam- as cum-, and
pom- as pum-. The apparently irregular occurrence of the subject enclitic
-up will be discussed in a later chapter since it involves issues too complex for consideration here.

    The following table shows the relative positions of the various elements
within a finite verb form. It should be understood that the analysis on
which this table is based is a preliminary one which will be modified,
sometimes radically, in subsequent chapters.

199.	I	II	III	IV
	ROOT	THEME	DERIVATIONAL AFFIXES	INFLECTIONAL AFFIX
		-i- or -a(x) (These may be replaced by -la and some causatives)	Internal ordering mainly determined by semantic criteria	Tense-Aspect suffix

POSITION I

Luiseño verb roots may be classified into those which allow one of the thematic affixes to follow them and those which do not. The majority of Luiseño verbs have one of the thematic affixes, -i or -a(x). They form the two major verb conjugations in the language. Many roots occur with either thematic affix. The remaining verbs can be classified into two major groups, primarily with respect to differences in the ways that their past punctual forms are constructed. The first of these, which we shall call SIMPLE VERBS, usually have verb roots ending in a consonant. A good number are monosyllabic. Many of them have quite "basic" meanings— "eat," "sleep," "drink," "go." The last group, which we shall designate DERIVED VERBS, contains old derivational affixes such as cu, tu, ta, la, ka, and ku, many of which serve to convert noun roots into verb roots. Many of these old affixes might once have been grouped together as environmentally conditioned variants of a single underlying element, but such regularities as can now be found are sporadic. They are, in any case, beyond the scope of this study. We show below four examples of each of the four verb groupings noted:

200.

-i VERBS		-a(x) VERBS		SIMPLE VERBS		DERIVED VERBS	
heey-i	"dig"	heel-a(x)	"sing"	yaw	"hold"	kii-cu	"build house" or "settle"
naaw-i	"write"	kupú'-ax	"sleep"	kup	"sleep"		
ƚe'i	"shoot"	se'-ax	"be shot"	qwa'	"eat"	peew-la	"marry"
tap-i	"finish"			mamayuw	"help"		
		tap-ax'	"be finished"			mom-tu	"(tide)" rise"
						'ow-lu	"bleed"

POSITION II

-i theme verbs are generally transitive, and active rather than stative. Some of them, like hang-i "hang," neekw-i "bend," and pið-i "break," seem to have a causative force. In such cases, there is usually a corresponding -ax form which is intransitive and which has either a stative or passive meaning.

-ax theme verbs are usually, but not always, intransitive. Although many have a passive or stative meaning, there are others, such as caqw-ax "catch," which cannot be so easily characterized this way. Nevertheless, if one comes across a "state" -ax verb such as ɫil-ax "be overflowing," one can predict with a reasonable change of success that there will be an -i form corresponding to it, such as ɫil-i, "spill something."

-la is a special derivational affix, a little like the Cahuilla -an distributive affix, which means approximately "V a lot." Unlike the derivational suffixes that appear in third position, this -la apparently occurs only after the verb root, and it occurs only with -i theme verbs. Almost any verb can be converted into a -la verb. Synchronically, at least, this -la is quite distinct from the old derivational affix -la, in peew-la, a denominalizing affix treated as part of the verb root. It is also quite distinct from the Position III variant -la "go and V" or "go in order to V," which will be discussed later in this chapter. Here are some examples of verbs with and without -la:

201.				
'oov-i	"give"	'oov-la	"give frequently"
ko'-i	"bite"	ko'-la	"bite often"
wot-i	"hit"	wot-la	"keep hitting"
caqw-i	"catch"	caqw-la	"catch a lot"
car-i	"tear" (a piece of paper)	caar-la	"tear many pieces" (one at a time)
ɔ́ar-i	"kick"	'ar-la	"kick repeatedly"
cung-i	"kiss"	cung-la	"kiss repeatedly or all over"

-xam is a causative affix which can also replace a thematic affix. It occurred only rarely in the speech of our consultants.

202. noo-nu-po   po-y   nec-xam-vicu-maan

     I-I-[-R]   he-ACC   pay-CAUS-want-DUR
                                           FUT

"I'll be wanting to make him pay for it. "

Kroeber and Grace (155) also report the following affixes occurring in this
position: -xami, -kixa(ni), -xani, all causatives, and a benefactive -xa(x).
The particular affix or combination of affixes occurring apparently
depended on the class of verb to which it was attached. We have been
unable to verify any of these with our consultants, though some recognized
the affixes as the way "the old folks used to speak. " The normal causative
affix employed by our consultants is -ni, which occurs in third position.
Two benefactive postpositions are used: -max and -qwaan(i). These occur
only on pronoun bases.

POSITION III

     The derivational affixes allowed in this position may occupy it alone
or in combination with other derivational affixes. The ordering of these
affixes relative to each other is determined primarily, though not completely, by semantic factors. The semantic scope of each affix is normally
the whole of the verb form preceding it, but not the affixes which follow it.
Furthermore, many of these interchangeable affixes may occur more than
once in a verb form, although we have no examples of the same affixes
occurring next to each other. The derivational affixes are as follows:

203.   -lu(w) or -la   "go somewhere and V, " "go there to V"

       -monáa   "come V-ing"

       -ni   causative, "make some $\begin{Bmatrix} \text{one} \\ \text{thing} \end{Bmatrix}$ V" .

       -ngi   "go away/back V-ing, " "go here and there V-ing"

       -vicu   "want to V"

       -vota or -lota   potentive, "can/may/be able to V"

The sentences following show various combinations and orderings of these affixes:

204. noo-n-il   wuqállax-vicu-muk

     I-I-[+R]   walk-want-RECENT
                         PAST

     "I wanted to walk."

205. noo-n-il   wuqálla-ni-vicu-muk   X̱waan-i

                   walk-CAUS-want-REC   Juan-ACC
                               PAST

     "I wanted to make Juan walk."

206. noo-n   no-wuqállax-lu-ni-vicu-ni-vuta-muk   X̱waan-i

     I-it   I-walk-go-CAUS-want-CAUS-POT-REC   Juan-ACC
                                            PAST

     "I was able to make Juan want to make her go there to walk."

207. noo-n   po-y   heelax-ngi-vicu-ni-vicu-q

     I-I   he-ACC   sing-go-want-CAUS-want-DUR
                                                   PRES

     "I want to make him want to go away singing."

POSITION IV

-q(a) and -wun are the present durative singular and plural suffixes respectively. The -q form is more common than -qa, but all our consultants accepted -qa on any verb stem they were given. Simple verbs were more likely to be used with -qa than any others, and this suffix was particularly common with monosyllabic verb stems. For the single stressless verb root in Luiseño, yax "say, tell," -qa is obligatory since this suffix must carry the word stress: ya-qá.

-qat is the recent past durative singular suffix. It is sometimes heard as -qut. The plural form is -qat-um, occasionally -qut-um. Like present durative forms, recent past durative forms do not normally occur with the [+R] enclitic -il.

-muk is another recent past durative suffix for both singular and plural forms. It is sometimes heard as -mok.

-ma is the usitative suffix. It indicates habitual actions, ones that occur repeatedly, and it is also used as a kind of durative, referring to actions begun in the past and continuing up to the time of utterance, or to the present. In the dialects of reservations north of Rincon, it sometimes occurs as -max. This suffix is homophonous to an affix, -ma, which is a variant of the derivational affix -monaa, which is optionally contracted before [q].

208. hax-ɟu-kun   miyx-ma   qay-ɟu-po   Taakwic
      who-DUB-QUOT   be-USIT   not-DUB-[-R]   Takwish

      "Who can it be, they say, if not Takwish?

209. 'iv-axáni-nik noo lovi'i-ma   —noo-n ya'ác nooti-kat
      this-do-after I   do-USIT   I-I   man   hunt-AGT

      "This is the way I do it—I'm a hunter. "

210. Xwaan-up   yu'pan   'oyóotu-ma   sinaval Maríy-i   poo-ngay
      Juan-he   again   steal-USIT   money   Maria-ACC her-from

      "Juan has been stealing money again from Maria. "

Verb forms with the -ma suffix are also used with various combinations of the enclitics -xu, -po, and -kwa as "irrealis" verbs (like the Cupeño usitative) in conditional sentences and "should have" sentences. For examples, see (205) and (207).

-maan is the future durative suffix. Since, like -ma, it appears on "irrealis" verbs as well, it is almost certainly -ma with the future ending -an.

211. noo-nu-po   pellax-maan
      I-I-[-R]   dance-DUR
                              FUT

      "I'll be dancing. "

212. 'om 'ooxa 'aa'-maan   pi   'om   cikwílax-maan
      you alone live-DUR   then you   sad-DUR
                       FUT   FUT

      "If you were single, you'd be lonely. "

-uk is the past usitative suffix indicating "used to V." For verbs ending in a vowel, this suffix becomes -k.

213. caam'   puyaámangay   ngoor-uk   yamayk

    we   always   run-USIT   once
                                  PAST

"Once we used to run all the time."

-quś is the past durative suffix, described by Sparkman as the "remote
past imperfect, back from two to three weeks ago" (Kroeber and Grace:
151). The suffix is sometimes realized as -xuś, -kwuś, or -wuś.

-ax, -ya, -yax, and -x are all used as simple past (i.e. past punctual)
suffixes. Although there is considerable variation for all four classes of
verbs, the following observations appear to be reasonably accurate for the
Rincon dialect:

    i. -i verbs have their final -i replaced by -ax or -yax. For example,
neqp-i "fight" becomes neqp-ax; pa'-i "drink" becomes pa'-ax or pa'-yax;
tiiw-i "see" becomes tiiw-yax, tiiw-ax, or tiiw-'ya. This last form is an
exception to our generalization. So is tan-a (or tan-'a), the simple past
forms of tan-i "dance Indian-style."

    ii. -ax verbs have their -ax replaced by -ya or -a. For example,
wil-ax "jump" becomes wil-ya; hatí'-ax "go" becomes hatí'-ya; pell-ax
"dance" becomes pell-ya or pell-a, but śawaq-ax "make bread or tortillas"
becomes śaśwaq-a, and ngoy-ax "wake up" (intr.) becomes ngoy-yax as
well as ngoy-ya.

    iii. Simple verbs ending in consonants and most ending in vowels
usually have reduplicated simple past forms. Monosyllabic stems with
long vowels have the vowel split into two short vowels separated by a
glottal stop. Since past forms like these are found in all three Cupan languages, the reduplicated past may be a relic of an older, probably pre-
Cupan, system. The verb 'aamo "hunt" becomes 'a'mo (probably via
*'a'amo), putí' "dream" becomes pupti', huulu "make arrows" becomes
huh(u)lu, and toomavcu "become deaf" may become tootmavcu, or
toomavcu-x (following the derived verb process described below) or even
toomavicú'-ya, as if there were an -ax verb toomavicú'-ax.

    iv. Derived verbs, whose stems normally end in a vowel, take an -x,
as do some other verbs whose stems end in a vowel. For example,

mamayuw "help" becomes mamayuw-x; 'elku "beg" becomes 'elku-x;
'oyóotu "steal" becomes 'oyóotu-x, and wiru/wiðu "play the flute" becomes
wiru-x/wiðu-x.

   -an, with the variant -n after all vowels except i, is the future suffix.
Quite often it is better translated "probably will" rather than just "will, "
for which the Luiseño inceptive is often used.   When -ax verbs are given
the future suffix, the final x of the stem is deleted, in the speech of our
consultants.   But it appears that earlier generations of speakers retained
the x, as is evident from some of the Kroeber and Grace texts, and from
J. P. Harrington's field notes.

214. caam-ca-po   po-y   yu'pan   tiiwi-n

      we-we-[-R]   he-ACC   again   see-FUT

      "We'll see him again, I hope. "

215. noo-ǂu-n   heela-an

      I-DUB-I   sing-FUT

      "May I sing? "

216. caam-ca-po   maǂa-an

      we-we-[-R]   lie-FUT
                    down

      "We'll lie down. "

   -lowut or -lut is the inceptive singular suffix, while the plural suffix
is either -kutum or -ktum.   They are usually translated "be going to V, "
"be about to V, " or even "will V. "   In embedded sentences they mean "in
order to V. "   For our Rincon and La Jolla consultants, -lut rather than
-lowut occurred on all but the simple verb class.   However, we encountered some inconsistency, and with speakers from other reservations,
-lowut was sometimes in free variation with -lut.   Moreover, we often
came across "intermediate" forms such as [lowt], so that it sometimes
seemed that there was a continuum rather than two quite separate forms.
Our findings are thus in disagreement with those of Kroeber and Grace
(32-33), who reported that -lowut was restricted to what we have labeled
"simple verbs. "   Malécot, whose experience with the language appears to
have been comparatively short, does not appear to have noted -lowut at all.

The plural -ktum suffix usually occurs when the stem ends in a vowel. Like the Cupeño inceptive verb forms, these Luiseño forms do not occur with the [-R] enclitic.

217. S.Lu   'o-y-op   mokna-lowut

           you-ACC-he   kill-INCEPT

           "He's going to kill you. "

218. S.Lu   noo-n   no-oxay   wokó'-a-q   tiiw-i-lowut

           I-I   I-alone   come-ax-DUR   see-i-incept
                                          PRES

           no-ta'-aȼ-i   Taakwic

           my-cousin-ACC   Takwish

           "I only came to see my cousin Takwish. "

219.   caam-ȼu-c   papavc-um   miyx-kutum

      we-DUB-we   thirsty-PL   be-INCEPT
                                      PL

    "Are we going to be thirsty? "

Imperative forms do not fit into the positional framework utilized so far for Luiseño verb forms. For singular imperatives the stem, plus the thematic affix if there is one, is the form used. Plural imperative verb forms have an additional -yam or -am suffix. The -yam is added if the singular imperative form ends in a vowel, and -am if it ends in a consonant. Sometimes the vowel quality varies, -yum, -um, and -yom, -om occur quite frequently. The first person plural exhortative ("Let's V") is expressed either with hani plus the first person plural subject enclitic form -ca and the durative present verb form, or just with -ca on the first word and then the durative present verb form. The examples following have been either provided or accepted by all of our consultants, regardless of their reservation:

220. SINGULAR   PLURAL   MEANING

     hati'-ax   hatí'-ax-am   "Go! "

     heey-i   heey-i-yam   "Dig!"

SINGULAR	PLURAL	MEANING
mamayuw	mamayuw-am	"Help (him)!"
'aamu-ngi	'aamu-ngi-yam	"Go hunting!"
pa'-i	pa'-i-yam	"Drink!"

The verb forms described below are not finite verb forms, although some of them are used in some constructions where they appear to be main verb forms rather than verbs in embedded constructions. However, this finite/non-finite distinction is not to be taken too seriously at this point. Some of the verb forms already described may turn out to be embedded, non-finite, verb forms upon a more thorough examination.

-vo and -pi are suffixes marking realized and unrealized events respectively. With plural subjects, -pi may be changed to -mi. Some speakers say -vi or -ve instead of -vo. Both -vo and -pi are usually suffixed to verb stems in embedded sentences.

First, -vo and -pi forms appears in complement sentences, usually as subject or object of a higher verb.

221. caam   yaa   wunáal   po-pell-ax-vo-y

     we   say   he   he-dance-ax-[+R]-ACC
               PAST

     "We said that he had danced."

222. caam   'ayál-i-wun   Felísita   po-pell-ax-pi-y

     we   know-i-DUR   Felicita   she-dance-ax-[-R]-ACC
               PRES

     "We know that Felicita will dance."

223. pi   loov-i-q   po-'aamo-qal-vo

     and   fine-i-DUR   he-hunt-DUR-[+R]
              PRES

     "It's good that he was hunting."

Secondly, both -vo and -pi appear on verbs forming part of a compound verb construction with the copular verb miyx "be, have." With -vo, the construction means "have V-ed," and with -pi, the construction means "have to V."

224. Maríya   hamú'   po-waaq-i-vo   miy-quƒ   no-wokó'-a-qala

     Maria   already   she-sweep-i-[+R]   be-DUR   I-come-ax-DUR
                                               PAST

     "Maria had already swept when I arrived."

225. caam-up   cam-waaq-i-pi   miy-q

     we-it   we-sweep-i-[-R]   be-DUR
                                   PRES

     "We have to sweep."

Thirdly, both suffixes occur in relative constructions in which the lower subject is not coreferential with the had noun phrase. While -vo appears on past relatives, -pi appears on future relatives.

226. tukwut   po   no-nonom-i-qal-vo   'atáax-m-i   qe'ée-k

     mountain   that   I-follow-i-DUR-[+R] person-PL-ACC   kill-USIT
       lion   PAST

     "The mountain lion that I was following used to kill people."

227. noo-n   'ayál-i-q   ponéy-m-i   'aa'alvic-um-i   po

     I-I   know -i-DUR   that-PL-ACC   story-PL-ACC   that
                      PRES

     Xwaan   po'aa'alv-i-pi   'exngay

     Juan   he-narrate-i-[-R]   tomorrow

     "I know the stories that Juan will tell tomorrow."

Very rarely, both -vo and -pi appear in relative constructions whose subjects are coreferential with the head noun phrase. In such constructions, the verb form takes on both the case and number properties of the head noun phrase.

228. noo-n-il   tiiw-yax   wunál-m-i   nánatmal-um-i

     I-I-[+R]   see-PAST   that-PL-ACC   girl-PL-ACC

     ponéy-m-ï   po   ne-y   pom-cung-i-v-um-i

     that-PL-ACC   that   I-ACC   they-kiss-i-[+R]-PL-ACC

     "I saw the girls that had kissed me."

Finally, both suffixes, which in all the constructions above had to have
a subject prefix attached to the verb form, occur on verb forms without
subject prefixes. In such cases these suffixes are realized as -vol and
-pic. These constructions can be noun phrase complements, with a passive
meaning, or a passive-like relative construction, or even what look like
main clauses.

229. wunáal   ʃu'íc-i   ma'ma-quʃ   po   qwa'-í-vol-i   waxáam

     that   rabbit-ACC   want-DUR   that eat-i-[+R]-ACC yesterday
                                PAST

     "He wanted the rabbit that was eaten yesterday."

230. ʃahóvit   tan'-i-vol

     war dance   dance-i-[+R]

     "The war dance was done."

231. 'iví-p   hilá'-i-pic

     this-it   eat-i-[-R]

     "This will be eaten" OR "This is for eating."

-qat and -qatum are the singular and plural suffixes that appear on
verb forms in present relative constructions. Both suffixes take accusative marking in the appropriate positions. The verb forms have subject
prefixes only if their subjects are not coreferential with their noun phrase
heads.

232. wunáal-up   ma'ma-q   kaváy-i   ponéy-i   (po)

     he-he   want-DUR   horse-ACC   that-ACC   (that)
                    PRES

     tooʃaxt-i   moyóo-ni-qat-i

     cottontail-ACC   eat-CAUS-REL-ACC
                         PRES

     "He wants the horse that is feeding the rabbit."

233. wunáal-up   ma'ma-q   kaváy-i   ponéy-i   (po)

     toočaxit   po-moyóo-ni-qat-i

     cottontail   he-eat-CAUS-REL-ACC
                           PRES

"He wants the horse that the rabbit is feeding."

-mokwic and -lut/-lowut serve as suffixes for singular verbs in past
and future relative constructions respectively. The plural forms are
-mokwic-um and -kutum/-ktum. All of these suffixes can be followed by
accusative marking. The subjects of these relativized verbs must be
coreferential with the noun phrase head.

234. wunáal-up   ma'ma-q   kaváy-i   ponéy-i   (po)

     toočaxt-i   moyóo-ni-qal-mokwic-i

     cottontail   eat-CAUS-DUR-REL-ACC
                        PAST

"He wants the horse that was feeding the rabbit."

235. wunáal-up   ma'ma-q   kaváy-i   poney-i   (po)

     toočaxt-i   moyóo-ni-lut-i

     cottontail-ACC   eat-CAUS-REL-ACC
                     FUT

"He wants the horse that is going to feed the rabbit."

-qala, which occurs only on verbs with subject prefixes, is a kind of
durative participial suffix on verbs in embedded constructions with a wide
range of meanings, such as "while X is/was V-ing," "before X finished
V-ing," "that X is/was V-ing," "on account of X V-ing," "no matter who
is V-ing," and many others. Unless there is a qualifying adverb such as
pitóowili "not yet," the time reference for the verb is the same as that for
the verb in the sentence into which it has been embedded. For convenience, we shall label it GER (for "gerund"), although these forms are not
strictly parallel to the English or Latin gerund.

236. Maríya   'oná-ni-vica-q   tee   'awáal po-wa'-i-qala

     Maria   know-CAUS-wish-DUR   if   dog   it-bark-i-GER
                         PRES

     "Maria wants to know if the dog is barking."

237. caam   tiiw-yax   hunwut-i   po-hulúq-a-qala

     we   see-PAST   bear-ACC   it-fall-ax-GER

     "We saw the bear as it was falling."

-qal is a durative suffix appearing on non-finite verb forms. It can precede other suffixes, as it does for example in 224, 226, and 233, or it can be in final position, as in the following sentence:

238. caam   tiiw-yax   hunwut-i   hulúq-a-qal

     we   see-PAST   bear-ACC   fall-ax-DUR

     "We saw the bear fall."

The logical subject of -qal forms like that in 238 is usually the nearest noun phrase preceding it. The time reference is that of the main verb, except where another suffix follows.

-nuk or -nik is suffixed to verb stems without subject prefixes. The meaning is approximately "after V-ing" or "having V-ed." The implied subject is always coreferential with that of the next higher verb. The same ending also appears on some manner adverbials where it seems to function rather like the -ly adverbial suffix in English.

239. noo   Xwaan-i   tiiw-i-nik   po-y   pat-ax

     I   Juan-ACC   see-i-after   he-ACC   shoot-PAST

     "When I saw Juan, I shot him"

-qanuk or -qanik are suffixes just like -nuk/-nik, except that the time reference of verb forms containing either -qanuk or -qanik is co-extensive with that of the higher verb. The approximate meaning then is "while V-ing." Such forms are thus not unlike the -qala forms discussed above, except for the more restrictive coreference limitation on -qanuk/-qanik forms.

240. noo   puyáamangay   piláac-i-ma   naqma-qanik

    I   always   learn-i-USIT   listen-while
                             PRES

"I always learn by listening."

-wunut, plural form -wuntum, is another suffix with a function like
that of the English -ing participial. Like -qanuk/-qanik it occurs on verbs
without subject prefixes. But, unlike these other forms, -wunut forms may
be marked for the case and number of the implied subject, which is coreferential with the subject noun phrase of the clause containing it. For
-wunut we use the abbreviated label ING.

241. noo   toy'-a-qat   'o-y   caqálaq-i-wunut

    I   laugh-ax-DUR   you-ACC   tickle-i-ING
             PAST

"I was laughing as I was tickling you."

-ic is a suffix converting verbs into nominal forms, as in heelax-ic
"song," from heelax "sing."

-lo(w) or -la(w) is a suffix converting verbs into action nominals or
abstract nominals. Thus cam-pa'-i-la means "our drinking," and
po-'aamo-low, either "his/her hunting" or, if the reference of the subject
prefix is indefinite, just "hunting." A less common use is in a kind of
relative construction. In this case, the forms just given would mean
"which we always drink" and "that we always hunt" respectively.

-aat, plural -aantum, is an adjective suffix, as in xway-aat "white,"
and koś-aantum "sweet (things)."

As in the other two languages, there are various reduplication processes affecting verb forms. Reduplication as a means of expressing past
time reference has already been noted. Additionally, many -ma usitative
forms contain reduplicated stems, where the reduplication serves to
emphasize the iterativeness of the act or event. In the sentence following,
the verb is a reduplicated form of cor-i "out":

242. Patti-xu-p-ko   corcor-i-ma   kulawut

    Patti-DES-[-R]-COND   cut-i-USIT   wood

"Patti should have cut the wood."

Reduplication is found in many verb forms with plural subjects, in
adjectival forms derived from verbs, such as xaláxlac "loose, " from
xàl-ax "be loosened, " and in other "distributive" verb forms as a way of
expressing frequency, intensity, and duration over a longer period of time.
Of course, some reduplicated forms have taken on specialized meanings,
as is common in many languages. The exploitation of vowel length is a
similar phenomenon to the use of reduplication. Here again some semantic
specialization is found. The verb root cor "cut, " again provides some
good examples.

243. cor-i   "cut a single piece of wood"

      cor-ii   "cut a lot of wood"

      coor-i   "cut wood with a buzz-saw"

      cocor-i   "cut very large amounts of wood"

Since Kroeber and Grace discuss such phenomena in detail (159-171), and
since these are only marginally relevant to this study, we shall pursue the
topic no further.

   Finally, there is a special verb form, yaax, meaning "try to, " which
always appears with subject prefix. Frequently, but not invariably, the
other verb form associated with it contains the desiderative affix -vicu,
which can also be used to mean "try to. " Both -vicu and yaax can sometimes be translated "begin V-ing. "

244. noo-n   no-yaax   Luseño   piláac-i-vica-q

     I-I   I-do   Luiseño   learn-i-want-DUR
                                              PRES

     "I'm trying to learn Luisenõ" or "I've started learning/studying
     Luiseño. "

245. S.Lu po-yaax   po-'o'nan-a-y   mica-'axáninuk

           he-do   he-know-NOM-ACC   how-doing

           po-taax   desfen ð eer

           he-self   defend

     "He tried to use his knowledge to defend himself. "

Although <u>yaax</u> usually precedes the other verbs, the reverse order is not ungrammatical.

III. SYNTACTIC RECONSTRUCTION AND THE DETERMINATION OF SYNTACTIC CHANGE

3.1 Introduction

The more immediate goals of the present study can be reduced to the following summary:

i. the reconstruction of Proto-Cupan syntactic structures by means of systematic analyses and comparisons of the modern Cupan languages;

ii. the determination, wherever possible, of the directions of syntactic change in Cupan through a comparison of structures reconstructed for Proto-Cupan with modern Cupan constructions.

Such an investigation in Cupan presents at least one obvious pitfall—that of circularity—one that is far less likely for a diachronic study of the Romance languages. For those languages, which have a time depth approximately the same as that of Cupan, there are written records of earlier stages, many of them dated. What reconstruction is needed is relatively simple compared with the situation in Cupan. The determination of the directions of syntactic change in Romance between, say, the tenth and the nineteenth centuries may be made through an analytical comparison of independently attested stages of each language together with a comparison of the changes in each language.

3.2 The Danger of Circularity

No such direct data are available for Cupan. What data we have are confined to the surviving languages as they are spoken in the twentieth century. The risk of circularity arises from the fact that we are using the modern languages as the bases for reconstructing earlier stages, which are then compared with the modern data used to reconstruct the earlier stages. The fact that the modern Cupan languages are likely to share important properties of the proto language is an obvious and trivial consequence of the way in which the proto language has been determined.

But such circularity is not inevitable. Where all the modern languages share a feature A, reconstructing such a feature A for the proto language is a safe conservative procedure. And no direction of change can be determined since there has been no change. A more ambitious and risky procedure is to postulate some other feature B for the proto language, a feature which, it might be claimed, developed into feature A in all the modern languages, independently. While such a development is possible, hypothesizing a feature B presupposes a strong claim about languages having feature B—that they are likely to change in the way described. In the absence of other evidence from the languages to justify such a presupposition, the claim must almost certainly be rejected.

3.3 Irregularity as Evidence for Reconstructions

The kind of evidence we are referring to is the existence of inconsistencies and irregularities within each language as well as across the languages. For example, Mountain Cahuilla, Luiseño, and Cupeño all have past, present, and future tense forms. It would seem quite reasonable on this basis to posit past, present, and future tenses for the proto language. However, an examination of verb forms in complement sentences and relative constructions shows that while there are neat, symmetric rules governing past and future forms of verbs in them, the rules for present tense forms are quite different, and, indeed, in two of the languages apparent present tense forms are often used to represent past time. In such constructions the present tense suffixes are used as if they are just durative aspect suffixes. Add to this the following facts:

i. There are two kinds of durative affix—those referring to realized action and those referring to unrealized action.

ii. In all three languages, some of the so-called future suffixes can be used to refer to past time if the event referred to was not realized, i.e. if it is reported as not having occurred.

iii. The two languages having temporal enclitics only use these enclitics for past and future time reference, and, in fact, the "future" enclitic, like the "future" suffixes, can refer to past time if the event represented was not realized.

iv. The past tense suffix in one language, Cupeño, is the same as the durative suffix in another, Luiseño, and also the suffix used in another dialect of Cahuilla to refer to present time.

Such evidence suggests that positing past, present, and future tenses for the proto language is not the only reasonable conclusion. The modern tense systems may have developed from a purely aspectual system whose temporal dimensions were restricted to representing actions and events as either realized or unrealized. In this case there has been a development, incomplete as it is for some constructions, from a relatively simple aspectual system to a more specialized and complex tense-aspect system. As will be shown later in the present study, this development—with some qualifications—may well have taken place in Cupan.

3.4 Evidence Relating to Stages in Cupan

A further consideration suggesting that circularity is not inevitable is the possibility, not just of establishing the existence of more than one stage in the development of Cupan, as reflected in differences among the languages, but of being able to assign specific linguistic features to these stages. The lexical, morphological, and syntactic data given in the previous chapter are more than enough to establish that these languages must have shared a common ancestor. In light of the manifold similarities at all levels, the contrary conclusion would be ridiculous.

But our Stammbaum diagram for the Takic languages in the first chapter embodies another claim about Cupan. The claim is that the ancestors of the present Luiseño-speaking Indians became separated from other Cupan speakers at a period considerably earlier than that in which the second split occurred—the one separating the ancestors of the modern Cahuilla people from those of the Cupeños. Here again, though none of the languages are mutually comprehensible, the striking resemblances between Cahuilla and Cupeño vocabulary and verb morphology contrast with the less striking similarity of either language to Luiseño. A parallel contrast can be found in the traditional myths of the three peoples. The Creation stories told by the Cupeños and Cahuillas have many common features not shared by the Luiseño creation stories. The same is the case for many of the traditional religious ceremonies—the funeral clothes-burning, the eagle-killing, and others. While these non-linguistic characteristics suggest a long-standing and close relationship between the Cahuilla and Cupeño peoples, the linguistic data indicate that the relationship was more than the result of cultural diffusion, that the two languages were probably dialects of a single language for some time after the Luiseño separation. We feel justified then in assuming the existence of the two major stages referred to above in the development of Cupan. This assumption appears to be the most conservative one on the basis of the linguistic data.

3.5 Further Criteria for Reconstruction

This two-stage assumption justifies a further assumption. Any characteristic noted for only two of the three languages may more reasonably be
ascribed to Proto-Cupan if the languages are either Luiseño or Cupeño, or
Luiseño and Cahuilla. This is because the linguistic data indicates that
there was no stage at which Luiseño and only one of the other languages
were a single language. If, however, only Cahuilla and Cupeño share particular properties, then such properties cannot necessarily be assumed to
have characterized Proto-Cupan—unless there is other evidence to suggest
this, evidence from Luiseño or possibly from such Takic languages as
Gabrielino, Morongo Serrano, and Kitanemuk Serrano. A further possibility is the reconstruction of some syntactic phenomenon for Proto-Cupan
even if it occurs in only one Cupan language. Such a reconstruction might
be reasonable if this same phenomenon were widely distributed among other
Uto-Aztecan languages, especially across the larger sub-groupings of Uto-
Aztecan. Such a phenomenon would, of course, be a strong candidate for
reconstruction for proto-Uto-Aztecan. A final possibility—separate and
independent development of the same phenomenon—is a very interesting one
which can almost never be excluded. Here considerations of the complexity
of the development are important. The more elaborate and complex the
phenomenon, the less likely it is to have developed independently in two or
more related languages.

In other words, the fact of a simple majority of the three languages
will not in itself be enough to establish Proto-Cupan reconstructions.
Further, where the gap between Luiseño and the other two languages is too
wide, it may be both necessary and desirable to reconstruct first the Proto-
Cahuilla-Cupeño structures.

These criteria regarding reconstruction for syntax are not, of course,
new. Much the same criteria have traditionally been used for phonological
and morphological reconstruction.

3.6 Cupan Enclitics

A brief consideration of Cupan enclitics here should illustrate how the
factors discussed may interact. Luiseño and Cupeño have active and quite
similar enclitic systems. In Cahuilla, syntactic enclitics occur infrequently
and most of the enclitic functions are filled by verb suffixes, special verbs,
or, in the case of interrogatives, by sentence intonation. What must have

been the situation for Proto-Cupan? The following major alternatives are clear:

i. Proto-Cupan may have had few or no enclitics. In Luiseño and Cupeño an enclitic system may have developed, perhaps from relatively insignificant Proto-Cupan forms, perhaps from other types of constituents. For example, the Luiseño and Cupeño dubitatives ʂu and ʂə may have developed from a Proto-Cupan noun *sun "mind, heart," or from a verb derived from it, *sunax "believe, suspect." In Cahuilla, however, the original Proto-Cupan situation has most nearly been preserved.

ii. Proto-Cupan had an enclitic system carrying out major syntactic functions, just as in modern Luiseño and Cupeño. Cahuilla enclitics are vestiges of this earlier system.

Alternative ii is altogether more likely. Otherwise we would be claiming it as no more than a coincidence that two languages which became separated from their common core at different times independently developed remarkably similar enclitic systems. Moreover, Gabrielino and both Serrano dialects, as well as Hopi, have enclitics and in Serrano, at least, they function very much like the Luiseño and Cupeño ones.

Furthermore, as Steele (1972) has shown, there is ample evidence to support the reconstruction of an enclitic system for Proto-Uto-Aztecan. The Cahuilla enclitics then seem to be gradually disappearing vestiges of a more elaborate system like that of Cupeño.

But Steele goes further than just reconstructing Proto-Uto-Aztecan enclitics. She suggests an interesting relation with verb suffixes. If subject and object enclitics are not considered, there are two main enclitic positions with distinct semantic functions. The verb suffix position may be regarded as a third position since, she claims, in Proto-Uto-Aztecan,

> every morpheme of the tense-aspect-modality system could occur
> in any one of three positions, and each of these positions had a
> particular semantic function.
>
> (p. 1)

Steele associates the first position with modality, the second with aspect and the third with tense.

While this semantic correlation with position works out quite well for Luiseño and Cupeño, it should not be surprising that it does not always work. Some verb suffixes in Luiseño have primarily modal or aspectual functions. But what is particularly interesting is that none of these suffixes are shared with Cupeño, although the particular enclitics used often correspond to Cupeño enclitics, as the previous chapter has shown. The suffixes appear to be innovations. Kroeber and Grace confirm our own impression that, in Luiseño, the enclitics are falling into disuse. They comment:

> In 1909 when Kroeber reorthographed Sparkman's texts and secured the text of a new letter, the syntactic enclitics constituted a characteristic idiom of Luiseño. By 1951, they were evidently disappearing; their use was somewhat scattering and inconsistent.
>
> (p.63)

Our major Rincon consultant, a very intelligent and precise person, used them in careful speech. But when she conversed with her brothers and others we noticed that, with the frequent exception of the realized and unrealized enclitics, most of the enclitics were omitted. Other speakers revealed the same characteristics even in careful speech.

In Cupeño, on the other hand, enclitics occur far more often, and the potentive enclitic qwə, unlike the Luiseño kwa and xu (both related to qwə), is almost never omitted. In Cupeño, however, there are considerably fewer mode-aspect endings for verbs.

Luiseño appears then to be replacing enclitics with verb suffixes. Consequently some verb suffixes may have important roles as indicators of modality or aspect. Cahuilla, which has almost lost its enclitics, has gone furthest in this respect, as might be expected. Cupeño, the most conservative as to enclitic retention, is also the only language not to have nondurative future or past suffixes. Indeed even the durative past and future suffixes appear to have once been purely durative affixes, as our seventh chapter will show. We see here a not atypical "trade off" relation between enclitics, suffixes, and the development of a tripartite time-reference system from a binary realized/unrealized aspectual system. The situation is, as always, more complex than this discussion suggests, as the treatment of past tense forms in the next chapter will show.

IV. VERB STRUCTURE IN
PROTO-CAHUILLA-CUPEÑO

4.1 Some General Considerations

In this chapter, morphological and syntactic evidence will be used to
determine the structural characteristics of the Proto-Cahuilla-Cupeño
forms that later became finite verbs with past time reference. The two
major alternatives are these:

i. The earlier forms were finite main verbs much like the modern
forms.

ii. The earlier forms were nominalized structures with higher copular predicates.

If the second alternative is the correct one, the Proto-Cahuilla-Cupeño
surface structures will resemble the complex abstract structures proposed
in semantically based generative theories (as in McCawley, 1971). A
similar kind of development must have occurred in English, with the
modern auxiliary plus verb combination. For example, the English may
fight corresponds to Anglo-Saxon constructions like mæg feohtan in which
mæg is a main verb originally meaning "have the strength to." The infinitive verb feohtan is part of an embedded sentential structure functioning
as the noun phrase object of the main verb, or, in certain contexts, as the
sentential subject. Interestingly, just as happened in Cupan, the mæg verb
lost its physical strength meaning as it became a surface auxiliary verb
rather than a main verb. We will discuss the Cupan counterpart of this in
chapter VII.

Unfortunately, there are no records of earlier forms of the Cupan
languages. To establish the second alternative as the correct one, we
would need, for example, evidence from the modern languages suggesting
that these verb forms had characteristics found otherwise only in nominal
structures. Cupan nouns are either possessed or non-possessed. If
possessed, they normally have a possessive prefix. If non-possessed,
they normally have an absolutive suffix—c after an i, otherwise t or l

(Luiseño also has <u>ca</u>, <u>ta</u>, and <u>la</u> as variants). Cupan nouns have -(V)m
suffixed to show plural number and -<u>i</u> to show accusative case.

4.2 Cahuilla and Cupeño Verbs with Past Time Reference

Cahuilla main verbs, whatever the time reference, all have subject
prefixes.[1] If the verb is transitive, an object prefix always precedes the
subject prefix. But more significant for our purposes are the Cupeño
facts. In Cupeño, subject markers appear on past tense verbs but not on
present and future tense forms.[2] On the surface there appears to be no
reason why past tense verbs alone should have such markers. Object
markers are optional, they are found on past, present and future tense
forms, and they rarely occur when the object is singular. What was the
likely situation in Proto-Cahuilla-Cupeño (henceforth PCC)? We shall
take up the object prefixes first.

Neither Luiseño nor any other Takic language for which we have data
has object prefixes on verbs. But there is other evidence to suggest that
object prefixation was a later development restricted to PCC. In the Kupa
dialect of Cupeño there is a phonological rule shifting word stress on
so-called "stressless roots" (see Hill and Hill for discussion) onto a prefix
if there is no suffix. This rule has become optional in the now defunct
Wiláqalpa dialect and might have disappeared if this dialect had survived.
So, corresponding to Wiláqalpa

1.   nə'- əp   nə -t$\underset{\sim}{\acute{ə}}$w   'axwác-i
     I-[+REALIZED]   I-see   he-ACC
     "I saw him."

is the Kupa dialect form

2.   nə'-əp   n$\underset{\sim}{\acute{ə}}$-təw   'axwác-i

The same rule applies to stressless nouns in the Kupa dialect. But there
is one exception to this rule. The stress is not shifted if the prefix is an
object prefix:

3.   nə'-nə̀-pə   mi-t$\underset{\sim}{\acute{ə}}$w
     I-I[-REALIZED]   them-see
     "I will see them."

---

[1]An apparent exception to this statement is the absence of any subject prefix on verbs
with third person singular subjects. Fuchs identifies this prefix as a ∅ morpheme. But

This strongly suggests that object prefixation was a later innovation in PCC alone, probably an incorporation of either a preceding independent object pronoun or of an object enclitic. This chronology would also explain the OBJECT MARKER-SUBJECT MARKER ordering. Object enclitics are found in a number of Uto-Aztecan languages, most notably Serrano, and Cupeño itself shows traces of object marking on its enclitic complex. Indeed, in Cupeño there is a separate set of subject markers that appear with present tense transitive verbs but not with intransitive verbs.

In Cahuilla, this kind of incorporation has gone considerably further, making the language look quite different from the more conservative Serrano and Luiseño. But the incorporation of independent non-verb or verb elements into a main verb form is nevertheless a general character-istic of Cupan. Many of the verb suffixes listed in the second chapter correspond both morphologically and semantically to existing independent verbs. In Cahuilla, however, verbs not only have subject and object mark-ings, but also elements like the <u>'ax</u>- prefix, probably the Cahuilla counter-part of the "potential" <u>xu</u> enclitic in Luiseño, and the q^w_∂ equivalent in Cupeño. The process is evident in the contrast between the position of Cahuilla <u>pa'</u>- "there," and Luiseno <u>'ivá'</u> with the same meaning:

4. Ca   ...nanxanic-em   pa'-hem-cengen-ve
           man-PL   there-they-dance-[+REALIZED]

5. Lu   ...'ivá'   ya'áyc-um   pum-pelli-vo
           there   man-PL   they-dance-[+REALIZED]
        "...where the men danced."

The evidence points to at least a subject marker plus stem form for PCC verbs with past time reference. Object marking may have been optional. But there is one further difference between the two languages that requires some consideration. Cahuilla verbs clearly referring to past time, particularly distant past, have an additional affix, one not found on

there is considerable evidence for an underlying <u>he</u>- prefix which is deleted by a late phono-logical rule. A discussion of this matter appears in Appendix B of the present study.
[2]In Cupeño, of course, they occur as infixes on -<u>in</u> and -<u>yax</u> theme verbs. On embedded verbs, subject markers occur on both realized and unrealized verbs in all three Cupan languages.

Cupeño verbs.[3] We must find out whether this affix is a Cahuilla innovation or an old form that should be postulated for PCC. But first we need to understand more fully its role in Cahuilla.

4.3 The Cahuilla -'i Past Time Marker

The affix just referred to is -'i, which is used to mark past time reference. However, although we shall refer to it as the -i marker, the actual vowel quality varies according to its phonetic environment. In all Cahuilla dialects it is normally -'i on forms without durative affixes, except when the stem ends in [l] or [n]. On stems like 'e'nan "know" and qal "be there," the [i] vowel of the affix commonly becomes [e]. Thus the -'i becomes -'e in 6 and 7.

6. pe-n-'e'nan-'e
   him-I-know-PAST
   "I know him."

7. pa'-cem-qal-'e
   there-we-live-PAST
   "We lived there."

Since in Wanikik and Desert Cahuilla the durative affixes end in [l] or [n]—-qal and -wen— an -'i affixed after them has the form ['e]. There is, however, a variant form in which the glottal stop precedes the final consonant, as in

8. ne'   pe-n-walin-qa'le
   I   it-I-dig-DUR
                   PAST
   "I was digging it."

In Mountain Cahuilla there are forms like 6 and 7, above. But the combination of the durative affixes -qal and -wen with an -'i past time marker—a combination which was probably -qal'e ~ -qa'le and -wen'e- -we'ne at one time—changed its surface form. The forms -qal and -wen, which had no -'i marking, lost their final consonant and became -qa and -we respectively. Those with -'i marking lost both the final [e] and their

final consonant, becoming -qa' and -we', sometimes with an extra copy of
the vowel after the glottal stop, as in -qa'a and -we'e (the extra vowel on
the -qa' being more common than that on the -we'). This surface change
has not changed the deeper facts even for Mountain Cahuilla. There is a
single past morpheme -'i with a number of phonologically conditioned
variants.

4.4 External Support for a Cupan -'i

Evidence from other Uto-Aztecan languages indicates the existence
of such a -'i back before Proto-Takic. Thus K. Hill (1967:85) reports a
completive -'i for Serrano. He says that it "marks an event as terminated
before the point of common focus." Whorf (1946:173) mentions an "even-
tive" punctual -i, apparently with past time reference, for Hopi. Lamb
(1953) describes a punctual suffix -'i with past time reference in Mono.
Finally, Miller (personal communication) reports that there is such a
suffix in Comanche and Shoshone.

4.5 The -'i and -'a Suffixes in Cahuilla

In Cahuilla the suffix -'a presents some interesting parallels with -'i.
The examples 9 and 10 below differ in that the first contains an embedded
sentential structure while the second is an unembedded sentence:

9.   tavut   ne-sex-'a

        rabbit   I-roast-'a

        "the rabbit I roasted"

10.   tavut   ne-sex-'i [4]

        rabbit   me-roast-PAST

        "The rabbit roasted me."

While 9 need not refer to time previous to the utterance, it usually does.
This characteristic is the one we have labelled [+REALIZED] or [+R]. The
difference crucial to the present discussion is that -'a forms follow their
semantic object noun phrases while -'i forms follow subject noun phrases.

---

[4]The object marker ne looks like a subject marker here because the real subject
marker he has been deleted. See footnote 1 above.

Although the subject <u>ne</u> "I" is specified in 9, constructions with -'<u>a</u> do not require the specification of a subject for the verb:

11.   tavut   sex-<u>a</u>-t

         "the rabbit which was roasted"

Compare

12.   tavut   'e-sex-'a

         "the rabbit which you roasted"

Note that when there is a subject prefix, there is no final <u>t</u>. When there is no subject prefix, there must be a final <u>t</u>. The subject prefix has the same shape as a possessive prefix, and the construction is, at least in this sense, a nominalized one.[5] The final <u>t</u> is one of the three absolutives that go on non-possessed nouns. In the appropriate environments these constructions also take the usual plural and accusative endings for nouns. However, unlike true nouns, they "agree" in case and number with the inherent features of some real noun or pronoun. Yet they can and do function syntactically as noun phrases, as we shall soon show.

If we are to show that the -'<u>i</u> constructions bore anything more than a superficial resemblance to the -'<u>a</u> forms, we must produce some evidence that they were nominals. The problem is that there is no evidence that these -'<u>i</u> forms have ever taken plural or accusative endings. And finding some other noun-like qualities in them (such as noting that their subject prefixes are homophonous with possessives) will not be enough. We must be able to explain <u>why</u> these -'<u>i</u> forms never occur with plural or accusative endings.

We have shown that the -'<u>a</u> forms with subject markers are really possessed nominals and that the -'<u>a</u> forms without such markers (and without a glottal stop) but with a final <u>t</u> are really non-possessed nominals. If the -'<u>i</u> forms discussed are likewise possessed nominals, then there should be other non-possessed -'<u>i</u> forms with absolutive endings, in fact with the particular absolutive <u>c</u>, since this is the one that normally follows

---

[5] We have no explanation as to <u>why</u> a subject form becomes a possessive form in these embedded structures. Claims for the Genitive as the unmarked case provide no real explanation for this very widespread, almost universal, phenomenon in human language. Obviously a wider definition of Genitive is needed, one providing a plausible semantic characterization of the Genitive relation in all its manifestations. Some special kind of topicalization relation seems to be involved.

<u>i</u>. That is, since there is both a <u>tavut ne-sex-'a</u> and a <u>tavut sex-a-t</u>, there should be, corresponding to <u>tavut ne-sex-'i</u>, another construction— like this:

13.   *tavut   sex-<u>i</u>-c

        rabbit   roast-PAST-ABS

        "the rabbit which roasted. ..."

with an object for <u>sexic</u> since the verb is transitive. And there is such a construction:

14.   tavut   'isil̄-i   sex-<u>i</u>-c   'ípa'   'ax-kup-ne

        rabbit   coyote-ACC   roast-PAST-ABS   there   will-sleep-FUT

        "The rabbit which roasted the coyote will sleep there."

The -'<u>i</u> form here allows plural and accusative endings, just as we would expect for a nominalized form:

15.   me-n-tew-'i   tavt-am   'isil̄-i   sex-i-c-emi[6]

        them-I-find-PAST   rabbit-PL   coyote-ACC   roast-PAST-ABS-
                                                       PL-ACC
        "I found the rabbits that roasted the coyote."

The evidence thus supports the hypothesis that the earlier forms that became finite main verbs were nominalized structures. But no explanation has yet been provided for the lack of accusative or plural noun suffixes on the possessed -'<u>i</u> nominals, i.e. those with subject prefixes and without absolutive endings.

4.6 Why Possessed -'<u>i</u> Nominals Lack Accusative and Plural
     Suffixation

One major difference between -'<u>a</u> constructions and -'<u>i</u> constructions has not yet been discussed. When -'<u>a</u> forms without subject markers are used (for example, <u>sexat</u>), no <u>specific</u> subject or agent is understood. But when -'<u>i</u> forms such as <u>sexic</u> lack a subject prefix, they are still

---

[6]Forms like <u>sexicemi</u> normally become elided as, for example, <u>sexćami</u> or <u>sexcemi</u>.

understood as having a specified subject, one coreferential with their head noun phrase in the next higher sentence.

The following underlying structures for <u>tavut sexat</u> and <u>tavut 'isili</u> <u>sexic</u> capture this distinction:

16.

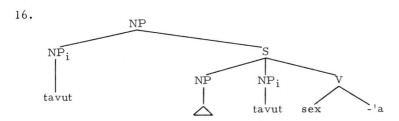

"the rabbit which was roasted"

17.

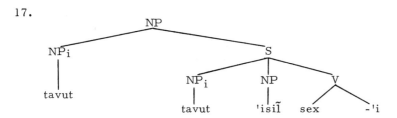

"the rabbit which roasted the coyote"

The △ in diagram 16 represents the unspecified subject, and the subscript <u>i</u> marks coreference.

Three of the transformations required to generate embedded constructions in both Cahuilla and Cupeño are particularly relevant here. They are the following ones:

    i.   Coreferential or "Equi" NP Deletion;

    ii. Subject Copying;

    iii. Case-Number Marking.

The first transformation, henceforth EQUI, deletes coreferential noun phrases almost exactly as in Relative Deletion in English. The other two transformations, which are agreement transformations, apply fairly late in the grammar. SUBJECT COPYING attaches a pronominal copy of a specified lower subject to its verb. The lower subject, if a personal pronoun, may then be deleted. CASE-NUMBER MARKING copies the case and number features of a head noun phrase onto the lower verb provided that no specified subject noun phrase intervenes.

EQUI applies to both 16 and 17 to delete the lower <u>tavut</u>. SUBJECT COPYING is blocked for both because neither structure now has a specified subject noun phrase. The original specified subject has been deleted in 17, and the subject in 16 is unspecified. CASE-NUMBER MARKING may be applied to structures like these, and it will generate structures containing forms like <u>sextami</u> and <u>sexcami</u>.

Where an -<u>'a</u> form has a specified subject noun phrase, as in 18, below:

18.

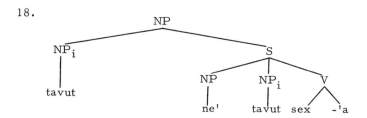

"the rabbit that I roasted"

EQUI applies to generate 16:

19. *tavut ne' sex-'a

Then SUBJECT COPYING generates 17:

20. tavut ne' ne-sex-'a

and the pronoun may be deleted:

21. tavut ne-sex-'a

Then CASE-NUMBER MARKING may apply, since there is no specified subject noun phrase intervening.[7] If, for example, the noun phrase dominating 21 had been an object noun phrase, then <u>ne-sex-ay</u> (where the <u>y</u> represents the accusative <u>i</u>) would have resulted.

Now if sentences like 22:

22. nanxanic-em   hem-taxmu-'i

    man-PL   they-sing-PAST

    "The men sang."

[7] For some speakers, this restriction has become optional.

are really nominalized forms and hence part of a higher sentence, there should be some other candidate for the position of main verb in the higher sentence. Such a verb would have little semantic content of its own since the major semantic content would be carried by the embedded sentence. Verb forms meeting these conditions will be discussed in the next chapter. In the meantime we shall use the general term COPULA to represent this higher verb. The evidence presented suggests the following underlying structure for 22:

23.

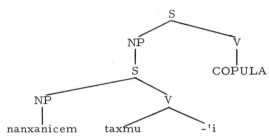

"The men sang."

EQUI cannot apply to 23. SUBJECT COPYING generates 24:

24. nanxanicem hem-taxmu-'i COPULA

But CASE-NUMBER MARKING cannot apply because there is no head noun phrase with features to copy. After COPULA DELETION, a transformation discussed in more detail later, sentence 22 is generated.

So possessed -'i constructions do not have accusative or plural marking because these structures do not meet the structure index for the CASE-NUMBER MARKING transformation, a transformation with independent justification since it is also needed for various relative and complement constructions (see chapter VIII, below). Moreover, this analysis has been carried out within a synchronic framework and justified in terms of the modern language. Postulating such underlying structures for earlier stages of a language is much more reasonable if these structures can be shown to be valid synchronically.

Since we seek to reconstruct these structures for a stage at which Cahuilla and Cupeño were a single language, it would be desirable for us to show that these underlying structures are synchronically valid in Cupeño as well. But Cupeño has no -'i for its finite main verbs with past time reference.

4.7 Justifying These Underlying Structures for Cupeño

Constructions just like the Cahuilla -'a forms also occur in Cupeño, as the following examples show:

25. nə-'isnin-'a   'isnin-ə-t [8]

     I-write-[+R]   write-[+R]-ABS

     "what I wrote"   "what was written"

26. nə-max-'a   max-a-t

     I-give-[+R]   give-[+R]-ABS

     "what I gave"   "what was given"

27. cəm-puy-'a   puy-ə-t (~puyat)

     we-eat-[+R]   eat-[+R]-ABS

     "what we ate"   "what was eaten"

Verbs with -in themes have the subject marker infixed, but the subject markers are still clearly possessives since no absolutive endings occur when the markers are infixed. The verb hum-in "paint" is just such a verb:

28. hum-pə-n

     paint-he-IN

     "He painted (it)."

29. hum-pə-n-'a

     "what (sg.) he painted"

30. hum-in-ə-t

     "what was painted"

[8]In word-final position, Cupeño ə and Mountain Cahuilla e are often realized as [a]. But in some cases the [a] realization has led to a reanalysis of non-word-final ə or e as a. Although we have labelled these forms as -'a forms, the Cupan vowel correspondences (the Luiseño vowel is [o] or [u]) and other considerations to be discussed in Chapter Six all suggest that the underlying vowels may be ə and e, with *ə as the Proto-Cupan vowel. We will retain -'a as a convenient designation.

Like the other -'a forms, both the possessed and the non-possessed
nominals take accusative and plural endings:

31. nə'-əp   nə́-təw   pə'   hum-pə-n-a-m-i

    I-[+R]   I-see   what   paint-he-IN-[+R]-PL-ACC

    "I saw what (pl.) he painted."

32. Xuliyo-pə   təw-nac   kic-im   hum-in-ə-t-m-i[9]

    Julio-[-R]   see-DUR   house-PL   paint-IN-[+R]-ABS-PL-ACC

    "Julio will be seeing the houses which were painted."

Now Cupeño also has the same kind of -'i construction with an absolutive as Cahuilla has:

33. nə'-qwə-n   tə́'ə'əw   naxánic-i   pə'   haw-in-i-c-i

    I-[+POT]-I   see[+POT]   man-ACC   that   sing-IN-PAST-ABS-ACC

    "I can see the man that sang."

34. nawícmal   pə'   puy-nin-i-c   'awál-i

    girl   that   eat-CAUS-PAST-ABS   dog-ACC

    "the girl that fed the dog"

But there is no non-possessed form 35 corresponding to 34, no -'i form
without an absolutive:

35. *nawícmal-əp   pə-puy-nin-'i

    girl-[+R]   she-eat-CAUS-PAST

    "The girl fed (him)."

[9]Note that only the last word shows accusative marking. This limitation of accusative marking to the last form only of an object noun phrase is found in all three Cupan
languages although multiple accusative marking does occur, most frequently when the
affected words are not in their normal positions.

However, there is a grammatical sentence identical with 35 except for
the final -'i:

36. nawícmal-əp   pə-puy-nin

    girl-[+R]   she-eat-CAUS

In fact, corresponding to Cahuilla constructions with -'i we find synonymous Cupeño sentences without -'i. Like the Cahuilla forms, the Cupeño
stems have subject markers with the shapes of possessives. They differ
in lacking the -'i ending, and in occurring with a [+ REALIZED] enclitic
(just as PCC probably did). Furthermore, the parallel -'a construction
in Cupeño, as shown earlier, occurs both with an absolutive and without.
In the latter case a possessive subject marker occurs. The following
table summarizes the -'i and -'a data for Cahuilla and Cupeño:

37.

	[+POSSESSIVE] [-ABSOLUTIVE]	[-POSSESSIVE] [+ABSOLUTIVE]	[+POSSESSIVE] [-ABSOLUTIVE]	[-POSSESSIVE] [+ABSOLUTIVE]
CAHUILLA	-'i	-ic	-'a	-at, -et
CUPEÑO	Ø	-ic	-'a	-at, -ət

It seems likely from the foregoing that PCC had such an -'i. When
Cahuilla lost its [+REALIZED] enclitic, -'i was the only element indicating
that the verb was [+REALIZED], especially since subject markers now
appeared on [-REALIZED] verbs too. Cahuilla might therefore have been
expected to retain its -'i. Cupeño, however, retained its [+REALIZED]
enclitic and restricted subject markers on main verbs to those with past
time reference. Consequently it would have been much more likely to lose
the highly redundant vowel suffix.

4.8 The Proto-Cahuilla-Cupeño Structures

The resemblances between the -'i/-'a constructions in Cahuilla and
those in Cupeño are so strong and so detailed that we have to posit such
constructions for PCC. What appear in the modern languages to be finite
main verbs with past time reference are really nominalized constructions

embedded as subjects of higher copula verbs. The following tree
represents these constructions as we believe they were in PCC:[10]

38.

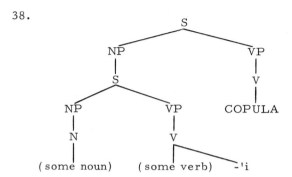

The -'i/-'a contrast is particularly interesting. In the modern languages the -'i forms stress the agent-action relation while the -'a constructions seem to emphasize the resulting state, the goal of the action.
Thus, even without subject markers, the -'i forms must be interpreted as
having a specified subject. But when the -'a forms lack a subject marker,
no such interpretation is possible. From Faye's 1920 field notebooks on
Cupeño it appears that he was not aware of most of these constructions.
But he did notice an -ət on durative verbs and he noted that such a form

> expresses a quality assumed by the subject in the past with a cer-
> tain degree of permanency

and Harrington's Cahuilla notes comment on the "static" quality of these
forms, calling them "perfect passive substantival" forms. However, he
also applies this label to the -ic forms and to certain action nominal -VI
forms that we have not considered here. Confirming this "state" characterization of -'a is the fact that many of the -'a forms are systematically
ambiguous. Cupeño tə'náan-a-t means both "what was planted" and "the
plant." Cahuilla wes-a-t means "what was sown" and "the seed." Cupeño
nə-hawin-'a means "what I sang" and "my song." There is, in addition,
an intriguing parallel between the -'i/-'a contrast and an -in/-yax contrast
(see chapters V through VI), about which we shall have more to say later.

----

[10]For ease of exposition we have omitted from the tree such elements as enclitics,
which we suspect should be represented as higher predicates in representations considerably more abstract than example 38.

[11]Kenneth Hale (personal communication) reports that in Papago, a more distant
relative of the Cupan languages, the */-a/, */-i/ endings also appear, but are phonologically determined in the main—with some irregularities. The /-i/ often appears in
derived adjectivals, the /-a/ never does.

In general, then, the following criteria appear to determine whether -'a or -'i is chosen as the subordinating affix:

i.   If the head noun phrase of a relative construction is coreferential to a non-subject noun phrase in the relative, then -'a is chosen.

ii.   If, in a noun phrase complement, the underlying subject (usually the agent) is not the surface lower subject, or if the lower predicate is stative (e.g. "be happy," "be green," "be crooked"), then -'a is normally chosen.

iii. Otherwise, whether the construction is a relative or a complement, -'i is normally chosen.

4.9 The -'i Constructions and Sentence Embedding

With the exception of the non-possessed -'i forms, the -'i/-'a constructions considered in this chapter have turned out to be relative constructions. The following general characteristics have been noted for these constructions:

i.   When a lower subject noun phrase is not coreferential with the noun phrase head of the construction, a subject marker is affixed to the lower verb.

ii.   When the lower subject noun phrase is either unspecified, or is coreferential with its noun phrase head, a subject marker does not appear.

These characteristics ensure that any lower subject not present in surface structure is recoverable. Absence of the subject marker in -'i constructions always means that there is a matrix noun phrase head coreferential with the underlying subject of the lower sentence.

But since verbs with -'i can only be embedded beneath noun phrases coreferential with their subjects, it follows that they can never occur with subject markers in such constructions. The subject marker indicates for these constructions that there is no higher sentence head noun phrase, that these -'i forms are in noun phrase complement constructions. What is predicated is the entire lower sentence. Within a framework in which tense or aspect is a higher predicate with a lower sentence as subject, it would not be surprising if this particular -'i construction, rather than the other three considered, had come to denote past time on the verb. But it appears that the next higher predicate for these nominalized subjects is not

tense or aspect but a copula verb.   The nature of this higher copula will
be discussed in the next chapter.

V. COPULA VERBS AND PROTO-CUPAN

5.1 Some General Considerations

In the previous chapter it was shown for both Cahuilla and Cupeño that what appeared to be main verbs with past time reference were really nominalized forms. These nominalized forms were embedded as subject noun phrases with copula verbs as their predicates. The underlying structures for these constructions were seen to be the same in both languages, and the processes required to generate the surface forms were very much alike too. Therefore we felt justified in reconstructing the same kind of underlying structure for Proto-Cahuilla-Cupeño (PCC) with transformations like EQUI, SUBJECT COPYING, and CASE-NUMBER MARKING also being required to generate the PCC surface structures. For convenience we reproduce the reconstructed PCC underlying structure here:

1.

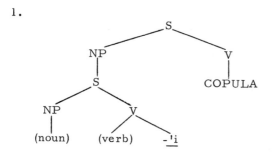

In this chapter we shall try to extend the findings of the previous chapter to Luiseño as a necessary prerequisite for reconstructing them for Proto-Cupan.

But first we must remedy a gap in the PCC reconstructions. Details of the higher copula verbs were left unspecified. We shall examine modern copula forms in the three languages, particularly as they relate to the representation of tense or aspect, and we will look for an explanation of their absence in the modern forms that we have already studied. We shall then look at Luiseño verbs with past time reference to see if there is justification for assuming that they too are, or were, nominalized structures and to find out whether the -'i/-'a contrast is valid for this language. If these findings hold for Luiseño, then they can be reconstructed for Proto-Cupan, since independent development of such a situation in three separate languages is highly unlikely.

5.2 The Modern Cupan Copula Verb mí-yax

In all three languages there is a copula verb mí-yax containing a mi-prefix that normally appears on interrogative or indefinite words meaning "how?" "somehow," "where?", "somewhere," "when?", "sometime" and sometimes "why?" and "for some reason." These copula verbs appear to be quite old. This is indicated by the fact that although they take the tense/aspect suffixes -qa(1) and -we(n)/wə(n), in Cahuilla and Cupeño, these suffixes do not as elsewhere serve to differentiate singular forms from plural forms. Instead they mark a rarer and certainly older contrast between "active" verb forms and "stative/passive" ones, c.f. Cupeño tul-qa "(he) is finishing" and tul-wə"(it) is completed" as well as "(they) are finishing." On these copula verbs, this distinction appears as the difference between "happen" and "do" on the one hand, and "be" on the other. The old interrogative meaning of the mi- prefix still appears on a few copula forms. The following examples illustrate the characteristics just discussed:

2. Cu   miyaxwənət   "How are you?"

3. Cu   nə'ən mi-yaqa   "What happened to me?"

4. D.Ca   hice'a ku pe' mi-   "What's going on there?"

             yax-qal   (Seiler, Texts:39)

5. D.Ca   mi-yax-wen   "What is the situation?"

                                   (Texts:116)

Another verb, Cupeño 'ixan, Cahuilla 'exan, both meaning "do," also allows mi- prefixation:

6. Cu   nə'ən 'ixaqat   "I'm gonna do it."

    Cu   nə'ən mixaqat   "What am I gonna do?"

But in general the copula verb has no such interrogative meaning, as the following examples from all three languages show:

8. Ca   siwma'   tamet   mi-yax-we'e

         hot   day   be-PAST

         "It was a hot day."

9. Ca   siwma'   tamet   mi-yax-wen-ne

         hot   day   be-FUTURE

         "It will be a hot day."

10. Ca   siwma'   tamet

         "It's a hot day."

11. Cu   Loola   'a'cimal   pə-mi-yax-wən

         Lola   beautiful   she-be-PAST

         "Lola used to be beautiful."

12. Cu   Loola   'a'cimal   mi-yax-wən-i-qat

                                                        be-INCEPTIVE

         "Lola is going to be beautiful."

13. Cu   Loola-'am   'a'cimal
                              3rd
                              SG

         "Lola's beautiful."

14. Lu   'onu-p-il   no-tukmay   mi-y-qut
                      3rd

         that-SG-[+R]   my-basket   be-PAST

         "That was my basket."

15. Lu   'onu-po   no-tukmay   mi-yx-maan
                 [-R]   be-FUTURE

         "That will be my basket."

16. Lu   'onu   no-tukmay

     "That is my basket."

Sentences 10, 13, and 16 show that, in all three languages, present
time reference is the unmarked time reference. A copula verb may be
added to these sentences, but it rarely is, unless an emphatic assertion is
required. The COPULA DELETION rule discussed in the previous chapter
appears to be a generalized form of this process. The unmarked character
of present time reference for copula verbs has been noted for many unrelated languages. Unbegaum (1957:285), for example, reports that in
Russian:

> the copula "to be" is hardly employed except in the past (<u>byla</u>) and
> future (<u>budet</u>). In the present, the copula ... is rare ... .

5.3 mi-yax as Predicate for Nominalized Verbs

The next step is to show that <u>mi-yax</u> can have the kind of function we
ascribed to the COPULA in the underlying structure of 1, above. The
Cupeño inceptive, like the other Cupan inceptives, is a nominalized form
ending in the <u>t</u> absolutive, i.e. it is a non-possessed nominal:

17. nə'ən   hiwcu-qat

    "I'm going to learn."

In the appropriate environments, this verb form can take plural or accusative suffixes like any other noun. The following sentences suggest that
there is an underlying present copula form in 17:

18. nə'-əp   hiwcu-qat   pə-mi-yax-wən

    I-[+R]   learn-INCEPT   it-be-PAST

    "I was going to learn."

19. nə'-qwə-n   hiwcu-qat   mi-ya'a

    I-[+POT]-I   learn-INCEPT   be
                                 [+POT]

    "I might be going to learn."

Note that in 18, a <u>third</u> person singular (rather than first) subject marker is prefixed to the copula verb. This pǝ- can only be a pronominal copy of the lower sentence. Much more common is a periphrastic past or "perfect" construction consisting of a possessed nominal and a copula verb:

20. Ca ne-taxmu-ve   mi-yax-we

        I-sing-[+R]   be-PRES

        "I have sung."

21. Cu 'axwác-i-ǝp   cǝm-tǝwí-vǝ   pǝ-mi-yax-wǝn

        that-ACC-[+R]   we-see-[+R]   it-be-PAST

        "We had seen that."

22. Lu hamú'   no-waaqi-vo   mi-y-q

    already   I-sweep-[+R]   be-PRES

    "I've already swept."

The same kind of construction occurs with an unrealized marker on the lower verb. The following Cahuilla sentence typifies this common Cupan construction:

23. Ca ne-taxmu-pi   mi-yax-we

        I-sing-[+R]   be-PRES

        "I am to sing, I have to sing."

In Luiseño especially, the realized suffix may be omitted without apparently affecting the meaning. Note that the third person enclitic in the Luiseño sentence below indicates that, although the lower verb has "we" as its subject, the copula has the entire lower sentence as its subject.

24. Lu cam-ngorax-up   mi-y-q

      we-run- 3rd   be-PRES
             SG

    "We have run."

The underlying structure of this last sentence, like that of the other
sentences we have been considering, is the same as that reconstructed for
PCC on the basis of Cahuilla and Cupeño main verbs with past time
reference:

25.

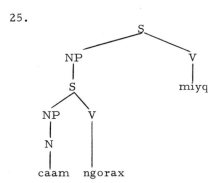

This structure, like that of 1, is for a sentence with past time reference.
The same set of three transformations can be tested here. EQUI is not
applicable, SUBJECT COPYING attaches a pronominal copy (in possessive
form, i.e. cam, not caam, the independent non-possessive form) to the
verb, and the pronominal subject noun phrase may be deleted. CASE-
NUMBER MARKING does not apply.

We have thus shown that there is a copula verb in Cupan, one that can
certainly be reconstructed for Proto-Cupan, that not only can fill the role
of the COPULA posited in the last chapter but actually does fill this role
in certain constructions, constructions very much like that for which we
originally posited the COPULA. However, all that we have established is
a reasonable likelihood, since there is no morphological trace of this
copula verb remaining on the verbs discussed in the last chapter. Moreover mi-yax is not the only candidate that should be considered. There are
other yax forms that merit discussion here, if only because they also
appear in the positions we might expect of such a copula as the one we have
proposed.

5.4 The yax Copula

The root yax goes back to a form reconstructed for Proto-Uto-Aztecan
by Miller (1967) as *ya , *yas "sit." Miller reports a cognate Serrano verb
yein "be alive, live," and in Hopi, yeese "sit, live." Like other copula
verbs in Uto-Aztecan then, yax can be related to an older location verb.
Whorf (1960:172) gives a ya in Hopi as a plural subject suffix which,

significantly, is a constituent that he describes as being in certain
constructions "similar to a suffix, but even more like an auxiliary verb in
close-phrase contact with the predicator" (171). The singular subject
suffix (or "annex" as Whorf labels this particular usage) is ni, probably
related to the Proto-Uto-Aztecan causative *ina. We shall see later in
this discussion that the Cupan cognate of this caustive replaces the yax
forms in some environments. The Hopi ya also occurs within the verb
stem in a position that would in Cupeño mean that the verb has a stative or
passive-like interpretation. Unfortunately, Whorf gives no details of the
Hopi function.

In Cupan there are several unprefixed yax forms, all of which might
perhaps be reduced to a single underlying form with conditioned realizations. The verb yaax in Luiseño and Wanikik Cahuilla, and yáya(x) in the
other Cahuilla dialects and in Cupeño, most commonly means "try to V,"
or "start V-ing," as in the following synonymous sentences:

26. Cu nə-yayax-nə-pə   tan-in

       I-try-I-[-R]   dance

27. Cu nə'-nə-pə tan-in   nə-yaya(x)

       "I'll try to dance."

It is rather like an English auxiliary verb in that its form lacks most of the
normal verb inflections. We might show the underlying structure of 26 and
27 below:

28.

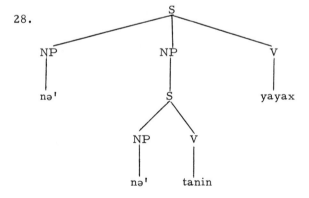

But, like the English auxiliary may, the verb yayax may also have a
sentential subject, be an epistemic modal:

29. nə'-nə-pə tan-in pə-yayax

    I-I-[-R] dance it-be

    "I'll dance for sure."

which could be represented thus:

30.

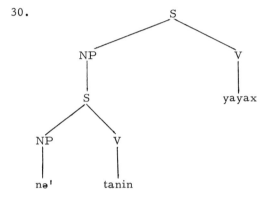

The pə- is a pronominal anaphor for the lower sentence. Note then that
in Cupeño SUBJECT COPYING applies to the higher verb, attaching a
pronominal copy of the sentential subject. It is particularly interesting
that in doing this a surface contrast between 27 and 29 is created, one
which is isomorphic with the root/epistemic modal opposition. Presumably
an interpretive theory of the kind proposed by Jackendoff would have to
treat this contrast differently for Cupan from the treatment for English, or
else have to duplicate the grammatical processes needed for Cupan with
basically the same processes in reverse for the interpretive component.
The root/epistemic opposition is quite clear here and does not depend just
on the pə. The third person enclitic that appears in sentences like 31 cannot be accounted for unless it is recognized as a marking for the embedded
sentence:

31. nə-naqma-'a-m pə-yayax

    I-hear-'a- 3rd it-be
           SG

    "Of course I've heard it."

However, if the yayax/yaax forms are like the copula forms discussed earlier in this chapter it seems strange that there should be such a radical semantic contrast for the root and epistemic forms as that represented by "try to V" and "of course X will V." In fact, these semantic differences are really conditioned by the realized or unrealized marking on the lower verb. The situation is a little more complex than our present discussion suggests but for our purposes we can reasonably assume that the copula, when present in surface structure, serves to re-assert the realizedness or lack of it of the event represented by the lower sentence.

In Wanikik Cahuilla, for example, if yaax is used with an unrealized lower verb, one with, say, the potentive ("may, might, can") suffix, -pil̃, a quite different emphasis is conveyed by the epistemic modal:

32. ne'   tuku   ne-cengen-pil̃   yaax

    I yesterday   I-dance-POT   (it-) be

    "I should/could have danced yesterday."

These yayax/yaax forms, though, which do not take any tense or aspect inflection, appear to be a special case of a more main-verb-like yax, just as the English desiderative auxiliary will (as reflected in "He won't come") does not take person inflection but is a "frozen" variant of a main verb will which can take person inflection:

33. Do what he wills.

5.5 The Gradual Incorporation of the yax Copula

In addition to the forms discussed in the previous section, there are clear indications of an earlier yax in Cupan which started off as an independent inflected copula verb, gradually became incorporated into the lower verb, and eventually became the "theme" suffix -(y)ax in two of the languages. It is this yax that appears to have been the higher copula verb for the past constructions considered in the fourth chapter.

This older yax appears as a main verb in Cupeño in a rather rare construction that requires special elicitation. There is a prefixed form 'í-yax which means "be like," as in

34. mə-ƛ̣ə-'ət Felísita   pə-'í-yax-wən

    and-DUB-she   she-like-be-PAST

    "Was she like Felicita?"

When native speakers were asked to use the Spanish-derived <u>kumu</u> "like" in the Cupeño sentence, they used <u>yax</u> even though they seemed to be unaware of <u>yax</u> as a <u>be</u> verb, i.e. they always recognized <u>yax</u> as if it were a (homophonous) verb which means "say, speak." Yet the <u>yax</u> was quite clear in

35. mə-ʂə-'ət   kumu   Felísita   pə́-yax

     and-DUB-she   like   she-be

     "Was she like Felicita?"

and was also noted by Faye in 1920.

But an inflected <u>yax</u> survives in unincorporated form in Cahuilla, with a specialized meaning "V a little," "only V" that is similar to the <u>yayax/yaax</u> forms discussed earlier. Seiler (1967:138-139), writing about this construction in the desert dialect, characterizes it as occurring primarily in the language of "old timers." In this construction, the <u>yax</u> takes all the tense and aspect inflection that might otherwise be expected to appear on the other verb, and it can also take the derivational affixes, like -<u>ici</u>, "while going along."

36. Ca taxmu   hem-<u>yax</u>-'i

       sing   they-be/do-PAST

       "They sang a little."

37. taxmu   'ax-hem-ya-ne

     sing   POT-they-be/do-FUT

     "They'll sing a little."

The same kind of construction appears in Wiláqalpa Cupeño except that the <u>yax</u> has become suffixed to the other verb. Thus, corresponding to

38. C.Cu   Xwaníta-əp   pə-tə́w   naxánic-i

        Juanita-[+R]   she-see   man-ACC

        "Juanita saw the man."

is

39. W.Cu   Xwaníta-əp   təw-pə-<u>yax</u>   naxánic-i

                    see-she-be/do

         "Juanita glanced at the man."

Stress and the impossibility of any word intervening before the <u>yax</u> make
it clear that the <u>yax</u> form is suffixed.

     But in both dialects of Cupeño, the <u>yax</u> appears in full in the regular
past tense forms of the so-called -<u>yax</u> theme verbs like ha𝑓ax, "go." Thus,
the past tense form corresponding to the verb in 40, below,

40. Cu   nə'ə-n   ha𝑓a-qat   Paala-yka

      I-I   go-INCEPT   Pala-to

      "I'm going to go to Pala."

has -<u>yax</u> in this example :

41. nə'-əp   há𝑓i-nə-<u>yax</u>   Paala-yka

      I-[+R]   go-I-be/do   Pala-to

      "I went to Pala."

Evidence from other constructions, some of which will be presented later,
shows that the infixed subject marker belongs to the preceding verb root,
not to the affix. In present and future tense forms, the -<u>yax</u> is not separated from the rest of the verb stem but appears as an ordinary affix, -<u>ax</u>,
or sometimes -<u>yax</u>.

     This kind of partial incorporation of a higher verb has been noted for
other languages. In the Romance languages, for example, the future tense
forms consist of the verb infinitive plus a suffix clearly related to the
indicative of the verb "have." In Portuguese, according to Pardal, one
could, until approximately the seventeenth century, say in literary prose
<u>dar hei</u> for "will give." The forms were written as separate words and
pronouns could appear between them. In modern Portuguese this future
has become <u>darei</u> "I will give," <u>darás</u> "you will give," etc. The disappear-
ance of the <u>h</u>, and other changes in the plural forms, have made the link
with <u>haver</u> a tenuous one. But one link remains. In an affirmative main
clause, object pronouns are infixed in future verbs. Thus "you will give

me ..." is dar-me-ás, where the me pronoun is inserted between the original lower verb dar and the original higher verb ás.

But if the yax verb rather than the mi-yax verb served as the higher copula carrying the inflectional marking for past or [+REALIZED] aspect, we should expect to find in Luiseño, as well as the other languages, some signs of this, and not merely the appearance of absolutive-like endings on past tense verbs—which would suggest an old nominalized form—but signs of a yax with past tense forms.

5.6 The Luiseño Past Punctual

Luiseño has a multiplicity of past tense paradigms. This is a surprising situation in view of the simplicity of the other Cupan languages, as well as Hopi, Serrano, and Tubatulabal. Of all the paradigms, only two, those with -qat and -quś suffixes, look as if they were once nominalized forms. But neither can be reconstructed as Proto-Cupan past forms. The -qat forms allow regular noun plural making but do not permit any copula to occur with them in the way that the -qat inceptives do in the other languages. Their occurrence as recent past durative forms is unexpected, and when -qat forms appear in relative constructions they have present rather than past time reference. The -quś distant past durative forms end in a consonant that may once have been a c absolutive, suggesting an early -qwic or -kawic ending. This allows the rather tenuous possibility of a connection with the past relative suffix -mu-kwic. Aside from this, this distant past does not correspond to any tense either in any other Cupan language, or in the larger Takic family, although, admittedly, our information on some of the languages is very incomplete. Of the other paradigms, all but one can be related to non-finite forms in the other languages—participial or adverbial constructions. What is left is the past punctual, the form that speakers proficient in Luiseño and another Cupan language most often use when they translate from the other language into Luiseño.

As in Cupeño, the past punctual forms—and only the past punctual forms—vary according to the verb class. The transitive -i theme verbs have their final -i replaced by -'ax or -yax in the Rincon dialect. However, La Jolla and Soboba speakers, including Adan Castillo, Harrington's informant, often use -yax instead of -'ax. Many speakers from all reservations drop the final x off both forms. Similarly the -ya or -'ya endings replacing the theme in -ax theme verbs was sometimes realized (for the same verbs) as -yax, -'yax, or -'a in the speech of most of our consultants, even our somewhat prescriptively oriented Rincon consultant. Finally, the so-called "simple" verbs, some of which allow reduplicated past forms, also allowed -ya, -yax, -'ax, -'ax, -'a , and -a suffixes for past time reference. Thus, for 'ohó'van "believe," we elicited, often from the same consultant, 'ohó'van-ya, 'ohó'van-a, 'ohó'van-ax, and 'ohó'van-yax. Malécot (1963:199-201) lists many of the same variations for the speech of his La Jolla consultant. But he identifies the forms as marking two distinct past tenses—preterite and remote preterite. In most cases the forms with y are the remote preterites while the forms without are the ordinary preterites. Where, however, there was no yax ending, as for reduplicating verbs, the -ax suffixes were identified as remote preterite. None of our own consultants made this distinction, nor, apparently, did those of Sparkman, Harrington, Kroeber, or Grace.

This being so, we feel justified in relating all these past punctual endings to a yax. The correspondence in both forms and uses to our PCC copula verb *yax is too close to be a coincidence. We thus conclude that in Proto-Cupan the modern past tense forms were nominalized verb constructions which served as sentential subjects for higher copula verbs. Since the modern Luiseño verb has no prefixes when it is a main rather than embedded verb, there is now no strong direct Luiseño evidence as to whether the nominal was indeed a possessed nominal.

5.7 Nominalized Forms and the -'i/-'a Contrast in Luiseño

There is, however, a small amount of indirect evidence. Some few verb forms, forms obviously cognate with forms in the other languages, are possessed verb nominals functioning as surface main verbs:

42. noo-p   no-ma'max   Xwaan

    I- 3rd   I-like   John
      SG

    "I like John."

and the potentive -vutax mode verbs are also possessed:

43. caam-up   cam-toyax-vuta-q

    we- 3rd   we-laugh-POT-PRES
       SG

    "We can laugh."

The presence of the third person singular subject enclitic in both examples
and the appearance of the singular ending in 44 indicate that the surface
main verb is part of the underlying sentential subject of a higher verb
(which in 43 is probably -vutax rather than a copula).

There is also evidence for a Luiseño i with "realized" if not past time
reference. Luiseño has -ic forms that take nominal case and number
inflection and look very much like the Cahuilla and Cupeño forms:

44. Ca   ne' pe-n-teew-'i   'á'wal-i pe'   mi-mamayaw-i-c-i

45. Cu   nə'-əp nɔ́-təw   'awál-i pə'   mi-mamayəw-i-c-i

46. Lu   noo-n-il   tiw -'yax   'awáal-i po'   mamayuw-i-c-i

However, there is a distinct meaning difference between the Luiseño and
the other two languages. The sentences 44 and 45 mean "I saw the dog
that helped them," while the Luiseño sentence means "I saw the dog that
was helped." Verbs ending in -ic occur also as surface main verbs:

47. Lu   tukmal-um tap-i-c-um

    "The baskets are finished."

48.   'awáal   xec-i-c

    "The dogs are beaten."

49.   kic kuláw-tal   lo'x-i-c

    "The house is made with wood."

The last three examples occur in contexts where the semantic stress
appears to be on the "realized-ness" or accomplished state rather than on
the "pastness" of the action referred to. In fact, when a speaker wants to
refer specifically to a time removed from the time of utterance, he uses a
copula verb such as miyquɕ "was," or miyxmaan "will be."

Indeed, all these -ic constructions in Luiseño appear to be more like
the -'a plus absolutive t constructions in the other languages. For many
of these Luiseño constructions there is an almost completely synonymous

one which looks very much like the corresponding -'a forms in Cahuilla
and Cupeño:

50. Lu   'awaal   xecaat

    "The dog is being beaten."

51. tukmal tapaat

    "The basket is finished."

Our Luiseño consultants were fairly consistent in claiming that tapic was
the same as tapaat, but most felt that xecic was a little different from
xecaat. The clearest description came from a La Jolla consultant:

> If you were outside a house and you could hear a stick going and
> dog howling, you might say xecaat, but if you passed by and saw
> the dog bleeding and running away you could say xecic. But tapic
> tapaat, if it's finished, it's finished.

The verb "finish" refers to a state necessarily achieved at a particular
POINT in time, while "beat" refers to action occurring over a period of
time. The distinction looks like one between durative and non-durative
aspect verbs, a distinction that would be neutralized for verbs that are
inherently point of time verbs. As will be seen later, there is good reason
to suspect the presence of an underlying durative element in the -aat constructions. What looks like the -'a element or a [u] variant also appears
in other Luiseño constructions, but they always contain a durative affix:

52. po-hulúqa-qal-a

    "as he was falling"

53. hulúqaq-wun-u-t

    "falling"

Remove the possessive-like po-, and the a has to go too:

54. caam tiwyax   hunwuti   hulúqa-qal

    "We saw the bear fall."

The Cahuilla and Cupeño equivalents for 53 would end in i rather than a.

It appears clear that we can safely reconstruct a nominalized verb construction as the Proto-Cupan ancestor of the Luiseño past punctual and the Cahuilla-Cupeño past forms. It also appears clear that there was a Proto-Cupan i which marked verb forms as representing realized events. The existence of -'a forms in Luiseño indicates the possibility in older forms of Luiseño that an i/a opposition like that in the other languages also occurred in this one, and hence in Proto-Cupan.

There are, however, some difficulties. First, it is not obvious that -'i was a Proto-Cupan past time suffix. The Luiseño -ic forms can, through their higher copula verbs, refer to future time. However, such usages all refer to the realization of the lower verb's action prior to the time reference of the copula. The question is not so important since it is quite reasonable for the [+REALIZED] marker to take on past time reference. But in Luiseño the -'i and '-a forms appear to be suppletive forms of the same underlying grammatical element, one which marks forms that are [+REALIZED]. The -'i is restricted to non-durative stems while -'a occurs only on durative forms. Both are used only when the lower underlying subject is a deleted proform. This difference in Luiseño would seem to be a later development. But there is some evidence that such a conclusion might not be correct, and that the limitation of -'i to non-durative environments might be an older one. The -ic relative constructions in Cahuilla and Cupeño, unlike the other relative constructions in the languages, cannot have durative aspect, although semantically this should be possible. The equivalent Luiseño construction does allow durative aspect, but instead of -ic a suffix -mokwic is used which may or may not contain the -ic. The rather scanty non-Cupan evidence also suggests such a limitation. The Serrano -'i apparently occurs just with non-durative forms (though this is not so stated in K. Hill's description). And the Mono, Comanche, and Shoshone -'i forms were reported earlier as being basically punctual.

5.8 Proto-Cupan

A safe reconstruction for the underlying structure in Proto-Cupan of
the constructions that later became past time reference forms is the
following:

55.

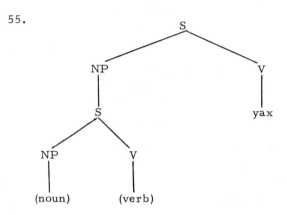

A pronominal copy of the lower subject is prefixed to the lower verb and a
suffix added if the verb is [+REALIZED], its form being determined eventually by the presence or absence of a durative suffix. The [+REALIZED]
suffix would most probably have been i, which, after the final l or n of a
durative affix, would have become [ə]. This [ə] retained its particular
vowel quality in Cupẽno except word-finally, when it becomes [a] preceded
by a glottal stop. In Cahuilla, ə became [e] and, in word-final position,
['a].

VI. ON FROM PROTO-CUPAN

6.1 Introduction

In the two previous chapters we traced back to Proto-Cupan both
Cahuilla and Cupeño past tense forms, as well as the Luiseño simple past.
We traced all these back to a Proto-Cupan construction containing the verb
as a possessed nominal (with the [+REALIZED] -'i suffix). The possessive prefix stood for the subject of the embedded verb. The whole nominal
was a noun phrase complement sentence embedded as the subject noun
phrase of the copular verb yax. This construction, whose surface form is
shown here thus,

1.   POSSESSIVE - VERB - 'i   yax
       PREFIX

would have prior to subject copying and nominalization the following
(approximate) underlying structure:

2.

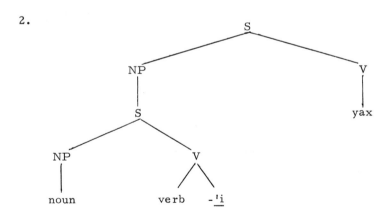

The -'i suffix had the form -'i for non-durative forms and probably -'ə or
-'a for duratives.

In the course of working back to Proto-Cupan we temporarily omitted
from consideration such phenomena as the -i/-ax dichotomy for most
Luiseño verbs, and the corresponding -in/-yax division of verbs in Cupeño.

137

We shall consider these phenomena in the present chapter. We start in this chapter with the reconstructed Proto-Cupan forms and follow their development through various stages up to the present time.

6.2 The Proto-Cupan Copular Verb

It seems likely that at one stage of Proto-Cupan the possessed nominal construction with yax was used only to represent realized action or events—or past time, if pastness was grammatically represented then—and possibly in command sentences and minor constructions such as the "V a little/try to V" ones still surviving in the modern languages. Data from Luiseño and Cupeño support our claim. We do not regard the absence of Cahuilla evidence as of major import, in keeping with the criterion for reconstruction presented in our third chapter and repeated here for convenience:

> Any characteristic noted for only two of the three languages may more reasonably be ascribed to Proto-Cupan if the languages are either Luiseño and Cupeño, or Luiseño and Cahuilla. This is because the linguistic data indicates that there was no stage at which Luiseño and only <u>one</u> of the other languages were a single language.

The evidence supporting our claim is as follows:

i.   In Luiseño, the occurrence as a suffix of one or other of the yax variants—<u>ax</u>, -<u>yax</u>, -<u>a</u> , -<u>ya</u>, or -<u>x</u>—is not restricted to -ax theme verb forms. But when such a suffix occurs on either derived or -<u>i</u> theme verb forms, these verb forms are always either past tense forms or imperatives.

ii.   In Cupeño, an -<u>ax</u>, -<u>yax</u>, -<u>ya</u>, or -<u>a</u> variant of <u>yax</u> occurs as a suffix only on -<u>yax</u> theme verb forms. But only on the past tense forms of such verbs does the -<u>yax</u> occur, almost as a free form, separated from the verb root by an infixed pronominal subject marker.

At the stage of Proto-Cupan that we are discussing, <u>yax</u> was a separate verb, much as it is in constructions like the following:

3.   Ca   cung   ne-yax

       kiss/suck   I-do

       "I kiss a little."

where the cung can be separated from ne-yax by other constituents of a
sentence. Similar constructions occur in Wiláqalpa Cupeño. The next
step was probably incorporation of the two verb stems into one, as in this
form:

4. Cu   cung - nə - yax

         kiss - I - do

         "I kissed a little."

No constituents can intervene now between the cung and the rest of the verb
form.

    The next stage may have started just prior to the Luiseño split, when
the three modern languages were probably three major dialect divisions.
This next step was full incorporation into the verb stem, as in this modern
example:

5. Lu   noo-n-il   Xwaan-i   cung-ax

         I-I-[+R]   Juan-ACC   kiss-PAST

         "I kissed Juan."

6.3 The Introduction of -in

    At about the same time, another element began to replace yax for cer-
tain verbs. This element, derived from the Proto-Uto-Aztecan causative
*-ina, can, for Proto-Cupan, be reconstructed as *-in. We can show it as
-in rather than *-in because it still survives as -in in Cupeño and Cahuilla.
In Luiseño this suffix is now -i. To highlight the shared properties we
show the two forms as IN and YAX in our morpheme glosses for all three
languages.
    This -in replaced yax on non-stative, mainly transitive verb forms.
The yax remained on stative, mainly intransitive forms, and its meaning
narrowed from "do, be, happen" to "be" or to the passive equivalent of the
-in form. Thus, in Cupeño, cung-in means "kiss," and cung-ax, "be
kissed." But, like yax, -in appears to have been treated as a verb-like
element. Possibly this was so because its functions so closely paralleled
those of -yax. That such a parallel was felt is evident from the "V a little"
constructions in Cahuilla, which were reported by Seiler (1967:138-139) as
used by "the old folks." Our sentence 3 is just such an example. The
actual verb in Cahuilla is cung-in "kiss." The in affix is the only affix that

may be omitted when the free verb form yax is used. Other examples are
hiv pi-yax-'i "He took a little" from the verb hiv-in, hat pi-yax-'i "He
made some light" from the verb hat-in, wal 'ax-pi-yax-ne "He'll dig a
little" from wal-in "dig."

This deletion of -in when yax appears was always carried out by our
two consultants over seventy-five, but appeared to be optional for our
younger Cahuilla consultants. Since other derivational endings do not
undergo such deletion, it is reasonable to assume that speakers felt—and
some still feel—that the -in affix duplicates in some way the function of the
yax.

A further indication of this can be seen if these yax constructions in
Cahuilla are compared with the very rare Cupeño equivalents, which,
interestingly, occur only as past tense forms. We have come across only
three, one of the occurrences being in a traditional text, the others from
elicitations based on the text. Here are the forms in Cahuilla and Cupeño:

6.

Cahuilla	Cupeño	English
qwa' pe-m-yax-'i	pi-qwa-pə'-ma-n	"They ate a little of it."
eat it-they-YAX-PAST	it-eat-they-PL-IN	
teew pe-m-yax-'i	pi-təw-pə'-ma-n	"They glanced at it."
see YAX	see IN	
pa' pe-m-yax-'i	pi-pa'-pə'-ma-n	"They drank a little of it."
drink YAX	drink IN	

In each case where yax is used in Cahuilla, -in is found in Cupeño.

Finally, the specialization or narrowing of the meaning of yax referred
to earlier in this chapter is readily seen from the following Cupeño and
Luiseño contrasts:

7.   Cu   nə'-əp   pi-cung-nə-n

          I-[+R]   her-kiss-I-IN

          "I kissed her."

8. Cu   nə'-əp   cung-nə-yax

    I-[+R]   kiss-I-<u>YAX</u>

    "I was/got kissed."

The -<u>in</u> seems to denote the active "do," while the -<u>yax</u> indicates the passive or stative "be" or "get."

9. Lu   paala   ɟil-a-qa

    water   spill-<u>YAX</u>-DUR
                       PRES

    "The water is spilling over."

10. Lu   hax-ɟu   paal   ɟil-i-qa

    who-DUB water   spill-<u>IN</u>-DUR
        [+ACC]   PRES

    "Who is spilling the water?"

The Luiseño examples show a stative/causative contrast.

6.4 The Extension of IN and YAX

As examples 9 and 10 show for Luiseño, one final development in Proto-Cupan was the extension of IN to non-past forms. The following example illustrates this same development in Cupeño.

11. W.Cu cinga-nə-pə   qaawi   man   'əməm-pə ni-səx-in

    if-I-[-R]   die   then   you- -R   me-burn-<u>IN</u>
                                PL

    pəta'əma-y

    everything-ACC

    "If I die, then burn all of me."

Here an unrealized enclitic and a verb without a tense suffix are used to indicate the non-durative future. The next example illustrates the use of IN in a non-past form in Cahuilla:

12. Ca   'ax-pe-m-hat-in-wen-ne

            FUT-it-they-light-<u>IN</u>-DUR-FUT

            "They'll probably be lighting it up."

Except for Luiseño past forms, IN and YAX become thematic affixes in the two languages, marking off the two largest verb conjugations in each language. No such YAX and IN conjugations are found in Cahuilla, despite the existence of verb forms like 12 above. Since this difference almost certainly arises from a later development affecting Cahuilla alone, we shall reserve further comment for a separate discussion later in this chapter.

It is interesting that another causative affix, -<u>ni</u>, found in all three languages, may also be derived from Proto-Uto-Aztecan *-ina. It differs from -<u>in</u> in the following respects:

     i.   It is a derivational affix without any apparent copular function. Hence it does not disappear in Cahuilla <u>yax</u> constructions like the "V a little" ones referred to above. Nor does it allow subject marker infixation, as -<u>in</u> does in Cupeño.

     ii.   It denotes only causation, regardless of the root to which it is attached.

We cannot be sure as to whether -<u>ni</u> was incorporated into verb forms earlier or later than -<u>in</u>. But the varying semantic functions of -<u>in</u> suggest that, if indeed it is derived from *-<u>ina</u>, this element has been incorporated longer into verb forms in Cupan, especially since it participates in some highly idiosyncratic constructions like the rare "V a little" ones in Cupeño, which have been found for only six verbs. Furthermore, in Cupeño, verb forms with -<u>ni</u> must also have -<u>in</u> immediately after the -<u>ni</u> (resulting in -<u>nin</u>). These special -<u>nin</u> forms often have no corresponding non-causative -<u>in</u> form. Thus <u>puy-ni-n</u> "feed, make eat," has no corresponding -<u>in</u> form *<u>puy-in</u>, but simply <u>puy</u> "eat, dine." The -<u>nin</u> forms do not behave like regular -<u>in</u> forms in allowing subject marker infixation. It may be that when -<u>in</u> lost its consistent function as causative, -<u>ni</u> filled the other element's function but was felt to need the -<u>in</u> element's "do" function. The merger into -<u>nin</u> resulted in the creation of a new affix not subject to the same processes as -<u>in</u>.

Our account of -in fails to provide a satisfactory explanation as to why such an element descended from a Proto-Uto-Aztecan causative affix *-ina should have become a verb-like element like yax, which is itself a descendant of a Proto-Uto-Aztecan verb. In all three languages, the IN element appears in most environments as just an ordinary derivational affix, just as its ancestor *-ina is presumed to have been. Why should this -in have become a verb-like element in the special constructions noted? If the answer is that it has replaced the old copular verb yax in just these constructions, then we still need to understand why -in, an affix, should have replaced the old copular verb yax in these constructions, and why it should have filled the role of yax on so many non-stative verb forms when yax certainly denoted both the non-stative "do" and the stative "be"—as it still does in some constructions. Our present account provides few if any clear answers for these questions. It must be recognized, however, that this kind of failure is not restricted to Cupan studies. It reflects a more general ignorance concerning the nature of syntactic and morphological change in language, and of the forces motivating such changes. We shall return to the Cupan aspects of this problem later in this chapter.

6.5 The -'i Suffix Shift

The modern Cupan forms indicate that as the yax copular verb was becoming more and more closely associated with the verb stem, the past of [+R] suffix -'i shifted to the right of the yax (or to the right of the -in that replaced yax for some verbs). We might reconstruct the following as an early Proto-Cupan verb form:

13. *pə-wal-'i   yax

    he-dig-[+R] YAX

    "He dug (it)."

14. *pə-wal   yax-'i

    he-dig   YAX-[+R]

and/or

15. *wal   pi-yax-'i

    dig   he-YAX-[+R]

in which the subject pronominal marker is prefixed to the auxiliary yax
rather than to the main verb. 15 looks like the modern Cahuilla form

16. Ca   wal   pi-∅-yax-'i

           dig   it-he-YAX-[+R]

           "He dug it a little."

However, as we explained in our fourth chapter, there is good reason to
believe that the object incorporation observable in 16 was a later
development.

　　Probably both 14 and 15 were acceptable expressions. A similar
phenomenon is to be found in modern Cahuilla, where, as Seiler has shown
(1967:138), derivational affixes may occur either on main verbs or on aux-
iliaries in sentences like the following, from Seiler (138):

17. D.Ca   kus-<u>ngi</u>   pi-yax-e-qal

           take-go   it-YAX-<u>e</u>-DUR
                around

           "He takes it (a little) one by one."

18. D.Ca   kus   pi-yax-<u>ngi</u>-qal

           take   it-YAX-go-DUR
                             around

           "He takes it (a little) one by one."

　　It may have been about this time, or perhaps just a little later, that the
affix -<u>in</u> took over from <u>yax</u> in many non-stative verbs. The present range
of translations possible for -<u>in</u> in Cupeño is a not unlikely consequence of
the use of a causative for a function previously carried out by <u>yax</u>, meaning
roughly "behave." When -<u>in</u> was introduced for this function, <u>yax</u> must have
been either almost an affix, or perhaps already one, as in

19. *wal-pi-yax-'i

    dig-he-YAX-[+R]

from which sentences like the following are descended:

20. Cu   wal-pi-yax

       "It was dug."

With the substitution of -in, verb forms like these may have developed:

21.   wal-pə-n-'i

           dig-he-IN-[+R]

22.   pi-wal-in-'i

           he-dig-IN-[+R]

which may be compared to the following modern forms:

23. Cu   (pi-)wal-pə-n

          (it-)dig-he-IN

          "He dug it."

24. Ca   pi-∅-wal-in-'i

          it-he-dig-IN-[+R]

          "He dug it."

In the dialect of Cupan that later became Luiseño, however, the yax affix must have kept its position in past tense forms, since it still survives in simple past tense forms. Perhaps -in and -yax forms alternated in past forms, with only the yax forms surviving in Luiseño. Certainly these Cupan past tense forms, whether they contain IN or YAX, appear quite different from all other Cupan forms containing IN or YAX. The absence of adequate information about earlier stages of these languages makes it difficult to choose any one of the various alternatives. However, the evidence suggests that the introduction of IN and YAX on non-past forms preceded the occurrence of these affixes on past forms. If we accept this, then we can assign the development of past forms with -in to PCC. Since the Luiseño split from the Cupan core would have preceded this development, we can predict that simple past forms with IN would not appear in Luiseño— as indeed they do not. However, forms with IN do occur for other Luiseño past tenses. Since these developed later, we might attribute their

occurrence to the generalization of the IN pattern from the non-past forms,
or, alternatively, to the adoption of non-past verb forms, probably non-
finite forms, for past tenses. While we prefer this last alternative, it is
clear that in our present state of knowledge such choices are often arbitrary
and might more properly be regarded as informed speculation.

Fortunately, some of our conclusions can be more soundly based. Our
claim that -'i, the realized suffix, moved rightward was based mainly
upon Cahuilla evidence. Cupeño and Luiseño evidence for this shift is to
be found in the following sentences in which -'i occurs to the right of the
-in or -yax morpheme:

25. Cu   pə'   kiimal.   pə'   tuku   'axwác-i

          the   boy   that   yesterday   that-ACC

          haw-in-i-c   has-ax-qat   'a-yka

          sing-IN-[+R]-ABS   go-YAX-INCEPT   that-to

          "The boy that sang that yesterday is going to go there."

26. Cu   nə'-nə   hiwcu-qa   kiimal-i   pə'   pə

          I-I   know-DUR   boy-ACC   he   that
                    PRES

          tuku   'a-yka   has-ax-i-c-i

          yesterday   that-to   go-YAX-[+R]-ABS-ACC

          "I know the boy that went there yesterday."

27. LJ Lu noo-n   'ayál-i-q   ponéy   po   heel-ax-i-c

           I-I   know-IN-DUR   that   that/which   sing-YAX-[+R]
                    PRES

          "I know the song that was sung."

28. LJ Lu noo-n-il   tiiw-yax   wunáal   wicat   ponéy   po

           I-I- +R   see-PAST   that   rope   that   that/which

           xal-ax-i-c

           loose-YAX-[+R]-ABS

          "I saw the rope that had been loosened."

Evidence for Luiseño forms with IN is not easy to find since after the older -in became -i, any subsequent -i merged with it, as in

29. Lu   tukmal-um   tap-   i-c-um

basket-PL   finish- $\underset{[+R]}{\text{IN}}$ -ABS-Pl

"The baskets are finished."

The form tapicum is derived from the verb tap-i "finish," which contrasts with tap-ax "be finished." The i, it might be argued, is clearly the IN element—there is no trace of a [+R] suffix -'i. However, there is an alternative form with about the same meaning, tapaxicum, where the i is obviously the [+R] suffix -'i rather than an IN element.

Unless it was followed by an absolutive ending, the [+R] -'i suffix was dropped from the dialects that were to become the Luiseño and Cupeño languages. We have already noted that this loss occurs in the languages retaining a [+R] enclitic, while the suffix survives without an absolutive in Cahuilla, which now has no [+R] enclitic.

However, we cannot be sure as to the existence of this enclitic in the Proto-Cupan dialect that later became Cahuilla. The partial loss of -'i in the other dialects may have made it more difficult to distinguish the realized forms from the others unless the enclitics were retained. Moreover, it may have led to the creation or preservation of distinctive past forms in Cupeño and Luiseño, forms quite different from the very regular ones in Cahuilla. The fact that the realized enclitic in Luiseño is much more often omitted in this language than in Cupeño may arise from the retention of the distinctive yax in past tense forms. This, however, is no more than a speculation.

6.6 Some Conclusions as to the IN Phenomenon in Proto-Cupan and
      Proto-Cahuilla-Cupeño

Despite the previously mentioned lack of data, what we have suggests the following as the sequence for the spread of IN:

i.   IN replaced YAX on non-past forms of certain non-stative Proto-Cupan verbs.

ii.   After the Luiseño separation, IN replaced YAX on non-stative past forms in PCC. Luiseño retained YAX for its simple past tense forms.

This appears to be the most satisfactory way to account for the differences among the languages since it involves making few assumptions not clearly supported by available data.

6.7 Languages and Dialects

In this study we have frequently expressed ourselves in such a way as to suggest that clear boundaries distinguish dialect groupings within a language from groupings of closely related languages. In fact there are no such clear boundaries since each member of a family of related languages may on the basis of a number of internal isoglosses be considered as constituting a family of dialects, and some dialects of language A may well be closer in some respects to language B than they are to other dialects of language A. This is clearly not the case with the Cupan languages because major phonological, morphological, lexical, and syntactic boundaries set off each of the three modern languages.

Yet it must once have been the case that the differences were slight, that the languages were once dialects or groups of dialects constituting a single language. The incorporation of IN and YAX into verb forms appears to be the last major syntactic change that we are aware of that is reflected in all three of the modern languages. Later changes affect only one or two of the entities that became the modern Cupan languages. The first of these stages marks the emergence of Luiseño as a separate language.

Nevertheless we should be aware that linguistic change is rarely if ever an overnight phenomenon and that speakers of Luiseño and PCC could probably communicate with each other without much trouble for quite some time after separate Luiseño and PCC changes had begun to occur. It is interesting that some Cahuilla speakers claim that they can understand Cupeño but not Luiseño even though they do not speak Cupeño. Tests we have run—having a Cupeño speaker recite to Cahuillas a traditional tale occurring in both languages—show this claim to be quite false, yet the claim persists. The claimants intuitively perceive the greater degree of likeness between these two languages and are sometimes aware of the sound correspondences linking all three languages. Our experiments have also shown, as might be expected, that the more radical sound correspondences linking Cupan to Serrano are not perceived by either Cupan or Serrano speakers.

6.8 Some Changes in Luiseño

One early change in Luiseño was a phonetic one—the dropping of the final <u>n</u> in the -<u>in</u> thematic affix. As the Cupeño potentives and imperatives indicate, this <u>n</u> was probably deleted in Proto-Cupan for certain modalities. In Luiseño this deletion was generalized.

More important than this was the dropping of subject prefixes and hence of the distinction between realized possessed and non-possessed nominalized verbs. After this, these verb forms, which had already lost their -'<u>i</u> suffix, could no longer be considered as nominals morphologic- ally and the surface connection with -<u>ic</u> forms disappeared.

Some verb forms still retain their nominalized status. They have either a possessive subject marker or an absolutive, and they allow case and number marking. If these verb forms occur without a copular verb, they are understood as referring to present time, or, alternatively as forming part of a subordinated construction such as a relative or a gerun- dive form. Inceptive verb forms like <u>toonav-lut</u> illustrate one type. With- out a copula, this verb form means "is going to make baskets." The com- bination <u>toonav-lut miy-qu$</u>, containing a copular verb with a durative past suffix, means "<u>was</u> going to make baskets." Forms like the -<u>ic</u> forms considered in the last chapter and those in examples 28 and 29 in this chap- ter are of the second type—they cannot normally serve as main verbs. Finally, verb forms with -<u>vo</u> and -<u>pi</u> appear to have the characteristics of both types. As we have shown in chapter II, these forms occur not only with copular verbs, but also in such embedded constructions as noun phrase complements and relatives. As we suggest in chapter VIII, all of these verb forms are actually in embedded constructions whether there is a copular verb or not.

However, not all of the apparently nominalized Luiseño verb forms conform to the foregoing generalizations. This failure does not refute the generalization; rather it indicates on-going changes in both morphology and syntax, changes of the type needed to account for many of the idiosyncratic properties of Cupan verb forms. Luiseño -<u>qat</u> is a suffix indicating recent past durative when it occurs on main verbs but present time on verbs in relative constructions. Verb forms with this suffix look very much like nominals. The final <u>t</u> appears to correspond to the phonologically appro- priate absolutive ending. In relative constructions an accusative suffix may be attached, and the regular noun plural suffix -<u>um</u> may occur whether the

verb form is a main verb or a relative construction verb. Yet verb forms
with -qat differ in two significant ways from regular nominalized verbs:

    i.   They do not occur with copular verbs.

    ii.   They allow a subject prefix to co-occur with the otherwise regular
absolutive ending.

    These forms provide valuable information regarding the development
of finite, tense-marked main verbs from embedded nominalized verbals
of the type described in the previous two chapters. The -qat forms in this
language, unlike those in Cupeño, are approximately midway in their development. The former possessive pronominal prefixes which served as subject markers have now lost their identity as possessives. The absolutive
suffix might alternatively be regarded as no longer an absolutive but simply
as part of a CVC recent past suffix. The non-occurrence of any copular
verb, past, present, or future, indicates that these verb forms can no
longer be regarded as surface structure embedded nominalized verbs. We
shall have more to say about these qat forms in the following chapter, where
we treat in detail Cupan duratives.

    Yet another past tense form indicates further developments which have
almost completely obliterated surface evidence of an older identity as a
nominalized verb form. Verb forms having the -quʂ past durative suffix do
not correspond in form to any inflected finite verbs in Cahuilla and Cupeño,
or indeed to any in Serrano and more distantly related languages such as
Hopi and Tubatulabatl. This -quʂ, recorded by Kroeber and Grace as -kwuš
or kwaš (1960:137), contains the only final ʂ in the language according to
our data. This claim is supported by the absence of any counterexamples
in Bright's dictionary, Malécot's lexicon (1964:18-31), or Harrington's
notes. Such a situation strongly suggests that this ʂ was an innovation,
probably replacing an earlier [š]. A similar process has occurred in a
number of Cupeño forms where the introduction of ʂ either differentiated
forms now homophonous except for a ʂ/š contrast (as in huʂ-pə-n "he
smoked," and huš-pə-n "he skinned (it)") or indicated that the consonant
could never be replaced by [č].

    We claim that this ʂ may well have been a c absolutive on a nominalized
verb form. As this verb form, like the other past forms already discussed,
lost its nominal identification and became a main verb, it also ceased to
allow plural and accusative marking. Since it was thus invariably realized
as [š] rather than [č], this failure to alternate with [č] and to take plural
marking with plural subjects led to a re-analysis. This [š] sounded like the

absolutive variant [š] but was somehow not quite the same. The [ȼ]
consonant also sounds like the variant [š] but never becomes [č]. So this
strange [š] became ȼ.

Such an argument would be more satisfying if there were nominalized
verb forms to which these -quȼ forms could be linked, just as the Proto-
Cupan past forms with -'i can in all three languages be linked to past relative verb forms having the -ic suffix. There are such forms—the past relative verb forms with the -mokwic/-makuc/-makwic suffix. The parallel
to the connection between the non-finite past relative form with -ic and a
finite past tense form is not an accidental one. In fact, as we shall show
in a later chapter, the so-called "present" relative suffix -qat is really a
[+R] suffix allowing past time reference. The link between this -qat and
the recent past -qat is of the same type, the latter -qat being a more recent
development.

We conclude then that the Luiseño simple past, past durative, and
recent past durative verb forms developed out of non-finite forms with
past time reference. We have noticed the beginning of a like development
in Cupeño where the non-finite -və verb forms are used, though rarely, as
finite past tense main verbs. In the case of the -mokwic/-makuc development, speakers must have re-analyzed the -kwic part of the ending as
being the past tense marker.

We cannot as easily provide an explanation for the other Luiseño past
tense forms with -uk/-k, the past usitative or distant past suffix, and with
-muk, the recent past durative suffix. These tenses also have no equivalents in Takic, Hopi, or Tubatulabatl, although there is a Gabrielino -mok
recorded by Harrington on past tense verbs. This language appears, from
Harrington's very limited data, to be more like Luiseño than is any other
non-Cupan language. The Luiseño -muk may be a borrowing which fitted
in rather neatly with the existing -uk distant past. Or it may have come
from a combination of the affix -ma and -uk. The affix -ma serves elsewhere as a durative (as in -maan) and as a usitative which, according to
Hyde (1971:102) "indicates that an action is continuous over a period of
time," action which appears always to end at the present and begin in the
recent past.

Our first explanation for -muk—borrowing—is no more elegant than our
second, although it is strange that these two Takic languages alone should
have the same past tense ending, one different from past tense suffixes in
any other Takic languages for which data are available. Our second explanation still leaves the -uk to be accounted for. If these -uk forms, which
so often refer to distant past, are like the other Luiseño past forms already

discussed, they too should be derivable historically from a non-finite
verb form.

The most obvious candidates as ancestors of the -uk forms are the
non-finite -nuk/-nik forms. Since the equivalent Cupeño and Cahuilla
suffix is -nuk, we reconstruct *-nuk as the Proto-Cupan form. In all
three languages, verb forms having this suffix are usually translated into
English as "having V-ed" or "after V-ing." Thus such verb forms always
have a time reference prior to that of the main verb, whether the latter
has present, future, or past time reference. Given the Luiseño tendency
to convert non-finite past forms into finite past tense verbs, these -nuk
forms, whose time reference is always more past than that of accompanying main verbs, are likely candidates for conversion into finite "super-past"
verb forms.[1]

In sentences like the following:

30. S.Lu pomóm   wukó'i-nuk   ṣungáal-i   tiiw-'yax

     they   arrive-after   girl-ACC   see-PAST

     "When they had arrived, they saw the girl."

the form wukó'i-nuk might easily be interpreted as a main verb, as the
alternative translation for 30, "They arrived and (then) saw the girl,"
indicates. The uk part of -nuk might thus have been interpreted as a past
tense suffix. This hypothesis, which is much like our earlier one deriving
-quṣ from -makwic, suggests one additional possibility. At the time this
development occurred, the IN element might still have survived as -in
rather than -i in some environments. This would allow the following
possible breakdown of the verb form:

        wukó'-in-uk

        arrive-IN-PAST
                DISTANT

---

[1]-nuk itself presents some problems because it is almost certainly the same -nuk that
occurs as a suffix on manner adverbials in all three languages. A probably related form is
the nk cluster occurring for example in Cahuilla penkic and Luiseño 'ankic, both meaning
"like it, him, her." K. Hill (1967:36) reports a -nq ending on manner adverbs, translated
as "so-doing." From our own work on Serrano and from a very small amount of other
Takic and Hopi evidence, we suspect that -nuk was a pre-Takic form, perhaps *ni-yi-k,
meaning "it was done (thus)," containing a predecessor of Proto-Cupan *yax.

We might note here the comment of Kroeber and Grace (152) that

> our material indicates that some of the "tenses" given here actually
> are aspectual in meaning. In the texts collected in 1951, tenses 4,
> 5, and 6 the past durative, the -uk distant/usitative past, and the
> simple past are all used to refer to the time of the recounted
> events. The distinctions were clearly aspectual; tense 4 was dura-
> tive, 5 was usitative, and 6 punctual.

We found a number of examples where an -uk verb was not used in the
usitative sense, but rather in the sense of "way back when" or yamayk
"long ago," as the Luiseños say.[2]

It would seem then that the Luiseno simple past developed from an
embedded nominalized verb with a copular verb, and that at least two of
the other puzzlingly numerous past tenses are also descended from nominalized constructions. All of the past tenses appear to have developed
from non-finite verb forms of various types, many of them in much the
same way that the normally non-finite English verb form done has become
a finite past tense verb form in some dialects, as in

31.   I done it for laughs, I did.

Two other characteristics of the changes described are worth noting
here:

     i.   Analytic forms (i.e. periphrastic constructions) have been replaced
by synthetic forms (i.e. single inflected forms) with surface structures less
like the underlying abstract structures that might reasonably be assigned
to them.

     ii.   The -qus and -uk forms, if our analyses are correct, show a shift
from time reference relative to the time reference of some other verb form,
to time reference relative to the speaker's time perspective. This is, of
course, one natural consequence of the change from a non-finite subordinate
form to a finite main verb.

     6.9 The Multiplicity of Past Tenses in Luiseño

As to why so many past tenses have developed in Luiseño, we have no
answer. We have noticed that, as might be expected, -uk forms usually

---

[2]In fact, one early hypothesis of ours, afterwards rejected as overly speculative, was
to relate the -uk to -yuk/-ik "to, toward," as in ya-má-yk "towards when it was," "long
ago." There is some reason to link the inceptive ka'/kat suffixes to the directional -yka.

appear in narratives, and that speakers using -qat appear not to use -muk;
indeed we do not recall any of our consultants using -muk except when we
asked them to. A fairly thorough examination of the thirty-seven pages of
text in Kroeber and Grace failed to uncover any qat forms and only one,
highly dubious, -muk form, (recorded as -mik). Not all of these texts are
traditional narratives—some are letters, personal reflections, and recollec-
tions. A similar examination of texts collected by ourselves and by
Harrington yielded no such forms at all. Despite the theoretical availabil-
ity of many past tense forms, speakers usually make use of no more than
three—the simple past, the distant or usitative past, and the durative past—
each with its quite distinct aspectual meaning. If the recent past is to be
emphasized, -qat is sometimes used but present durative forms are
occasionally used in their place.

6.10 Proto-Cahuilla-Cupeño (PCC)

The major development that can with reasonable certainty be assigned
to PCC concerns the Proto-Cupan *-'i realized (or past tense) suffix. As
we have shown in chapter V, it is very likely that there was in Proto-Cupan
a [+R] suffix *'i which appeared as *-'i or *-ic (with an absolutive) on non-
durative verb forms and as *-ə or -'a on durative verb forms. The vowel
quality of the suffix on the durative verb forms required the absolutive
ending to be t rather than c.

These [+R] suffixes are realized as i and either o/u or a in Luiseño,
as i and either ə or a in Cupeño, and as either e or a in Cahuilla. The
vowel qualities correspond exactly to the sound changes postulaged by
Langacker (1969:8), for example. We summarize the relevant processes
here:

i.   Proto-Cupan *i becomes i in all three languages.

ii.   Proto-Cupan *ə becomes o or u in Luiseño, ə in Cupeño, and e in
Cahuilla.

iii. Proto-Cupan *a becomes a in all three languages.

From the alternations between o/u and a in Luiseño, between ə and a
in Cupeño, and between e and a in Cahuilla, we conclude that there must
have been a *ə/*a alternation in Proto-Cupan. And, of course, at the
morphophonemic level the Proto-Cupan *-'i and *-ə/-'a were conditioned
variants of the same morpheme.

In PCC these forms must still have been *-'i and *-ə/-'a. At this point, for what reason we cannot tell, the difference between *-'i and *-ə/*-'a (henceforth referred to as just *-'a) widened from one conditioned by the presence or absence of a durative affix to an opposition in which the *-'i forms represented the agent-action relation while the *-'a forms represented the resulting state, the goal of the action. As we saw earlier, the -'i forms in Cahuilla and Cupeño are used in relative constructions with subjects coreferential to the noun phrase in their head, while the -'a forms are used in relative constructions in which the agent noun phrase is not coreferential and may also be a deleted pro-form of the same type as that underlying "someone" or "anyone" in English. These contrasting relative constructions are a reasonable outcome of the opposition described above.

The factors motivating this rather radical development are as usual unclear. However, the new PCC contrast of primarily active *-'i with primarily stative *-'a appears remarkably parallel to the IN/YAX active-versus-stative contrast that had already developed in Proto-Cupan. The parallelism even extends to the vowel qualities of the elements. Possibly the relatively late Proto-Cupan active/stative contrast stimulated the semantic specialization of *-'i and -'a in PCC, a specialization fostered further by a sound symbolism perceived by PCC speakers. This change is at least partly responsible for other major differences between Luiseño and the other two languages, most notably in relative constructions, as will be seen in chapter VIII. It is interesting that the -'a in Cahuilla hen-hici-kat-em-'a, "I was going to go" may reflect the two Cupan changes described so far—the use of -'a to indicate a realized state and the possible first stages of the development of a new finite past tense from a nominalized embedded verb form.

6.11 Cupeño

The *-'i/*-'a split described above marks the last relevant change that we can clearly attribute to PCC. Later changes appear to be language-specific rather than shared by the two languages. It is true however that the loss of -'i in finite [+R] verb forms is shared by Cupeño and Luiseño and may either have begun in the parent dialects of these two languages or have occurred independently or by diffusion at some undetermined state. The otherwise almost isomorphic character of Cupeño and Cahuilla past verb forms, and the particular shapes of the durative suffix (to be discussed in the next chapter) persuade us that *-'i probably did not disappear completely from subject-prefixed forms until fairly well on into the PCC stage.

In some other respects, phonological as well as morpho-syntactic, Cupeño appears to be the most conservative of the three languages. The set of Cupeño pronouns and subject markers, for example, is just the set we would reconstruct for Proto-Cupan; the enclitics have been more tenaciously retained than in the other languages; and the past tense verb forms have preserved most of the surface and underlying properties claimed for Proto-Cupan. This is not to argue that Cupeño is generally more conservative. The next two chapters will show that in many respects, Cahuilla alone retains major features of Proto-Cupan.

6.12 Cahuilla

Five major changes must be noted for Cahuilla. But the changes, though greater than those in Cupeño, appear far less drastic than those described for Luiseño.

The major changes relevant to past verb forms are as follows:

i.   The Subject-Copying transformation was generalized to apply to non-past as well as past main verb forms. In other words, subject prefixes came to be required on all finite verb forms.[3]

ii. Object-Copying, optional in Proto-Cupan, became obligatory for finite verbs. Object prefixes came to be required on all finite transitive verbs, even those with sentential objects.

iii. Enclitics ceased being the significant factor in Cahuilla syntax that they are in Cupeño and Luiseño. The preservation of the various [+R] and [-R] suffixes accompanied the loss of the major [+R] and [-R] enclitics.

iv. The -in and -yax verb suffixes disappeared, except for a tiny group of verbs which have retained -in. We have noted seven, and there are probably a few more:

cung-in	"suck, kiss"
hat-in	"shine, make light"
hiv-in	"get"
kicúng-in	"kiss"
nam-in	"change" (mind)

---

[3]This is not quite correct since this transformation may be blocked by a special object incorporation rule attaching full object pronominals like ne'iy as prefixes to verb forms. This transformation, however, appears to be restricted to verb forms which are clearly surface nominalizations like the -ka' and -ic forms.

nu'-in   "rule, command"

pangal-in   "lasso"

The -in here is clearly the copular-like IN we described earlier, since this derivational ending alone may be dropped when yax occurs as in

32. peqe   cung   pe-yax-í-kt-em

    just   kiss   it-YAX-i-INCEPT-PL

    "They're just gonna kiss."

v.   The he- and hem- singular and plural suffixes replaced the older third person possessives or subject markers. The older forms may have been either PCC *pə- (c.f. the demonstrative pe') and *pəm- or early Cahuilla forms that, we surmise, were *pe- and *pem-. Since he- appears only under primary stress and such stress is rarely on prefixes, possessed forms usually have no subject prefix if the possessor noun phrase is third person singular. Only the absence of an absolutive suffix identifies such forms as possessed.[4]

6.13 Another Look at IN and YAX

Earlier in this chapter we noted that our account of -in as derived from the Proto-Uto-Aztecan causative affix *-ina failed to account for the verb-like quality of -in in various Cupan constructions. Why should the descendant of a Proto-Uto-Aztecan affix behave so much like the verb yax, itself derived from a Proto-Uto-Aztecan verb? And why should this active -in have appeared, when yax already served both as an active and a stative form? The result, as we saw, was a narrowing of the semantic role of yax so that it appeared with stative verb forms rather than active verb forms. Furthermore why should the PCC -'i/-'a contrast be so parallel to the -in/-yax contrast?

[4]One possible source for he- and hem- is an old Takic form which survives in Serrano as 'a- and 'am- "his" and "their." A third person singular 'a- also occurs in old Luiseño forms with the meaning "one's, someone's" and this may be related to the 'o- of the demonstrative 'ono. In Cupeño, there is a like third person element 'a or 'ə, as in 'axwáa'aw "over there," 'axwác "that," and 'ət and 'əv'at "it, the, that." In Cahuilla there is 'et and 'e-vá-t "it, the, that." The Cupan forms suggest Proto-Cupan *'a/*'ə with plural forms *'am/*'əm. The Cahuilla forms reflect only the *'ə- and *'əm variants, which would have been realized as *'e- and *'em- respectively. These prefixes are homophonous with the second person prefixes. So it seems likely that an h replaced the ', as it did in other environments. For example, the hen- prefix was once, as we shall demonstrate in the next chapter, 'en; the 'ax- future prefix is frequently heard as hax-; the hec- or -hic first person plural prefix for inceptives is frequently recorded by Seiler (19) as 'ec or 'ic in the desert dialect. For further discussion of he-, see our Appendix B.

We wish here to outline an alternative approach which we hope to explore in more detail in a later study of Serrano as well as of the Cupan languages. At present, however, although it provides an explanation for phenomena not accounted for in our earlier schema, this new schema also presents some new difficulties that we have not yet been able to resolve.

We postulated earlier in this study structures something like this for the Proto-Cupan ancestor of modern past tense or [+R] forms:

33.

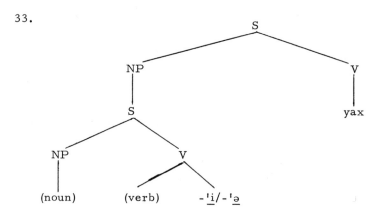

The *-ˈi, we noted, occurred on non-durative verb forms and the -ˈə on durative verb forms. Since durative aspect indicates <u>state</u>, while non-durative (or "punctual") aspect indicates <u>activity</u>, there must have developed an association of *-ˈi with <u>activity</u> and *-ˈe with <u>state</u>, one that developed more fully in PCC.

Now through some form of predicate raising (which will be described further in the next chapter), structures like the following must have developed:

34.

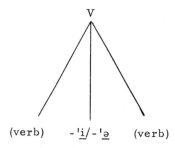

Structures such as 34 presumably occurred prior to the incorporation of
yax and the rightward shifting of the affix which has already been described.
In structures like 34 it is not at all unlikely that the *-'i/*-'ə affix might
be reanalyzed as a prefix to *yax rather than as a suffix to the verb. This
would lead to the development of verbs like *'iyax and *'ayax, the former
perhaps with a more active semantic association, the latter with a more
stative one. Note that this reanalysis does not exclude in realistic terms
the other analysis of *-'i/*-'ə as verb suffixes.

Obviously the existence of forms like *'iyax and *'əyax in the modern
languages would provide strong support not only for this analysis but also
for our earlier hypotheses regarding *-'i and *-'ə as Proto-Cupan suffixes
and *yax as the Proto-Cupan copular. In fact both Cahuilla and Luiseño
have such verbs. In Cahuilla 'iyax and 'ayax mean "be like, behave thus,"
with a tendency to use the i form for the non-stative meaning. In Luiseño,
'iyx and 'aax have about the same meanings as their Cahuilla counterparts,
except that, in our rather limited data, there appears to be a stronger
active/stative contrast. Thus, for English sentences like "I built my own
house and so did Juan," 'iix is used (... pi Xwaan 'iy-quš), while for
English constructions like "if you were single...," 'aax is used with the
"be in such a state" meaning ('om 'ooxa 'aa-ma-an). In Cupeño, there is
only an 'iyax, and this allows both meanings. Of course, both meanings
are closely linked: being like someone often entails behaving like someone.

But alongside the 'iyax verbs is another verb— 'ixan in Cupeño and
'exan in Cahuilla, meaning "do, behave," and sometimes "happen."
Luiseño does not appear to have such a verb, although it may have once had
a similar form with a, as the following set suggests:

35. Cahuilla   Cupeño   Luiseño   Meaning

    'exen(an)uk   'ixanuk   'axáninik   "thus"

The following Desert Cahuilla and Cupeño forms illustrate this verb. The
Cahuilla forms are all taken from Seiler's Texts.

36. D.Ca   pe-cem-'exan-nem

                it-we-do -FUT
                       like

             "Let's do it like this."

                                    (Texts:49)

37. Cu   nə'-əp   nə-'ixa-qal   'iví-y

     I-[+R]   I-do -DUR   this-ACC
            like   PAST

     "I was doing it like this."

38. D.Ca qa-miyax-wen   pe   pe-'exan-qal

     INDEF-be-DUR   it   it- do -DUR
                   like

     "What's causing this?"

                                      (Texts :121)

39. Cu   'atáx-am-qwə-l   yax-wənə   pə-'ixa(n)-pi

     person-PL-POT-SUBJ   say-USIT   it- do - [-R]
                                  like

     "People usually say it happens like this."

It seems clear that this verb with its more specialized meaning developed from *iyax, though we cannot be sure as to the source of the -an. In fact, in our earliest Cupeño work we transcribed 'ixan as 'iyaxwen and were corrected by our consultants when we read our transcriptions back to them. The Cahuilla and Cupeño forms, especially the latter, are often pronounced with a [y] glide, as in Cupeña ['iʸəxan], and we should probably use 'iyxan rather than 'ixan for this verb. Further evidence comes from the rare m- prefixation process for interrogation, illustrated in the following sentences:

40. Cu   nə'ə-n   m-iya-qa

     I-I   INDEF-be- DUR
              like PRES

     "What happened to me?" or "I am like what?"

41. D.Ca hice'a   ku   pe'   m-iyax-qal

     what   indeed   that   INDEF-be -DUR
                                like

     "What's going on there?"

                                    (Texts:116)

The only other verbs to which this m- can be prefixed are Cupeño 'ixan,
Cahuilla 'exan, as the following sentences show:

42. Cu   nə'ə-n   'ixa-qat

         I-I   do-INCEPT

         "I'm gonna do it."

43. Cu   nə'ə-n   m-ixa-qat

         I-I   INDEF-do-INCEPT

         "What am I gonna do?"

44. D.Ca   qa-hice'a   man   ne-m-exan-'i

         INDEF-what   CONJ   me-INDEF-do-[+R]

         "Something has happened to me."

                                        (Texts:53)

Up to this point, our hypotheses appear quite well motivated by the
evidence. We now wish to advance an additional and considerably more
radical hypothesis. This is the claim that the verb-like -in suffix was not
derived from the Proto-Uto-Aztecan causative *-ina but from the Proto-
Cupan and PCC verb *'ixan "do, behave," which replaced the older copular
verb *yax on most non-stative or active verbs. Such a development marks
the emergence of another semantic constituent as a surface structure
constituent and the consequent reassociation of semantic and surface
structures. It would further answer the following questions in the following
ways:

Question: Why is the -in affix so verb-like?

Answer: Because it comes from a Proto-Cupan verb, just as yax does.

Question: Why, if -in is derived from Proto-Uto-Aztecan *-ina, does
the -in affix so frequently seem to mean "do" or "happen" rather than
"cause"?

Answer: Because it is really derived from Proto-Cupan *ixan, which
had all these meanings, as do the modern independent verbs 'ixan and
'exan.

Question: Does this *'ixan hypothesis make the development of the modern Cupan languages seem more regular or less regular?

Answer: More regular. Almost all the verb suffixes, derivational and inflectional, can be related to independent verbs. We would also like to derive them synchronically from higher verbs. This hypothesis allows us to do both for -in. It converts a former irregularity into a further example of a regular historical process of verb incorporation in Cupan.

Question: What does this hypothesis do for Uto-Aztecan? There is a fairly general -i/-a division found for Uto-Aztecan verbs.

Answer: The -i/-a split in Uto-Aztecan verbs is the reverse of the -i/-a split in Cupan. Other Uto-Aztecan languages manifesting this split (which might well be reconstructed for Proto-Uto-Aztecan) show verbs ending in a to be transitive and verbs ending in -i to be intransitive. The reverse situation for Cupan appeared strange, especially if both endings were derived fairly directly from Proto-Uto-Aztecan. The present hypothesis provides an explanation for the Cupan difference.

Of course, to establish this hypothesis more firmly, we need evidence for phonological rules of the kind that would reduce 'ixan to -in. All the Cupan languages as well as Serrano have such a rule, one which, in general, deletes intervocalic x or h before an unstressed following vowel. All have vowel harmony processes which modify the quality of one of the vowels to match the quality of the other. Rules much like the x/h deletion described have been proposed by J. Hill for Cupeño (1966"194), by Seiler for Desert Cahuilla (1967:57), and by K. Hill for Serrano (1967:259). We present the following examples from each Cupan language:

45. Ca   'esáxane   ⟶ 'esán(e/a)   "I guess"

    Cu   pə-paha   ⟶ pə-pa(a)   "his father's sister"

    Lu   wukó'axan   ⟶ wukó'aan   "will come"

          yuvátaxot   ⟶ yuvátaat   "black"

    (These Luiseño examples illustrate diachronic and
    transdialectal variation.)

The change we have proposed, 'ixan ⟶ in, is a not unlikely development for a verb suffixed to another, especially since such suffixes lose their primary stress and, to some extent, their identity. The independent verb,

of course, retained its full form. A similar development can be noted in
Cahuilla where the "go" verb is <u>hici</u> as an independent form and -<u>ici</u> as a
suffix to another verb.

Nevertheless our alternative hypothesis presents problems of its own.
First it makes the resemblance between -<u>in</u>, which is so frequently causative, and the Proto-Uto-Aztecan causative *-<u>ina</u> merely a coincidence.
Secondly, it fails to take into account evidence from the Takic sister
language, Serrano, which has a causative -<u>ina</u> appearing in approximately
the same position in a verb form as our -<u>in</u>. Our Serrano examples are
taken from K. Hill (1967).

46. Se   tɨmɨ-m-<u>ina</u>-i-n

          shut-USIT-CAUSE-ACC-I

          "I keep shutting it."

                              (40)

Compare:

47. Cu   təm-<u>i</u>-qal-nə'

          shut-IN-DUR-I

          "I'm shutting it."

But according to K. Hill, Serrano has also an -'<u>n</u> verbalizer (42), and an
-'<u>n</u> or -'<u>na</u> stative affix (43, 115), as in

48. Se   'ɨcɨ-'<u>na</u>-i-n

          cold-STAT-ACC-I

          "I'm cold."

                    (115)

There is also a verb ñíhaa "do," but, as the following examples seem to
show, this verb also has a "be" meaning:

49. Se   ta-n   hou:nganic   ñi-:b

          DUB-I   poor one   do-FUT

          "I'll be poor."

50. Se   'ibi'   ti̵bac   'ubiht   mutu'   nama:'i   ñia:-w

      this   earth   long ago   still   soft   do-when

     "When this earth was still soft long ago. . . ."

                                (17)

As with the Cupan languages, it looks as though a more comprehensive generalization has been missed, but also as if the same analytic problems might present themselves. But it may be that Serrano, together perhaps with Hopi, with its own -ina and ya affixes, could provide us with some answers.

A further problem is the approximate dating of the 'ixan substitution—whether it was during the Proto-Cupan period or whether it took place in PCC. There is no Luiseño 'oxan. We have assumed a Proto-Cupan date, but the Luiseño -i verbs might well have drawn their -i from the 'iyax copular verb. The regular past suffix yax would then replace the i for simple past tense forms. The intransitive -ax/-yax verbs might likewise have drawn their suffix from 'ayax instead of yax. The whole matter obviously requires closer investigation.

Nevertheless, this alternative proposal accounts for apparently distinct phenomena in a unified way that fits quite harmoniously into the general framework of change that we have presented so far, and especially with our account of durative and tense affixation in the next chapter.

VII. TENSE, ASPECT, AND SEMANTIC PREDICATES

7.1 Introduction

We have shown in previous chapters that apparently finite past tense verb forms were originally—and in some cases still are—nominalized forms, some of them with a copular verb. Over a period of time, the copular verb yax "do," "be," or "get" was incorporated into some nominalized verb forms as an affix. The new verb forms no longer had surface structure identity as nominals with higher copular verbs. The semantic functions of yax narrowed when -in, which may also have been a higher copular verb, replaced yax on some forms. Indeed, in both Luiseño and Cupeño, the IN and YAX affixes now reveal some variation in their semantic contribution to the meaning of the whole verb form. This change appears to be a predictable outcome of the time depth of the incorporation. However, it is possible in most cases to assign a constant semantic value to these former verbs. We presume that a semantically based synchronic grammar might well treat these affixes as higher semantic predicates converted into surface affixes by means of PREDICATE RAISING, a syntactic process proposed for languages as various as English and Japanese (McCawley, 1971), and more recently for several Uto-Aztecan languages, including Luiseño and Cupeño (Langacker, forthcoming).

In this chapter we shall consider briefly PREDICATE RAISING and its relation first to English and then to the Cupan languages, expanding and extending the relevant parts of Langacker's arguments, with which we are in general agreement. Our own findings, as detailed in previous chapters, concerning nominalized forms and copular verbs, provide additional support for Langacker's case on both the diachronic and synchronic levels of analysis. We recognize that diachronic arguments are inadequate to sustain a synchronic argument, and vice versa. But given competing synchronic analyses of otherwise equal merit, we would favor that which also agrees with the diachronic facts. Indeed our diachronic investigations have established that what we would like to analyze synchronically as nominal sentences in underlying structure were morphologically nominal at some earlier stage. At this stage the facts of surface structure would have justified the synchronic analysis of lower verbs that we propose. We can also show that many of the surface affixes that we analyze as higher predicates actually had such a function at the surface level at some earlier stage of the language.

Our procedure for this chapter will first be to discuss PREDICATE RAISING and to motivate various other transformations required to generate surface forms from our underlying semantic forms. Then we will examine certain tense and aspectual affixes, try to reconstruct their forms and functions in Proto-Cupan, and, where possible, relate them to existing or former higher verbs of location. We shall consider other tense and aspectual affixes relatable to higher verbs of motion. Having shown that diachronically these forms were higher predicates, we shall provide further arguments for such an analysis synchronically.

7.2 Surface Structure and Complex Propositions

Apparently simple sentences may express quite complex semantic propositions, since the relation between surface structure constituents and semantic elements is not necessarily isomorphic. The English sentence 1 below:

1.   Juan wanted to feed Maria.

contains an embedded sentence (to feed Maria) which itself contains several semantic predicates. Thus 1 might be assigned the following approximate semantic representation in a semantically based grammar:[1]

2.

```
                              S
                               o
              ┌────────┬───────────────────┐
              V       NP                   NP
              │        │                    │
            WANT     Juan                   S
                                             1
                                 ┌───────────┼───────────────┐
                                 V          NP               NP
                                 │           │                │
                                DO         Juan               S
                                                               2
                                            ┌──────────────────┼──────────┐
                                            V                  NP         NP
                                            │                   │          │
                                          CAUSE              Juan          S
                                                                            3
                                                                     ┌──────┴──────┐
                                                                     V            NP
                                                                     │             │
                                                                    EAT          Maria
```

Such a proposal[2] embodies the claim that the relation between <u>feed</u> and the three lower sentences is not an arbitrary one but one reflecting various semantic and syntactic facts. For Juan to feed Maria involves Juan <u>DO</u>-ing something to <u>CAUSE</u> Maria to <u>EAT</u>. The DO notion has within its semantic

---

[1]Here, as elsewhere, we follow McCawley (1970) in positing VSO as the underlying order for English. Neither this discussion nor our others concerning basic verb final ordering in Cupan should be taken as expressing any theoretical commitment to an ordered base rather than an unordered base. For our purposes, we might have used an unordered base with a post-transformational linearization rule. The present state of generative theory is far too confused and the arguments based on too sketchy evidence to allow any such choice. For interesting arguments in favor of a non-linear base, see Hudson (1972).

[2]The semantic structure of 1 is, in truth, considerably more complex than that represented by the tree 2. We do not consider, for example, the internal semantic structure of the noun phrases, nor have we incorporated into this tree the semantic predicate "BECOME" although we agree with McCawley (1971:33) that "the notion of 'causing' which is relevant here is a relation between two events rather than between an event and a stage." But 2 is adequate for present purposes—such as defining the scope of each semantic predicate represented in 2. Furthermore, we shall consider here only the more <u>basic</u> meanings—who does what, when, etc.—rather than more subtle semantic

scope both the causing and the eating, with the kind of hierarchical relation represented in 2; the CAUSE notion has only the eating within its scope, while EAT, as its position in 2 indicates, has no other semantic predicate within its scope. WANT, on the other hand, has all the other predicates within its scope.

Moreover, the relation between WANT and the lower predicates is shown as no different in kind than that between DO and the predicates below DO. Yet DO and the predicates below it are lexicalized as a single verb in a sentence embedded as the object of <u>want</u>. It is quite conceivable that some other language might lexicalize WANT and DO as a single lexical item, or perhaps CAUSE and EAT. In 3 below, whose meaning is close to that of 1, four predicates have been lexicalized as separate verbs:

3.   What Juan <u>wanted</u> to <u>do</u> was to <u>make</u> Maria <u>eat</u>.

Within such a theoretical framework, where a surface verb may encode more than one predicate, a syntactic rule—PREDICATE RAISING—is needed to group the three lower predicates together as a constituent exhaustively dominated by V in this way:

4.

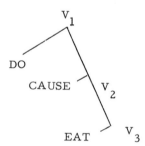

In 4, V_1 exhaustively dominates all three predicates, i.e. V_1 and only V_1 dominates all three and only those three. Consequently the single constituent V_1 can be matched with a lexical item, <u>feed</u>. Two other transformations, EQUI NP DELETION and SUBJECT RAISING, combine with PREDICATE RAISING to generate a surface structure from 2. We assume here rule ordering and cyclic rule application.

differentiations like those differentiating <u>feed</u> from <u>make eat</u> and both from <u>cause to eat</u>. We will thus consider <u>feed</u>, <u>make eat</u> and <u>cause to eat</u> as basically synonymous although, of course, they are not fully equivalent, and a grammar of English which achieves explanatory adequacy must provide an explanation for the meaning differentiations existing among these differing lexicalizations of the same basic semantic elements from morphemes corresponding to them. For further discussion, see McCawley (1971) and the references therein.

First, SUBJECT RAISING promotes <u>Maria</u> from S_3 to S_2.

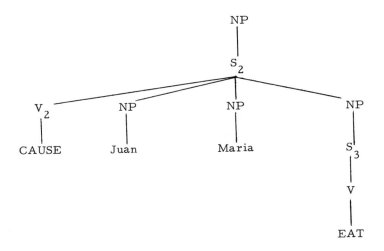

Next, PREDICATE RAISING daughter-adjoins the S_3 predicate EAT to the right of the S_2 predicate.

6.

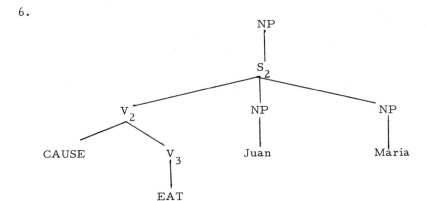

Then EQUI deletes <u>Juan</u> in S_2 by virtue of its coreferentiality with <u>Juan</u> in S_1. At this stage, the structure looks like this:

7.

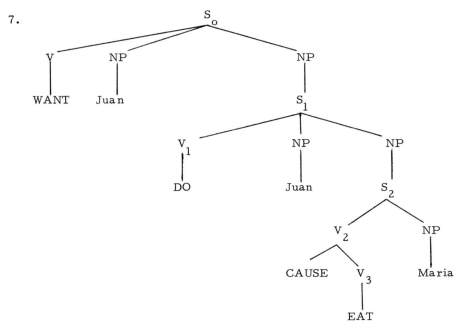

PREDICATE RAISING applies to the predicate in S_2, daughter-adjoining it to the right of the S_1 predicate. Now V_1 looks like 4, above. Then EQUI applies to delete <u>Juan</u> in S_1 because of the coreferential <u>Juan</u> in S_0. After unnecessary nodes have been pruned, the resulting surface structure is

8.

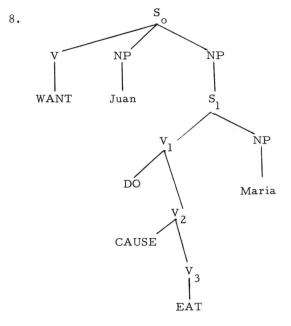

A post-cyclic V-NP inversion rule ensures normal English word order, and the lexical item <u>feed</u> replaces (DO(CAUSE(EAT))).

As Langacker has pointed out, SUBJECT RAISING and EQUI are well motivated rules with justification independent of the kind of construction we have been discussing. PREDICATE RAISING, however, is not so easily or directly motivated.

7.3 SUBJECT RAISING and EQUI in Cupan

Both of these transformations are well motivated for Cupan. In this section and the next we take our examples from Cupeño, although either of the other two languages would have done as well.

A subject raising rule is needed to account for the accusative <u>i</u> on nawícmali "girl" in 9 below:

9. Maríya-əp   pə-'ayəw-qal   nawícmal-<u>i</u>   pə-ngiy-pi

    Maria-[+R]   she-want-DUR   girl-ACC   she-go [-R]
                      PAST   away

    "Maria wanted the girl to leave."

Since <u>nawícmal</u> is the underlying subject of <u>ngiy</u> "leave," <u>nawícmal</u> might not be expected to have accusative marking. The fact that it does indicates that it has become an object noun phrase in the upper sentence.

EQUI accounts for the ungrammaticality of 10 as opposed to 11:

10. *Maríya-əp   pə-'ayəw-qal   Maríya-y   pə-ngiy-pi

    Maria-[+R]   she-want-DUR   Maria-ACC   she-go-[-R]
                    PAST   away

    "Maria wanted Maria to leave."

11. Maríya-əp   pə-'ayəw-qal   pə-ngiy-pi

    Maria-[+R]   she-want-DUR   she-go-[-R]
                      PAST   away

    "Maria wanted to leave."

7.4 Predicate Raising in Cupan

To generate the Cupeño equivalent of the English sentence

12. Juan wanted to feed Maria.

from its underlying structure 13

13.

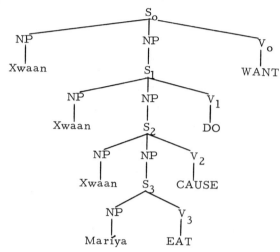

we must apply EQUI, SUBJECT RAISING, and PREDICATE RAISING.

First, SUBJECT RAISING promotes Maríya from S_3 to S_2 to the right of the S_2 subject NP.

14.

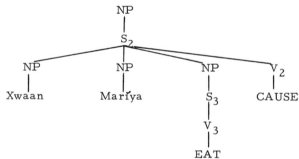

PREDICATE RAISING daughter-adjoins the S_3 predicate EAT to the left of the S_2 predicate.

15.

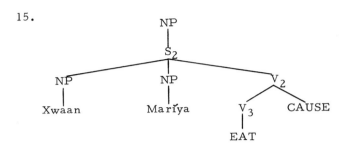

Next, EQUI deletes <u>Xwaan</u> in S_2 by virtue of its coreferentiality with <u>Xwaan</u> in S_1. At this stage, the structure looks like this.

16.

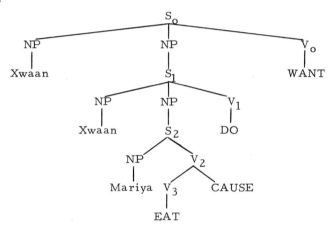

PREDICATE RAISING applies to the predicate in S_2, daughter-adjoining it to the left of the S_1 predicate. Now EQUI applies to delete <u>Xwaan</u> in S_1 because of the coreferential <u>Xwaan</u> in S_o. We could, after the usual node-pruning, stop here:

17.

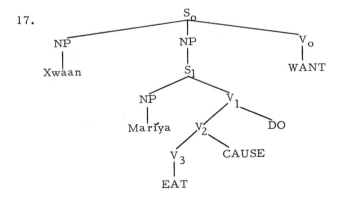

and apply the optional Cupan EXTRAPOSITION rule[3] shifting embedded sentences to the right.

18.

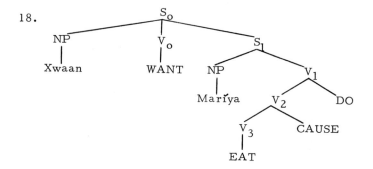

The sentence generated is 19:[4]

19. Xwaan-əp   pə-'ayəw-qal   Maríya-y   pə-puy-ni-n-pi

    Juan-[+R]   he-want-DUR   Maria-ACC   he-eat-CAUSE-DO-[-R]
                 PAST

    "Juan wanted to feed Maria."

The lexical item <u>puynin</u> has replaced EAT-CAUSE-DO in the surface structure, just as <u>feed</u> replaced the same three semantic predicates for

[3]Extraposition of embedded sentences accounts for the final position of embedded sentences in such varied constructions as the following (from Cupeño):

   (a) 'icáa   cəm-hiwcu-pi   cə'-mamalki-y
       good   we-know-[-R]   our-language-ACC

       "It's good for us to know our language."

   (b) naxanic-pə   haw-in   pə'   Maríya
       man-[-R]   sing-IN   that   Maria

       pə-mamayəw-qal-i-və   tuku
       she-help-DUR-i-[+R]   yesterday

       "The man will sing that Maria was helping yesterday."
                       or
       "The man that Maria was helping yesterday will sing."

   (c) miyax-wə   nə-haʂ-ax-pi   Paala-yka
       be-DUR   I-go-YAX-[-R]   Pala-to
       PRES
       "I must go to Pala."

[4]It should be noted here that, for simplicity of presentation, we have not considered here tense, enclitics, nor the suffixation of -pi, since these must await further discussion in this chapter and the next. Nor have we shown the SUBJECT COPYING transformation presented in our fourth chapter, although this rule is responsible for the subject prefixes in diagram 15. None of these matters are crucial to the present discussion, and they have therefore been excluded.

the English sentence 1. However, puynin, unlike feed, is not morphologically unanalyzable. It may be broken down into three morphemes which,
not coincidentally, match the order, scope, and function of the semantic
predicates. This Cupeño word, unlike the English one, consists of overt
isomorphic realizations of the semantic predicates. In other words, to
account for the particular morphology of puynin, we need to posit an
affixation process exactly corresponding to the PREDICATE RAISING
transformation already described. This is strong support for PREDICATE
RAISING in Cupan.

We might go further and predict that if the WANT predicate could be
lexicalized together with the other predicates, instead of separately, as
in 19, then it would appear just where PREDICATE RAISING would put
it—and where its relative semantic scope would require—to the right of the
DO affix. This is indeed what happens, since there is an affix -vicu
corresponding to WANT:

20. Xwaan-əp   Maríya-y   pə-puy-ni-n-vicu-qal

    Juan-[+R]   Maria-ACC   he-EAT-CAUS-DO-WANT-DUR
                                                          PAST

    "Juan wanted to feed Maria."

More complex forms are possible containing morphological representations
of additional semantic predicates, forms like the following:

21. puy-ləw-ni-n-vicu

    EAT-GO-CAUS-DO-WANT

    "want to make (him) go to eat"

22. puy-ni-n-vicu-n-Ø-lew

    EAT-CAUS-DO-WANT-CAUS-DO-GO

    "go to make (him) want to feed (her)"

23. pi-puy-ni-n-vicu-ngi-qa

    her-EAT-CAUS-DO-WANT-GO-DUR
                         AWAY PRES

    "He is going back wanting to feed her."

For Cupeño and, by extension, the other Cupan languages, PREDICATE RAISING relates surface forms to meaning in an insightful way, showing that the ordering of the verb root and affixes is not an arbitrary phenomenon but a natural consequence of underlying semantic relationships.

However, we have yet to consider the status of various tense and aspectual affixes as well as the role of enclitics with respect to the verb forms. And from the historical perspective we are also interested in any evidence that the various derivational and inflectional affixes that we may treat as higher verbs in underlying structure were ever surface structure verbs at some time in the past. Because some of the evidence related to this last consideration must also be considered for synchronic analysis we shall begin with the reconstruction of the suffixes on realized durative verb forms.

7.5 Proto-Cahuilla and the Tense/Aspect Suffixes on [+R] Forms

The following table shows the most common forms of affixes used to mark Cahuilla durative verbs with present or past time reference:

24.	M.Ca	W.Ca	D.Ca
	-qa	-qa(l)	-qal
	-we	-we(n)	-wen
	-qa'(a)	-qa'le (or qal'e)	-qa'le (or qal'e)
	-we'(e)	we'ne (or wen'e)	we'ne (or wen'e)

The forms in the upper half of the table, especially the Mountain Cahuilla ones, serve to mark present time reference. As we pointed out in chapter II, the time reference functions are less clear in Wanikik and Desert Cahuilla. The most reasonable Proto-Cahuilla reconstructions for the upper half would be *-qal and *-wen, since there is evidence for final consonant deletion in Cahuilla (for example in the nominative inceptive -ka' suffix as compared to the accusative -kati and plural -katem), and such reconstructions enable us to account for the specific form of the final consonant. There is considerable other evidence to support these reconstructions, evidence which will be presented later in this discussion. It seems reasonable to assume that speakers of Mountain Cahuilla generalized the more restricted consonant deletion rule of Wanikik Cahuilla.

The affixes in the lower half of table 24 are used for verbs with past time reference. The vowel repeated after the glottal stop in the Mountain Cahuilla forms is a purely phonetic phenomenon. But Mountain Cahuilla '̲ and Desert and Wanikik '(...)e (as in -qa'le) are, as we have shown in Chapter Four, variants of the past or [+R] affix -i̲. If these variants of -'i̲ are removed from the forms in the lower half of the table, we are left with a set of affixes identical with those in the upper half. We can thus reconstruct *-qal and *-wen as Proto-Cahuilla durative suffixes for real-ized events or actions, just as they are in Wanikik and Desert Cahuilla. The restriction of Mountain Cahuilla -qa and -we forms to denoting ongoing events or present time appears to be a later development towards a tense system from a more purely aspectual system.

Additional evidence supporting these reconstructions comes from the derived forms of verbs. The nominalizing [+R] suffix on non-possessed durative verb forms, -et̲, is attached after -qal or -wen in all three dialects, never after Mountain Cahuilla -qa or -we. Thus the embedded forms corresponding to the main verbs in

25. M.Ca   wa'ic-i   pe-∅-qwa-qa

          meat-ACC   it-he-eat-DUR

          "He's eating the meat."

26. D.Ca   wa'ic-i   pe-∅-qwa-qal

          meat-ACC   it-he-eat-DUR

          "He is/was eating the meat."

are the underlined forms in

27. M.Ca   pe-n-teew-qa   pe-qwa-qal-et-i   wa'ic-i

          him-I-see-DUR   it-eat-DUR-[+R]-ACC   meat-ACC

          "I can see him eating the meat."

28. D.Ca   pe-n-teew-qal   pe-qwa-qal-et-i   wa-'ic-i

          "I saw/can see him eating the meat."

Similarly, in all dialects, -qal and -wen are the durative affixes used with the -ve complementizing suffix, as in the complement sentences

pic-pe-qwa-qal-i-ve "that he is/was eating" and pic-pe-m-qwa-wen-i-ve
"that they are/were eating."

Synchronically, these facts suggest a revision of our description of
Mountain Cahuilla in the second chapter. Since -qa and -we appear only
on durative present forms, and -qa' and we' on durative past forms, we
might set up -qa and -we as purely durative affixes with Ø as the present
tense marker and -'i (realized as ['] on duratives) as the past tense affix.
The other two dialects would be treated as having no present tense forms,
merely [+R] forms without past time marking.

7.6 Cupeño [+R] Tense/Aspect Affixes

The situation in Cupeño is not too different from that in Mountain
Cahuilla. Although, on the surface, verb forms with past time reference
are distinguished from present time verbs by the presence of a final consonant instead of a glottal stop, nominalized durative verb forms have -qal
or -wən if they are [+R], regardless of whether past or present time is
referred to.

But there is other, stronger evidence for regarding -qal and -wən as
the underlying forms synchronically for present tense verbs. When
present tense verbs are sentence-initial, they may have suffixed to them
either the subject enclitics, or the nominative enclitics -ə, -əm, or -əl.
When any of these enclitics occur on such forms, the present durative
suffix becomes -qal or -wən as the following alternations show:[5]

29. 'axwác   mi-nəl-i-qa

    that   them-watch-IN-DUR

                  OR

    mi-nəl-i-qal-pə

    them-watch-IN-DUR-he

    "He is watching them."

---

[5]Apparent exceptions like nəli-qa-nə "I'm watching (it)" result from a phonological
rule (not noted in J. Hill 1966) deleting l before n. The same rule operates to delete the
final n of -in when the affix -ləw occurs after it, as in pi-caq-nə-Ø-ləw "I went to catch
it" versus pi-caq-nə-n "I caught it."

30. 'axwác-im   mi-nəl-in-<u>wə</u>

    that-PL   them-watch-IN-DUR

                 OR

   mi-nəl-in-<u>wə</u>n-mə

   them-watch-IN-DUR-they

   "They are watching them."

Note that these present tense forms with -<u>qal</u> or -<u>wən</u> are quite distinct from the past tense forms, which have subject markers prefixed or infixed. The past tense forms corresponding to the verbs in 29 and 30 are nəl-pə-∅-qal and nəl-pə'-ma-n-wən, respectively. At this deeper level, then, the -qal/-wən affixation appears to be a manifestation of durative aspect rather than of tense. We follow Hockett (1958:237) in defining aspect as having to do with the "temporal distribution or contour" of an event rather than just its location in time.

   7.7 Tense and Durative Aspect: PCC and Proto-Cupan Realized Verb
       Forms

   The table below shows our Proto-Cahuilla reconstructions together with the underlying durative affixes for Cupeño and the Luiseño present durative suffixes.

31. P.Ca   Cu   Lu

   -qal   -qal   -q(a)

   -wen   -wən   -wun

For PCC, *-<u>qal</u> and *-<u>wən</u> are the obvious reconstructions. They must have served as durative aspect markers for realized verbs.

   There appears, then, to have been a major realized-unrealized contrast for PCC verbs, one corresponding to the same contrast between two realization enclitics. This enclitic contrast survives in the opposition between Cupeño [+R] -əp and Cupeño [-R] -<u>pə</u> , and between Luiseño [+R] -<u>il</u> and [-R] -<u>po</u>. Apparently the realized forms could be marked with -'<u>i</u> for past time. A second major contrast is the durative-non-durative one, which is found in both [+R] and [-R] forms. However, the particular durative affixes occurring vary according to whether the verb is realized or unrealized. The [+R] or [-R] status of a verb, on the other hand, is not affected

by the durative or non-durative character of the verb form. This suggests
a direction of dependency that we will discuss further in this chapter.

The forms given in (31) are inadequate for positing both *-qal and
*-wən as the Proto-Cupan durative marker. The common past durative
forms in Luiseño -qat and -quś are of little help here except that the form
of the -qat suffix indicates at least *-qa as a basic durative element in
Luiseño. The Luiseño plural -wun is clearly cognate with the Proto-
Cahuilla and Cupeño forms, but we do not yet have enough evidence to
choose between -qa or *-qal as the Proto-Cupan durative singular form.

However, once again, non-finite forms provide useful evidence. Thus,
corresponding to

32. LJ Lu   wunáal   'awáal   wa'-i-qa

              that   dog   bark-IN-DUR
                                          PRES

              "That dog is barking."

is the lower verb form in

33. LJ Lu noo-p no-tiiw-i-vuta-q   'awáal-i po-wa'-i-qal-a

          I-it   I-see-IN-POT-DUR   dog-ACC he-bark-IN-DUR-[+R]
                       PRES

          "I can see the dog barking."

The same qal element appears in a non-possessed construction in 34:

34. LJ Lu   noo-n-il   naqmá-'ax   'awáal-i   wa'-i-qal

            I-I-[+R]   hear-PAST   dog-ACC   bark-IN-DUR

            "I heard the dog bark."

and in relativized durative verbs like wa'-i-qal-mokwic "who was barking."
The plural durative suffix -wun appears in forms like caqálaq-i-wun-ut
"tickling." It seems clear from this that -qal and -wun are modern reflexes
of the old Proto-Cupan duratives, and that we can reconstruct *-qal and
*-wən as these Proto-Cupan duratives.

7.8 Cupan Present Tense Forms

We cannot justify synchronically a *-qal as the form underlying the
present durative suffix -q(a). Indeed -qal and -wun are not, in modern
Luiseño, in suppletion as singular and plural forms in any construction.
The nominalizing suffix -ut converts caqálaq-i-wun into caqálaq-i-wun-ut
but caqálaq-i-qa ～ caqálaq-i-q never becomes *caqálaq-i-qal-ut, as we
might expect if -qal were the underlying suffix. Instead there is
caqálaq-i-qa-t ～ caqálaq-i-q-ut "(who) is tickling," in which the -qat-
-qut alternation is predictable from the -qa ～ -q alternation as present
durative suffixes.

Historically, the Luiseño present tense, like the Cupeño and Mountain
Cahuilla present tenses, developed from an unmarked form of [+R] verbs.
In Mountain Cahuilla, present tense verbs have almost the same forms as
past tense verbs. In Cupeño, the present tense forms originally had the
same durative suffixes and were probably distinguished from past forms
by the absence of -'i. The loss of the -'i differentiation may have been
accompanied by the loss of the realized enclitic for these forms. The
likeness of Luiseño present tense forms to the Cupeño ones is emphasized
by the close correspondence of the subject pronoun and enclitic complex
for them: Luiseño noo-n and Cupeño nə'ə-n. Despite their future time
reference, the same subject-enclitic forms may occur also for inceptives.
This suggests a development subsequent to the basic realized/unrealized
contrast, probably in late Proto-Cupan, since such similar present tense
forms are found in all three languages. Further indications come from
Serrano which has no overt present tense (K. Hill, 1967) and from Hopi
(Whorf, 1946:158-183), which also has the realized and unrealized contrast
(called "assertive" and "expective") and has unmarked verb forms allowing
either past or present time reference.

As we have seen, finite past tense forms are far more like future forms
than present tense forms. The same similarity is also found in derived
forms. As will be explained in more detail in the next chapter, derived
past and future forms in Cupan complement and relative constructions reveal
a neat symmetry, a symmetry lacking in forms presumed to be derived
from finite present tense forms. Moreover they allow wider time reference
range, permitting either past or present time reference, though this is less
true for some Luiseño forms.

The most likely kind of development that we can suggest for Cupan
present tense forms is that they were originally unmarked forms which
allowed past time reference. They co-occurred (and still do in most forms)

with an unmarked enclitic complex used with nouns and nominalized
forms, as the following examples show:

35. Lu   noo-n   kiháat

          I-I   child

          "I am a child."

36. Lu   noo-n   heel-ax-lut

          I-I   sing-YAX-INCEPT

          "I am going to sing."

37. Cu   nə'ə-n   Kiimal

          I-I   boy

          "I am a boy."

38. Cu   nə'ə-n   haw-i-qat

          I-I   sing-IN-INCEPT

          "I am going to sing."

39. Se   nɨ'ɨ-n   cicint

          I-I   boy

          "I am a boy."

40. Se   nɨ'ɨ-n   caatu-ka'

          I-I   sing-INCEPT

          "I am going to sing."

41. Lu   noo-n   heel-a-qat

          I-I   sing-YAX-DUR
                            R. PAST

          "I was singing."

42. Cu   nə'ə-n   haw-i-qal-ət

          I-I   sing-IN-DUR- [+R]

          "I am/was singing."

The same subject pronoun and enclitic combination occurred in
Cahuilla, but we have no evidence that it was ever used for a present
tense. The clearest evidence for the existence of the pronoun and
enclitic combination comes from the otherwise inexplicable pronominal
paradigm that occurs most commonly with intransitive inceptives:

43. hen-hici-ka'   "I'm going to go."

    'et-hici-ka'   "You (sg) are going to go."

    hici-ka'   "He's going to go."

    hec-hici-katem   "We''re going to go."

    'em-hici-katem   "You all are going to go."

    pe'em hici-katem   "They are going to go."

If the independent personal pronouns are placed before all these forms and
the whole set compared with Cupeño inceptives, the source of this strange
pronominal paradigm is quite clear:

44.

Cupeño haʂax "go"		Cahuilla hici "go"	
nə'ən	haʂaxqat	ne'	hen-hicika'
ḷə 'ət	haʂaxqat	'e'	'et-hicika'
pə'	haʂaxqat	pe'	hicika'
cəməc	haʂaxqatim	cem	hec-hicikatem
'əməm·	haʂaxqatim	'em	'em-hicikatem
pəməm	haʂaxqatim	pe'em	hicikatem

In each case the pronominal prefix to the Cahuilla form corresponds
exactly or very closely to the second syllable of the Cupeño pronoun-
enclitic combination. The second syllable must thus have been incorporated into the verb form and an initial h added to the first person forms.
Note that the Cupeño combination is the only one used for present tense
intransitives, and that the Cahuilla paradigm is also restricted to intransitive verbs. The same Cahuilla prefixes occur with nouns and other nominalized forms:

45. M. Ca   hen-kiyaat

    "I am a boy."

46. M. Ca   hen-kup-qal-et

"I had been sleeping."

Since, according to our data, Serrano, Kitanemuk, Gabrielino (and its close relative Fernandeño), and Hopi do not use as suppletive affixes pre-Cupan forms corresponding to the Proto-Cupan duratives *-qal and *-wən, we assume that this usage originated in Proto-Cupan. It remains for us to determine the source of these affixes in Proto-Cupan. It appears that they are related to verbs of location in each language.

7.9 Proto-Cupan *qal and *wən

The PUA forms are reconstructed as *katɨ "sit" and *wɨnɨ "stand". In Luiseño there are two main verbs with local meaning, qal "dwell," "sit," "be there," or "have," and wun "be there" or "have." The wun verb normally has only inanimate subjects when it means "be there." Sentences with wun meaning "have" do not have objects marked with accusative endings, as in

47. Lu   wunáal   po-miyx   muyuk   wun-q   cikáylic

     he   his-property   many   be have -DUR PRES   cane

This can be translated as

"He has many canes."

or

"Many canes are his."

The latter translation suggests that the subject may really be the inanimate noun phrase, and that wun, whatever its meaning, allows only inanimates as its subjects.

Both qal and wun are highly irregular verb roots. They can be used to refer to either past or present time, but not to the future (with one minor exception for qal). They occur with -quś, -qat, -uk, and -muk suffixes but, while qal may have -wun as a present tense suffix and wun may have q(a), qal does not allow -q(a), nor does wun allow -wun as a suffix. Consequently wun-q serves for both singular and plural subjects, while

qal-wun takes a suppletive verb form, 'aw-q[6], for singular subjects. For
the "have" meaning there is a qala singular form.

There are cognate locative verbs in the other two languages. Cupeño
qa "dwell," "be there," "lie," "have," and wə "be there," "lie" behave
just like the Cupeño affixes in adding -l and -n respectively on past tense
forms. But, unlike the Luiseño verbs, they take none of the inflectional
suffixes except for the nominalizing -və and -ət ones. While wə is used
for inanimates, qa is used for animates.

48. Cu   ṣawic   'amáy   wə   ivi'aw

      bread   today   be   here

      "There is bread today here."

49. Cu   kiyúl-im   pa-'aw   qa

      fish-PL   water-in

      "There are fish in the water."

As for Cahuilla, the location verbs qal "sit," "live," "be there,"
"lie there," and wen "be there," "lie there" both can be marked with the
past suffix -'i, usually realized as ['e]. In addition, qal takes -we or
-we'(e) if the subjects are plural and animate. Where Luiseño uses 'awq
and 'awquṣ, Cupeño has hiwqa and hiwqal and Mountain Cahuilla has hiwqa
and hiwqa'a. There is considerable meaning variation in each language,
variation conditioned by the animateness and/or number of the subject, and
the variations are not always the same for the two languages. In general
the qal forms are more likely to be singular or to have animate subjects,
while the wən/wen forms are likely to be plural or to have inanimate subjects. Again, with minor exceptions in each language, neither root is used
for future time reference.

It is fairly safe then to posit for Proto-Cupan, the main verbs *qal
and *wən. We shall refer to them as "location verbs."

---

[6]This Luiseño 'aw verb root is almost certainly related to the Cupeño -'aw locative
postposition. The reverse situation is found for -max which in Luiseño is a postposition
"for the sake of" and in the other two languages is a benefactive verb affix. Both are
related to the main verb max "give," which is found in all three languages, though our
Luiseño consultants labelled it an "old-time" word. Note that the Cupeño verb root mi'aw
"arrive" also contains this -'aw.

7.10 Location Verbs and Tense/Aspectual Suffixes

The Proto-Cupan durative affixes *-qal and *-wən are clearly related to the Proto-Cupan location verbs *qal and *wən. The affixes share too many properties with the main verbs—phonetic and semantic—for the like-ness to be accidental. In general, the Cupan reflexes of all of these four are restricted to present or past time reference, all the Cupeño forms lose their final consonant for present tense forms, and all share various idiosyncratic features—the association with singular number or animate activity with the *qal/*-qal forms, and of plural number or inanimate state with the *wən/*-wən forms. And, of course, the suppletion relationship between the two location verbs.

We have not yet shown the relation referred to between the affixes and the stative/active contrast. It is one found, though infrequently, in all three languages. Where it occurs, the *-wən affix does not also serve as marker of the plural, which is its usual function. Here are examples from each language:

50. Ca   ne'   ne-wi-lew-we

        I   I-fat-go-DUR
                    PRES

        "I am fat."

51. Ca   ne-wi-lew-qa

        "I'm getting fat."

52. Ca   pe-n-mu'aqan-qa

        it-I-pile-DUR
              PRES

        "I am piling it up."

53. Ca   mu'aqan-we

        pile-DUR
          PRES

        "It is all in a heap."

54. Cu   Xwaan   cawáyaxla'ac-i   kic   pə-huta-ngax   cəq-i-qa

        Juan   ladder-ACC   house   it-back-from   lean-IN-DUR
                                             PRES
        "Juan is leaning the ladder against the back of the house."

55. Cu   cawáyax-la'ac   cəq-yax-<u>wə</u>   kic   pə-huta-ngax

        ladder   lean-YAX-DUR   house   it-back-from
                                    PRES

        "The ladder is leaning against the wall."

56. Lu   po-up   huukapic   pið->i-<u>q</u>

        he-he   pipe   break-IN-DUR
                                            PRES

        "He is breaking the pipe."

57. Lu   huukapic-up   pið-ax-<u>wun</u>-ut

        pipe-it   break-YAX-DUR -[+R]
                                PRES

        "The pipe is broken."

7.11 The Luiseño -<u>aat</u> Forms

This stative function of the *-<u>wən</u> affixes underlies an unexplained
phenomenon referred to in chapter V. A Luiseño consultant, asked about
the difference between 'awáal <u>xecic</u> and 'awáal <u>xecaat</u>, both apparently
meaning "The dog is beaten," explained

> If you were outside a house and you could hear a stick going and a
> dog howling, you might say <u>xecaat</u>, but if you passed by and saw
> the dog bleeding and running away you could say <u>xecic</u>.

The contrast appeared to be a durative/non-durative one. The final -<u>at</u>
looks like the -'<u>a</u> plus an absolutive. As we saw earlier, -'<u>a</u> appeared on
Luiseño duratives and -'<u>i</u> on non-duratives. The -'<u>a</u> with an absolutive,
however, usually becomes -<u>ot</u> or -<u>ut</u>.

In fact, we have enough data from different periods and dialects to
observe an interesting phonetic change. In our second chapter, we
described -<u>aat</u> and -<u>aantum</u> as singular and plural adjectival endings.
Forms like xwáyaat, xwayaantum "white," koɬaat, koɬaantum "sweet,"
xalaat "loose," yuvataat "black"—and many others—have these endings. The
fact that stress is not on the long vowels is suspicious for Luiseño.

But Kroeber and Grace (150, 112) list rather different forms, for
example koɬaxot "sweet," xalaxut "loose," piðiviðaxot "broken." It
appears that forms ending in -<u>axot</u> ~ -<u>axut</u> became -<u>aat</u> through the phonological rule deleting intervocalic <u>x</u> before an unstressed vowel, a rule we
described towards the end of the previous chapter.

Harrington's field notes give Soboba Luiseño forms revealing yet another stage (we give his own transcription): yuváttahont "black," kóŝahont "sweet." Presumably a rule deleting n in a final consonánt cluster relates these forms to those given by Kroeber and Grace's consultants.

Finally, our own major consultant from Rincon gave us a few, more basic, forms like teetilla-wunut "talking" and mun-wunut "coming." We assume that the absence of x in the first form (which would otherwise have been teetillax-wunut) blocked a possible change to *teetillaat. These changes have not taken place in Cupeño. Compare, for example, Cupeño xway-ax-wən-ət "white" with Luiseño xwayaat "white." We assume approximately the following sequential changes from an older Luiseño -ax-won-ut

-axwonut > -axonot > -axont > -axot > -aat

The xecic/xecaat contrast was thus really a xec-ic/xecax-wun-ut contrast with the second form containing a durative, and specifying an action per-formed over a period of time rather than at one point of time.

7.12 Time and Space Correlation

Fairly stable correlations between temporal, spatial, and certain other real-world notions are found in most languages. The English pre-positions at and in occur in both locative and temporal expressions, but the native speaker feels some natural connection, some more general notion underlying the different usages. This more general notion might be described as "extension without direction"—but this phrase is also metaphorical, drawing from originally spatial terms. The English prepo-sitions from and to reveal the same time-location dichotomy but involve direction and hence movement. Furthermore, English from, like Cupan -ngax or -ngay, is used to express causation while to, like the reflexes of Proto-Cupan *-yəka, is used to express intention or purpose. If such correlations are as widespread as they seem, they should form part of a general semantic theory which would predict such correlations for specific languages as the unmarked situation. It is interesting that spatial notions so often appear to be the more basic ones. Proto-Cupan *qal is a reflex of Proto-Uto-Aztecan *kate "sit down," which Miller (1967:55) reconstructs as restricted to singular subjects, and Proto-Cupan *wən is a reflex of Proto-Uto-Aztecan *we or *wene "stand" (Miller 1967:58).

The connection between these non-directional (or non-motion) locative
verbs and the two affixes serving as durative markers is thus hardly surprising. If there are other durative affixes in the Cupan languages, we
might well expect these also to be related to locative main verbs.[7] As we
stated earlier, the modern reflexes of *-qal and *-wən are in general
restricted to realized events or, perhaps, events assumed by the speaker
to be "real," i.e. these forms would not appear in conditional or usitative
constructions, or verbs with future time reference. There are just a few
exceptions to this. In Luiseño, -qal appears in forms like pom-heel-a-
qal-pi "for them to be singing" instead of the expected pom-heel-ax-maan-
pi. In Cupeño and Cahuilla, the *-wən forms are used as plural suppletive
affixes for future durative forms. Cupeño -wənə, plural future durative
suffix, should be broken down into -wən, durative, and -nə, future, just
as the corresponding Cahuilla -wen-ne is. The same breakdown is suggested for the usitative plural -wənə. We might consider the two nə
suffixes as a single element denoting unachieved or unrealized action.

The other major affixes functioning as future durative markers are
Cupeño -naȿ (- -nac), Cahuilla -nac, and Luiseño -maan. This last affix
almost certainly contains a future suffix -an, as we pointed out in chapter II. Furthermore, an examination of Harrington's field notes reveals
that -maxan appears in future durative forms wherever -maan was used
by our Rincon consultants. Such forms are quoted in Kroeber and Grace,
e.g. monngimaxan "will be traveling" (142), who also note Pablo Tac's
early nineteenth-century transcription -maj-an (231). As the -ma usitative suffix is -max in these dialects, we shall consider -max as the more
basic form.

Since they appear in almost exactly identical environments with almost
exactly the same meanings, we can reconstruct for Cahuilla -nac and
Cupeño -naȿ - -nac, a PCC form *-nac. So PCC *-nac and Luiseño -max
are the two [-R] durative affixes. Based on our finding for the [+R] durative suffixes, we should expect to find main verbs of location corresponding
to these forms.

The Mountain Cahuilla verb form pa-cem-qal-'e "we lived there" has
as its corresponding future form, one containing a verb root max: pa-cem-
max-ne "we will live there." The same root occurs in Cupeño future
sentences like 'ivi'aw-əl-pə max "here they will live/be." The locative

<hr/>

[7]We noted, rather too late for inclusion in our discussion, an interesting Luiseño verb
stem wac (pl. waaca), with the meaning "several (inan.) be there" which is reported by
Kroeber and Grace (132). They list two examples thus: "wač-q-ap, pl. waača-xon-pom,"
but do not explain if the plural form refers to "being there on more than one occasion."

verb max, in these languages, is generally restricted to having plural
subjects and to denoting [-R] events. Corresponding to PCC *-nac, there
is another locative main verb nac in both Cahuilla and Cupeño, meaning
"sit," as in Cahuilla hem-nac-we "they sit," and Cupeño nə'ə-n nac-qa
"I am sitting." Like the other locative verbs, nac is replaced by other
roots in certain environments. We can reconstruct *nac "sit" for PCC.

For every durative affix, then, we have been able to find a modern
locative verb identical or almost identical in form. All three languages
also have "unreality" forms similar to these verbs. We summarize this
data below:

58.	Location Verb	Durative Affix	[+R] or [-R]	"Unreality" Suffix
	PC *qal	PC *-qal	[+R]	--
	PC *wən	PC *-wən	[+R]	--
	PCC *nac	PCC *-nac	[-R]	Ca -na (exhortative) Cu -nə (usitative)
	PCC *max	Lu -max	[-R]	Lu -ma (usitative)

The shape of the "unreality" suffixes suggests that there may be a
regular process deleting the last consonant of the underlying suffix word-
finally, just as happened with final l and n in Mountain Cahuilla and Cupeño
verbs, and as happens with suffixed verbs in Cúpeño, when imperative
forms are generated. The infrequent Cahuilla suffix, -nax(at) "the one
supposed to V," might also be considered related to the "unreality" forms,
or at least as a [-R] form in contrast with the usually [+R] -wet ending
that sometimes replaces it,[8] an ending usually signifying "one who V's
or is V-ing frequently."

Our analysis of Cupeño -naɬ ~ -nac as a [-R] durative suggests a
different analysis of future duratives from that in chapter II. There we
treated -naɬ as the singular future durative ending, and -wən as the
plural one, basically the analysis of J. Hill (1966). But we would prefer
to treat -naɬ and the -wən (of -wən) as suppletive durative affixes. So

---

[8]We suspect that -wet, probably a shortened form of -wenet, may be the same form
as the augmentative noun suffix -wet (with cognate forms in the other two languages). On
a regular noun, -wet indicates "bigness." The corresponding verb notion to "bigness" on
nouns might be "frequency." As an agentive ending, -wet would thus signify "one who frequently V's" and as an inflectional suffix for verbs, it would signify durativeness and
plurality of actions or actors.

the durative -wən is followed by the future suffix -nə, and -naɬ by a Ø
future suffix. This reanalysis has the following advantages:

    i.   We do not need to posit an extra -wənə durative element (but we
do have an extra Ø).

    ii. We capture a syntactic difference between -naɬ and -wən-nə.
Only the former can take an inceptive suffix (-qat). The -wən-nə form
has the maximum number (two) of aspect and tense suffixes; the -nac form
can and must be followed by a -Ø or a -qat.

    iii. The likely historical development is captured (see the paired
examples below).

    iv. The cross-linguistic likeness to Cahuilla is captured, as the
examples show.

59. Ca   Xwaan mamayaw-nac-ka'

    Cu   Xwaan mamayəw-naɬ-qat

        "Juan is going to be helping."

60. Ca   nanxanicem   mamayaw-wen-ne

    Cu   nanxacam-pə mamayəw-wən-nə

        "The men will be helping."

61. Ca   Xwaan   mamayaw-nac-ne

    Cu   Xwaan-pə   mamayəw-naɬ-Ø

        "Juan will be helping."

Note that if -naɬ is omitted from the last Cupeño sentence, the verb form
will still have future time reference, though not durativeness.

7.13 Other Verb Affixes and Main Verbs

If locative (non-movement) verbs are morphologically related to durative affixes, then to what kind of affix might we expect motion verbs with
meanings like "go" and "come" to be related; Matters are a little more
complex for these verbs.

    Seven of the twelve derivational affixes (excluding -ni) that we know
for Cahuilla can be related to modern Cahuilla main verbs. Of the nine

that we know for Cupeño (excluding -<u>ni</u>), six are relatable to Cupeño main
verbs and one to a Cahuilla verb. Of the nine mentioned for Luiseño, we
have found four, perhaps five, corresponding to main verbs in Luiseño.
The list below probably omits some verb affix connections because our
data, especially in Wanikik and Desert Cahuilla, are far from complete.
The meanings given are the most common ones.

62.

MAIN VERB		AFFIX	
Ca			
'ayaw	"want, try, begin"	-'ayaw	"almost V, try to V"
hick	"go"	-ici	"V while going, go to V"
max	"give"	-max	"V on behalf of"
ngiy, ngey	"go away, around, return	'ngi, -nge	"go away or around V-ing, V while going
neke(n)	"come"	-(va-)neken	"come V-ing"
pic	"arrive"	-pic	"arrive V-ing"
'exan	"do, behave"	-in	"do" (?)
Cu			
'ixan	"do"	-in	"do" (?)
max	"give"	-max	"V on behalf of"
mi'aw	"arrive"	-mi'aw	"arrive V-ing, come to V"
nəq	"come"	-(və-)nəq	"come along V-ing"
ngiy	"go away, around, return"	-ngi	"go away V-ing, V here and there"
yax	"do, be"	-yax	"do, be"
Cahuilla hici	"go"	-ici (rare)	"go to V"
Lu			
PC 'ixan	"do, behave"	-i	"do" (?)
max	"give" (also <u>maxani</u>)	(-max, postposition "on behalf of")	

munáa	"come"	-ma -munàa	"come V-ing" "come V-ing"
ngiy, ngey(m)	"go away, around, return"	-ngi	"go away or around V-ing"
yaax	"be"	-(y)ax	"be" etc.

Two of the affixes for which no main verb has been found are motion affixes—Cahuilla -puli "come here and V, come here in order to V" and the various forms reconstructable as Proto-Cupan *-ləw "go and V, go in order to V." There is a main verb puli in Cahuilla, but its meaning is "fall"; a connection would be hard to establish and not too useful for our purposes.

The connection between max "give" and -max "V on behalf of" seems straightforward enough. If you paint a house on behalf of someone, you are "giving" your act of house-painting to that person, for his benefit.

Although the other correlations between the verbs and the corresponding affixes appear to present few problems, we wish to discuss further some characteristics of the various motion affixes, including -puli and the various *-ləw forms. We shall refer to these forms as -ləw when we consider them as a group.

7.14 The Motion Verbs

These motion affixes are of two main kinds. First there are the huc ("hither") forms denoting movement toward the speaker. One other form, -ngi "go away, around, return, go here and there," which denotes non-directional or goal-less movement, can be grouped with the huc affixes.

These huc affixes— (-va)-neke(n), (-və)-nəq, -mi'aw, -ma, -munàa, and also -ngi—are likely to appear on verb forms denoting action while coming rather than action after coming. When, like most of the motion affixes, they lose their physical motion meaning and take on a more abstract sense, they express gradation of the main action represented by the verb form, or "becoming V-ed." In general, the occurrence of one of the two senses—gradation or becoming (where there is any difference)—is determined partly by the verb root and affixes preceding the motion affix, partly by the durativeness or non-durativeness and the realization status of the whole verb form. Examples are Luiseño yuvátax-munaa "it's getting black," Cahuilla wax-va-nek-'i "it dried up," and Cupeño haw-pə-ya-ngi "he became pimply," and pə-wax-mi'aw-qal-əp "it was drying up."

The second main group are the <u>illuc</u> ("thence") affixes denoting
movement away from the speaker. They normally qualify actions after
going rather than actions <u>while</u> going. As goal-oriented forms, they
easily take on a purpose sense, "go in order to V." The -<u>ləw</u> affixes are
particularly interesting. They are often used to represent future action
(future either relative to the speaker's perspective or to some other event)
at some place removed from the speaker. In Luiseño, one of the -<u>ləw</u>
forms is used as an inceptive affix to indicate future time reference, and
it loses altogether any sense of physical motion or of a removed location.
The same development may earlier have occurred with reflexes of the
Proto-Cupan postposition *-<u>yəka</u> "toward." These reflexes take on a
temporal sense and sometimes a purposive sense, as in Cupeño cəm-tan-
in-wən-i-yka "until we would be dancing," which is sometimes purposive,
sometimes merely temporal. The various inceptive forms with a suffix
reconstructable as *-<u>kat</u> for Proto-Cupan may be related to nominalized
verb forms once analyzable as containing a directional postposition.
Moreover, a deeper analysis of postpositions would suggest considering
them as predicates especially since they manifest certain surface characteristics otherwise restricted to verbs.[9]

All three Cupan languages (and Serrano) have *-<u>kat</u> forms for inceptives. But Luiseño inceptives are defective in their singular forms. They
have no singular -<u>kat</u> form. This form may have disappeared because the
-<u>qat</u> recent past forms made the existence of similar forms with future
time reference too confusing. What is particularly interesting is that a
nominalized -<u>ut</u> form with -<u>low</u> became the singular inceptive suffix
-<u>lowut</u>, sometimes shortened to -<u>lut</u>. So, from a motion with purpose
meaning, as in the Cupeño sentence

63. Cu   mə-nə-pə-n   qiingi-ləw   təmál

    and-I-[-R]-I   plow-go   earth

    "I'll go there to plow the land."

[9]For example, in Cupeño only -<u>yka</u> and certain other motionassociated postpositions
have an additional pronominal marker when their pronoun base is plural. This phenomenon
occurs elsewhere only on verbs.

there may have developed a closer association with purpose and a de-emphasis of the motion:

64. Cu   mə-nə-pə-nə   haʂ-ax   təmál   qiingi-ləw

       and-I-[-R]-I   go-YAX   earth   plow-go

       "I'll go to plow the land there."

Nominalized verb forms like the one in (65) below are not uncommon in Cupeño:

65. Cu   nə'-ən   puy-l̃əw-ət

       I-I   eat-go-[+R]

       "I'm going some place to eat."

In fact, in some Luiseño sentences it is hard to tell whether the -low-ut is an inceptive or whether it just signifies motion:

66. Lu   noo-n   kic   tiiw-i-low-ut

       I-I   house   see-IN $\begin{Bmatrix} \text{go-[+R]} \\ \text{INCEPT} \end{Bmatrix}$

       "I'm going to see the house."

The English gloss is likewise hard to interpret. Much the same kind of shift has occurred in English as well as in French. The French sentence below with va "go":

67. Fr   Il va voir la maison.

is a more common way of saying "He'll see the house" than is

68. Fr   Il verra la maison.

Likewise the English verb forms come to be, become and the French venir de and devenir show similar developments to those posited for the huc verbs.

    The absence of a main verb corresponding to the *-ləw affixes in any of the Cupan (or, for that matter, Takic) languages suggests that if there was indeed some such main verb, it would have to be reconstructed for some Pre-Takic stage.   Obviously related forms occur in Tubatulabatl and several other languages.

One final problem arises with the Mountain Cahuilla suffix -ne and the corresponding Cupeño suffix -nə, both future suffixes. In view of Luiseño -(a)n, Hopi -ni, Yaqui -ne, and Huichol -ni, all future suffixes, the Cahuilla and Cupeño endings look like reflexes of Proto-Uto-Aztecan. However, the corresponding Desert and Wanikik Cahuilla forms are -nem. There is a Cahuilla motion verb nem "go around" but it is not an illuc or goal-directed verb as we would expect. Related forms occur in the other two languages. However, in all three languages, reduplicated forms corresponding to this verb, and/or verbs having an IN affix, are goal-directed, for example Luiseño nonomi "follow" and Cupeño nənmin "chase." Without further evidence, we must consider the question as still open.

7.15 Higher Predicates and Enclitics

We have shown in this chapter that PREDICATE RAISING is a well-motivated syntactic process for the Cupan languages. An analysis positing a higher predicate semantic base and PREDICATE RAISING can account for the ordering and scope relations among the various affixes on a verb, as well as the scope relation between the verb root and the affixes. Other transformations complementing PREDICATE RAISING have also been motivated. Moreover, we have indicated at the synchronic level certain other directions of dependency—for example that the [+R]/ [-R] contrast determines whether -nac or -qal will mark durative aspect on singular verbs in Cahuilla. Furthermore, we have uncovered a considerable quantity of lexical and morphological evidence to support the diachronic counterpart of these synchronic claims—the claim that these predicate-like affixes were in fact higher verbs at some earlier stage of Cupan.

We would like to have shown that the [+R]/[-R] enclitics were, historically, higher verbs but, since enclitics go back to Proto-Uto-Aztecan, this would involve a very ancient change for which no morphological evidence survives. One enclitic, Cupeño -əp, which is [+R] has a counterpart which looks as though it has been nominalized with -ut, a process to which only verbs are subjected. The form 'əpút is usually translated "already," it never occurs with -əp despite the past time reference, and like the various verb forms with the t absolutive (-qat, -ka', -kutum) it co-occurs with subject enclitics normally used only for present time reference. Only present tense verbs occur with 'əpút. Of

the other enclitics, only the -san forms and yal in Cahuilla suggest a
morphological relation with verbs.

   A full synchronic analysis of syntactic enclitics would require a
discussion too lengthy and detailed for the present study. Our own data
suggest that the direction of semantic scope for enclitics may be directly
opposite to that for the affixes after the verb root. This ordering would be
what one would predict if there were some kind of transformation reversing
the position of an enclitic and the sentence within its scope. Extraposition
might be such a process. Our scope statement would imply a structure
something like the drastically simplified one below:

69.

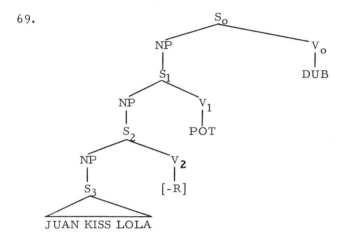

If S_3 were extraposed after V_2, then S_2 extraposed after V_1, and finally S_1
extraposed after V_0, the ensuing string would be

      DUB-POT-[-R]   Juan kiss Lola

If we filled in the Cupeño equivalents, and added a mə sentence introducer,
we would have a perfectly grammatical Cupeño sentence:

70. mə-ʃə-qwə-pə   Xwaan   Lola'a-y   cung-i

    and-DUB-POT-[-R]   Juan   Lola-ACC   kiss-IN

    "I wonder if Juan kisses Lola."

where, in Luiseño, the enclitic complex would be replaced by the single
element wuʃkapi. Of course, the analysis here is somewhat crude,

requiring considerable refinement and reanalysis, but it appears unlikely that such refining would affect the validity of our arguments.

7.16 Some Conclusions

What all this has been pointing to is a higher predicate analysis of enclitics and the verb forms within the semantic scope of the enclitics. We assumed that tense was not a predicate in Proto-Cupan. Tense developed later from aspectual and motion affixes which in turn had originated as location and motion verbs.[10] For one major stage of Proto-Cupan the Proto-Cupan form of the English sentence "We were laughing" might usefully be shown as having the following underlying representation:

71.

The highest verb in this abstract representation is realized as an inclitic in surface structure. It determines whether or not a realized affix will appear to the right of the durative verb (presumably by a segmentation process). It also determines which category of durative verbs will be available for the next verb node down. The next lower verb node, which dominates YAX, may represent the STATE or ACTIVITY quality of the lowest sentence, just as English <u>do</u> or <u>be</u> have been suggested for English verbs. At various stages of Proto-Cupan and Cupan different intermediate and surface structures must have existed, as well as differing lexicalizing

---

[10]In fact, of course, it is unlikely that languages ever have "pure" tense systems, i.e. verbs with time reference but without any aspectual qualities.

operations. Moreover, when a tense system developed in Luiseño the
semantic structures must have been amended to include a higher tense
predicate. At the stage prior to the development of the IN/YAX contrast,
when *-'iyax and *-ayax came into existence, an intermediate structure
something like 72 must be postulated. PREDICATE RAISING has already
operated.

72.

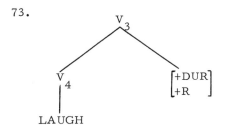

Processes which might be formulated as feature copying and segmentation
(as in Jacobs and Rosenbaum 1968:81-90) would copy the durative and [+R]
features onto V_3 which would have them attached as a segment to the right
of V_3.

73.

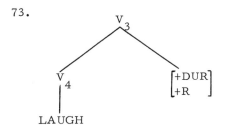

This would be lexicalized, say, as *sɘsɘm-'ɘ while V_1 and V_2 would
become *yax-qal. If the segment had also been attached to -qal, we would
have

74.   *sɘ́sɘm-'ɘ   yax-qal-'ɘ

—quite a likely Proto-Cupan form. Similar processes operating on trees
without a DURATIVE would generate either

75.   *sǝsǝm-'i   yax

or

76.   *sǝsǝm-'i   yax-'i

Presumably, through the appropriate applications of PREDICATE RAISING, V_3 (the '$\underline{i}$ or '$\underline{ǝ}$ predicate) could alternatively have been lexicalized together with V_2 and V_1, leading to forms like the following

77.   *sǝsǝm   'ǝ-yax-qal(-'ǝ)

or

78.   *sǝsǝm   'i-yax(-'i)

The precise formulation of these processes at the various stages is still somewhat problematic and must await more detailed investigation. What we have sought to show here is that the general framework we have pro-posed and the processes we have exemplified should be able to character-ize in a non-arbitrary way the detailed changes we have been describing. We have shown that there is considerable morphological and syntactic evidence to support such an analysis.

VIII. RELATIVE CONSTRUCTIONS, TENSE, AND ASPECT

8.1 Introduction

So far, we have been concerned primarily with <u>main</u> clause verb forms in modern Cupan. Many of these have been traced back to earlier constructions in which they were embedded as part of a <u>subordinate</u> clause. The nature of the specific subordinate structure in Proto-Cupan or in Proto-Cahuilla-Cupeño determined whether or not the verb form was marked for accusative case or plural number. Certain modern verb forms without subject markers—those with -<u>ic</u> and -<u>at</u> endings—all allow such case and/or number marking. We showed that at earlier stages as well as now these were non-possessed nominals in relative constructions, and that their case and number marking depended on the case and number marking of a head noun phrase. Similar verb forms are used as past tense forms in Cahuilla and Cupeño but these have subject markers and lack both consonantal endings and accusative or plural marking. This we have shown to be a natural consequence of their being possessed nominalized forms in <u>complement</u> constructions rather than in <u>relatives</u>. The lack of accusative or plural marking naturally arises from the lack of a head noun phrase with such marking.

We posited six major transformations to relate the underlying structures of the -'<u>i</u> and -'<u>a</u> forms to the surface forms. Three of these:

    i.   EQUI NOUN PHRASE DELETION

    ii.   SUBJECT RAISING

    iii.   PREDICATE RAISING

have already been justified as needed for other constructions in Cupan. But three others:

    iv.   RELATIVE NOUN PHRASE DELETION (RDEL)

    v.   SUBJECT COPY

    vi.   CASE-NUMBER MARKING

have not been so justified. In fact they are not in themselves adequate to
account for some of the -'i/-'a forms already described. We shall see that
a special Nominalization rule (NOM) is also needed to account for these
constructions and that a later rule, ABS, is necessary to account specifically for the presence or absence of an absolute ending on these verb
forms, a rule required in any case for ordinary Cupan nouns.

One goal of this chapter then is to motivate adequately those transformations not already so motivated. Since these are all used in relativization, we shall need to look more generally at relativization in modern
Cupan and to reconstruct for PCC and, if possible, for Proto-Cupan the
kind of relativization needed to account for the various modern forms.
In doing so we hope to find further support for our claim that the modern
tense systems developed from an earlier aspectual system with a basic
realized/unrealized contrast.

8.2 Relative Constructions in Cupan

Relative constructions in Cupan normally follow their head noun.
Immediately after the head noun is a pronominal element not unlike the
English relative particle that, called here the relative-demonstrative (RD).
The relativized verbs appear characterizable within a tripartite time reference categorization for past, present, and future time, frequently with
the option of durative aspect. Cross-cutting this division is one between
relatives having subjects coreferential with the head noun and those having
object or oblique noun phrases coreferential. Although our examples of
the latter group contain only coreferential objects, they differ from those
with coreferential oblique noun phrases only in lacking either an additional
pronoun marked for the particular oblique case or an additional suffix such
as -nga or -yka attached to the verb form.

8.3 Future Relative Constructions

Future relative constructions having subjects coreferential with their
noun phrase heads take the inceptive suffixes—though this statement must
be qualified for Cahuilla. Constructions with coreferential object or
oblique noun phrases have the [-R] suffix -pi.

The following are all relative constructions with coreferential subjects. All of then function as subject noun phrases in a main clause.

1. Ca   'awal   pe'   hunwet-i   mamayaw-nax(-ka')

         dog   RD   bear-ACC   help-FUT(-INCEPT)

2. Cu   'awál   pə'   hunwət-i   mamayəw-qat

         dog   RD   bear-ACC   help-INCEPT

3. Lu   'awáal   po   hunwut-i   mamayuw-lut

         dog   RD   bear-ACC   help-INCEPT

    "the dog that will help the bear"

The next three relative constructions also have coreferential subjects but they are all plural and all function as object noun phrases in a main clause:

4. Ca   'a'wal-em-i   pe'   hunwet-i $\left\{\begin{array}{l}\text{mamayaw-naxt-em-i}\\ \text{help-FUT-PL-ACC}\\[1em] \text{mamayaw-nax-kat-em-i}\\ \text{help-FUT-INCEPT-PL-ACC}\end{array}\right\}$

         dog-PL-ACC RD   bear-ACC

5. Cu   'awál-m-i   pə'   hunwət-i   mamayəw-qat-m-i

         dog-PL-ACC   RD   bear-ACC   help-INCEPT-PL-ACC

6. Lu   'awáal-um-i   po   hunwut-i   mamayuw-kut-um-i

         dog-PL-ACC   RD   bear-ACC   help-INCEPT-PL-ACC

    "the dogs that will help the bear"

The structure of these relative constructions appears quite uniform for all three languages. The Cahuilla -nax is almost certainly a later innovation since no such element is found in the other languages. Luiseño -lut (--lowut) is, as we saw in the last chapter, an innovation in the inceptive. The plural form -kut-um (--kat-um) indicates an earlier Luiseño singular suffix, either *-kut or *-kat, probably the latter, since the u seems to be a way of differentiating past -qatum from inceptive -kutum. We can reconstruct -kat for Proto-Cupan (cf. Serrano -ka).

The evidence indicates an underlying Proto-Cupan structure[1] something like the following simplified tree. We have chosen to exemplify an accusative plural construction:

7.

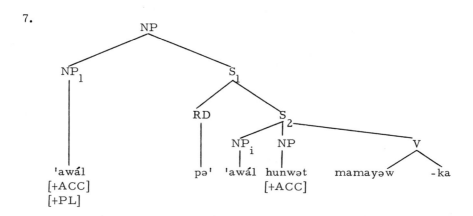

'awál
[+ACC]
[+PL]

pə'   'awál hunwət   mamayəw   -ka
           [+ACC]

The <u>i</u> subscript marks coreference. We have included the RD pə' in an S_1 because it and the constituents following are treated as an S by the EXTRAPOSITION rule described in chapter VII.

First, the RDEL transformation deletes the lower of the coreferential noun phrases. SUBJECT COPY cannot apply because there is no subject noun phrase in S_2 now. The resulting string is

8.   *['awál   [pə'   hunwət   mamayəw-ka]]]
        NP +ACC S_1 S_2 [-ACC] S_2 S_1 NP
              +PL

Now, if CASE-NUMBER MARKING were to apply to 8, the following string would be generated (after removal of the bracketing):

9.   *'awál   pə'   hunwət   mamayəw-ka
     [+ACC]   [+ACC]   [+ACC]
     [+PL]   [+PL]

---

[1]These are, in fact, intermediate structures here as elsewhere in the chapter. We do not know just how to represent the underlying structure of relatives either in English or Cupan, but we suspect that they originate as conjoined propositions. There is some good Cupan evidence on this for non-restrictive relatives (which we do not consider here) but not for the restrictive relatives.

which would be realized as

10. *awál-əm-i   pə'   hunwət-i   mamayəw-ka-m-i

    "the dogs that will help the bear"

However, this should not happen. Relativized verb forms in all three
languages are treated as nominals. If they are possessed, i.e., if SUB-
JECT COPY has affixed a pronominal marker, no absolutive ending is
required. But if they are non-possessed, an absolutive must be attached.
The particular examples we generated in chapter V, using RDEL, SUBJECT
COPY and CASE-NUMBER MARKING happened to have <u>possessed</u> relativized verbs, and therefore no absolutive was required. Even so, our formulation failed to capture the nounness of the relativized verb. Had we
generated forms with *-<u>ic</u> or *-<u>ət</u>, we would have had to formulate processes to mark the change to nominal status and to account for the presence
of the absolutive.

   We therefore posit NOMINALIZATION (NOM) as a transformation converting the V in S_2 into a nominal. This transformation must precede
SUBJECT COPY and CASE-NUMBER MARKING, which are later agreement rules. We assume in this discussion that NOM will follow RDEL, but
nothing crucial to the present discussion hinges on this assumption. The
actual absolutive marking process (ABS)—a general one affecting all non-
possessed nominals—is another late rule, and it will most conveniently follow SUBJECT COPY (which will block ABS), and precede CASE-NUMBER
MARKING. So, after NOM, the ABS transformation converts the lower
verb into *<u>mamayəw-kat</u>. Finally, CASE-NUMBER MARKING marks this
nominal for the accusative and plural features of the head-noun. After
these features are segmentalized, the following terminal string is
generated:

11. PC   *awál-əm-i   pə'   hunwət-i   mamayəw-kat-əm-i

    "the dogs that will help the bear"

which is a reasonable Proto-Cupan reconstruction. The same set of transformations applied to the appropriate underlying structures is valid for all
three modern languages.

   The next three examples illustrate future relative constructions with
coreferential <u>object</u> noun phrases. In our examples, all of these happen to

function also as object noun phrases in the sentence in which they are embedded.

12. Ca   'a'wal-i   pe'   hunwet   pe-mamayaw-pi-y[2]

13. Cu   'awál-i   pə'   hunwət   pə-mamayəw-pi-y

14. Lu   'awáal-i   po   hunwut   po-mamayuw-pi-y

        "the dog that the bear will help"

These constructions pose few problems for reconstruction. We reconstruct for Proto-Cupan the following underlying structure, one essentially the same as that which we posited for the -'a constructions in chapter IV, example 15:

15.

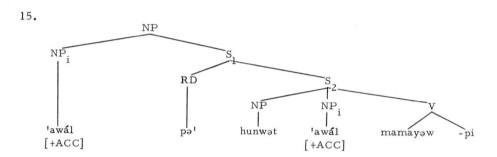

We can now apply the same set of transformations to 15. First RDEL removes the lower coreferential noun phrase from S_2. Next NOM converts the V in S_2 into a nominal. Then SUBJECT COPY attaches pə-, a pronominal copy of the S_2 subject, to the verb. Finally CASE-NUMBER MARKING copies the accusative feature of the heat noun onto the nominalized verb. The eventual output is

16. PC   *'awál-i   pə'   hunwət   pə-mamayəw-pi-y

        dog-ACC   RD   bear   he-help-[-R]-ACC

        "the dog that the bear will help"

---

[2] The pe- prefix in the Cahuilla form is not the ordinary subject prefix, which would be zero, indicating an underlying he-. There appears to be a surface restriction on -pi forms (but not on the corresponding -ve forms) requiring a prefix if the verb form is possessed. Where no other prefix is manifested, pe- must be used. We shall not consider this specifically Cahuilla development in the present analysis.

However, Cahuilla plural forms differ from the Cupeño and Luiseño in one significant respect. Only in Cahuilla is the plural feature of a head noun copied onto the relativized verb, resulting in forms like pə-mamayaw-pi-m, or with accusative marking pə-mamayaw-pi-m-i. In the other two languages it appears that the presence of a lower subject noun phrase blocks number agreement. Indeed, in the other languages, number agreement does, rarely, occur on -pi forms (and also on the reflexes of *-və forms, which have the same characteristics). But such occurrences are limited to relative constructions with coreferential subjects

17. Lu   noo-n   'o'na-q   pom-'aac-m-i   ponéy-m-i

       I-I   know-PRES   their-animal-PL-ACC   that-PL-ACC
                DUR

       po   ne-y   pom-ko'-i-pi-m-i

       that   I-ACC   they-bite-IN-[-R]-PL-ACC

    "I know the dogs that will bite me."

In 17 there is no subject noun phrase intervening to block the number agreement. Since this blocking of number agreement by an intervening subject occurs in both Luiseño and Cupeño we are inclined to attribute it to Proto-Cupan.

The *-pi suffix then generally occurs in relatives in which a coreferential object or oblique noun phrase has been deleted. The *-kat suffix indicates that a coreferential subject has been deleted. The presence or absence of a subject prefix is quite functional. If it is present, as in the -pi constructions discussed, speakers assume that the head noun phrase is not the semantic subject of the relativized verb. If there is no subject marker, then we might expect speakers to assume that the semantic subject is the nearest non-accusative noun phrase preceding the verb.

The *-kat suffix never occurs without its absolutive, and its subject is always coreferential with the subject of the next highest verb. This is true even of complement constructions where *-kat forms mean "in order to V." In this respect they are like the English "in order to" constructions and unlike the English "in order that" ones which need not have a complement subject coreferential with a higher subject.

It would seem then that, in relative constructions, -pi marks a specific kind of switch-reference. The presence of a subject prefix seems to have the same function. But if subject prefixes (or infixes for Cupeño in and yax verbs) were always present when such switch-reference occurs then it would be impossible to determine whether the subject affix or the *-pi form (or both) had the switch-reference function.

In fact, subject markers do not appear in one kind of relative construction with a -pi, one occurring in all three languages. These relatives are like the English relative construction who will be V-ed, in which the semantic subject or the agent noun phrase is a deleted proform:

18. Ca   hunwet   pe'-pe   mamayaw-pi-c

    bear   DEM-DEM   help-[-R]-ABS

    "the bear that will be helped"

Note that the absence of a lexicalizable subject noun phrase means that SUBJECT COPYING cannot apply and therefore that the ABS transformation has to attach an absolutive. The absence of a subject prefix in this case has not caused hunwet to be interpreted as representing the semantic subject.

8.4 Past Relative Constructions

A [+R] suffix reconstructable as *-və for Proto-Cupan appears on relativized verbs which have an object or an oblique noun phrase coreferential with the noun phrase head of the construction. In Cahuilla and Cupeño, -'a forms appear to have much the same role. The basic difference is that the -'a forms refer to an achieved state whereas the -ve or -və forms refer to completed action. The difference is more noticeable for some verbs. The two senses are almost the same as the two major meanings of the ambiguous English sentence

19. The window was broken last Tuesday.

where the actual shattering of the window may or may not have taken place last Tuesday. The meanings are not quite the same since, in Cupan, the state meaning also allows the window to have been shattered on the Tuesday, i.e. to have arrived at the state of being broken. Consequently, an agent noun phrase can be present in the Cupan forms although the agent-action relation appears de-emphasized.

Constructions with the Cupan reflexes of *-və (henceforth *-və constructions) are almost exactly like the *-pi constructions except of course for the [+R] sense of *-və, which makes such forms normally refer to past time. The likenesses should be clear from the following examples, which are all object noun phrases in the sentence in which they are embedded:

20. Ca   'awal-i   pe'   hunwet   mamayaw-ve-y

21. Cu   'awál-i   pə   hunwət   pə-mamayəw-və-y

22. Lu   'awáal-i   po   hunwut   po-mamayuw-vo-y

      dog-ACC   RD   bear   he-help-[+R]-ACC

      "the dog that the bear helped"

23. Cu   hunwət-i   pə'   mamayəw-və-l-i

      bear-ACC   RD   help-[+R]-ABS-ACC

      "the bear that was helped"

The Cahuilla -ve forms, like the Cahuilla -pi forms, are the only ones which can have plural marking. One minor difference between -pi and -ve in Cahuilla is that there is no surface structure restriction for the latter requiring a subject prefix to be present when there is no absolutive.

    The underlying structure we propose for these past relatives is exactly that which we posited for the -pi forms, with the important difference that the [+R] *-və suffix replaces the [-R] *-pi. The same set of transformations applies in the same ways.

    Past relative constructions with coreferential subject noun phrases appear to have the same basic structure and undergo the same transformations as the corresponding future forms with *-kat. But, as the following examples indicate, it is far less easy to reconstruct the precise Proto-Cupan forms. Each of the constructions below functions as the object noun phrase of the next higher sentence.

24. Ca   'a'wal-m-i   pe'   hunwet-i   mamayaw-i-c-m-i

      dog-PL-ACC   RD   bear-ACC   help-[-R]-ABS-PL-ACC

25. Cu   'awál-m-i   pə'   hunwət-i   mamayəw-i-c-m-i

      dog-PL-ACC   RD   bear-ACC   help-[-R]-ABS-PL-ACC

26. Lu   'awáal-um-i   po   hunwut-i   mamayuw-mokwi-c-m-i

        dog-PL-ACC   RD   bear-ACC   help-PAST-ABS-PL-ACC
                                        REL

    "the dogs that helped the bear"

    The Luiseño -<u>mokwic</u> suffix, the odd man out, appears to be an inno-
vation since no element like it appears in relative constructions in either
the other Cupan languages or Serrano. This conclusion does not, however, necessarily establish -<u>ic</u> as the appropriate Proto-Cupan suffix for
this kind of relative construction. If we leave this problem aside for the
moment, all three sentences reveal the same kind of underlying structure
and appear to undergo the same transformations. These transformations,
the same ones discussed in our treatment of the other relative forms,
generate surface structures apparently differing only in ways trivial for
the purposes of this study. We thus reconstruct the underlying structure
shown in 27 for Proto-Cupan. The abbreviation REL will be used for the
relative suffix.

27.

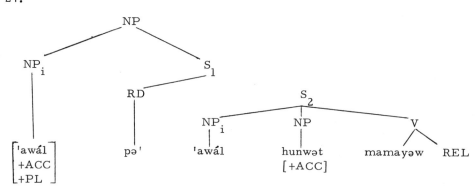

    RDEL deletes the lower coreferential noun phrase, NOM converts the
verb into a nominal. SUBJECT COPY cannot apply since there is now no
subject. ABS adds an absolutive to the nominalized verb form since it is
not possessed, and finally CASE-NUMBER MARKING is able to mark the
relativized verb for both case and number, since no lower subject noun
phrase intervenes. The string generated is

28. PC   *'awál-m-i   pə'   hunwət-i   mamayəw-REL-ABS-m-i

        dog-PL-ACC   RD   bear-ACC   help-REL-ABS-PL-ACC

    "the dogs that helped the bear"

For PCC we can reconstruct the same underlying structure and forms, as our fourth chapter showed, except that we can substitute *-'i for REL on the tree and *-i-c for -REL-ABS in 28.

8.5 The *-'i Problem

But we cannot be sure that *-'i was also the appropriate Proto-Cupan suffix, although Proto-Cupan had a realized -'i suffix for relatives. The difficulty lies in the fact that Luiseño -ic occurs in relative constructions in which an object or oblique noun phrase is coreferential with the head noun phrase while in the other two languages it is always the subject noun phrase that is coreferential. Moreover, the Luiseño -'i indicates achieved state or result rather than activity. Thus heel-ax-i-c means "that which is (always) sung," i.e. "song" while heel-i-vo-l means "which was sung." The contrast is reinforced by the rather typical use of the YAX affix for the 'i form and the IN affix for the -vo form.

As we have already shown in chapter V, it is likely that *-'i was used in Proto-Cupan for non-durative forms while the *-'ə variant appeared on duratives. So forms like the following may have occurred:

29. PC   ? *'awál pə'   mamayəw-i-c

               dog   RD   help-[+R]-ABS

30. PC   ? *'awál pə'   mamayəw-qal-ə-t

               dog   RD   help-DUR-[+R]-ABS

But we do not know whether the verb forms in 29 and 30 meant "helped" and "was helping" respectively, or "was helped" and "was being helped."

We can, however, suggest some tentative solutions to this problem on the basis of the following four considerations:

i. The apparent Luiseño reflex of 29 indicates realized state rather than past action. Forms with this -ic are often translated by consultants with "is V-ed" rather than "was V-ed."

ii. The apparent Cahuilla and Cupeño reflexes of 30 are used as present relatives rather than past relatives.

iii. Present tense suffixes were probably derived from realized aspect durative affixes which did not distinguish between past time reference and present time reference.

iv.   Cupeño and Cahuilla now lack past time reference relative forms with durative aspect, although Luiseño, which also has a more elaborated past tense system, does have such forms, forms with the -qal-mokwic endings.

We shall posit a paradigm illustrated in the following sentences, one in which there are no past tense forms and in which the crucial distinctions are between possessed verbal nominals whose subjects are not coreferential with the relative clause head, and non-possessed forms with subjects understood to be coreferential with the clause head. These non-possessed forms have undergone subject deletion. The SUBJECT COPY rule has therefore not applied and absolutive endings have been added.

31. *'awal   pə'   mamayəw-i-c

    "the dog that $\begin{cases} \text{helps} \\ \text{helped} \end{cases}$ "

32. *'awal   pə'   Xwaan   pə-mamayəw-'i

    "the dog that Juan $\begin{cases} \text{helps} \\ \text{helped} \end{cases}$ "

33. *'awal   pə'   mamayəw- $\begin{cases} \text{qal} \\ \text{wən} \end{cases}$ -ə-t

    "the dog that $\begin{cases} \text{is} \\ \text{was} \end{cases}$ helping"

Note that the particular semantic characteristics of the notion "help" make it unlikely that 31 and, possibly, 32 were used for present time references since helping is of its nature a durative activity. Hence, 33 and 34, below, would probably have been used instead. Facts like these indicate a likely trigger for reinterpretation of the durative affixes.

34. *'awál   pə'   Xwaan   pə-mamayəw- $\begin{cases} \text{qal} \\ \text{wən} \end{cases}$ -a

    "the dog that he $\begin{cases} \text{is} \\ \text{was} \end{cases}$ helping"

Construction 31 became the Cahuilla and Cupeño past relative with -ic, a predictable development given the shift from [+R] aspect to past tense. Construction 32 contains the form which became the ordinary

PCC past form, although it is likely that it was the occurrence of this
form in a complement construction that is reflected in the past tense use.
However, the modern Luiseño -ic form with its passive meaning came not
from 31 but from 32. The nominal status of the verb form in 32 led to an
absolute c being added whenever the subject was a pro-form and therefore subject marking was not triggered. This exactly mirrors the modern
difference between Luiseño -ic and Cahuilla-Cupeño -ic. The former
results from deletion of a pro-form, the latter from RDEL. 33 became
the Cahuilla-Cupeño present relative, singular and plural (and these forms
are also used as past tense forms, though rarely). In Luiseño the *-wən
reflex became a gerundial form for active verbs—mamayuw-wun-ut
"helping"—and a stative adjective for stative verbs—yuvát-ax-
wun-ut ~ yuvátaat "black, being black." Finally, the *-qal form of 34
became the Luiseño po-mamayuw-qal-a participial.

Note that only Luiseño -mokwic allows a durative prefix to precede it.
The lack of a durative -ic would appear to be a gap in a tripartite tense
system with durative aspect. All three languages have relatives with
future durative verbs and future non-durative verbs. But despite the striking similarities of past relative forms among the languages, only Luiseño
has the expected durative/non-durative contrast for past relatives. In
Cahuilla and Cupeño, however, present tense relative forms fill this gap,
i.e. the same forms are used for past and present duratives.

This suggests two possibilities. Either Cahuilla and Cupeño originally
had such past durative forms and then lost them, or there was no such
separation between past and present time reference for relatives, and the
primary contrast was a realized/unrealized one with a lesser durative/
non-durative contrast. The evidence of our earlier chapters all supports
the second possibility. Luiseño, which went furthest in developing a tense
system with rigidly restricted time reference, has allowed other suffixes
such as -mokwic to be introduced, suffixes filling obvious gaps in the new
time reference system. In Cupeño and in Mountain Cahuilla, where the
tense system was less developed and less rigidly constrained as to time
reference, the "gap" in the relative constructions was less noticeable. In
the other dialects of Cahuilla, the "gap" does not exist at all since the
realized/unrealized contrast still predominates and there is little "tense."

Note that our Proto-Cupan reconstructions here have enabled us to link
otherwise apparently random constructions with unexplained affixes (such
as the -a on Luiseño -qal-a). Moreover, this has been done without our
having to posit either a new grammatical elements or implausible historical developments. Moreover, the very comprehensiveness and neatness

of the reconstruction strengthens our hypothesis regarding the development
of the modern tense system from an earlier system with a basic realized/
unrealized aspectual contrast, two stages which are parallel to the
abstract synchronic analysis implied in this study: underlying aspect
becomes surface tense marking in some of the languages and dialects.

8.6 Present Relative Constructions

Without the aspect/tense hypothesis just referred to, it would be hard
to account for many of the details of the present relative forms below, as
well as their time reference. The examples just below contain constructions with coreferential subjects:

35. Ca   'awal   pe'   hunwet-i   mamayaw-qal-e-t

36. Cu   'awál   pə'   hunwət-i   mamayəw-qal-ə-t

37. Lu   'awáal   po   hunwut-i   mamayuw-qa-t

         "the dog that is helping the bear"

38. Ca   'a'wal-em   pe'   hunwet-i   mamayaw-wen-e-t-em

39. Cu   'awál-im   pə'   hunwət-i   mamayəw-wən-ə-t-im

40. Lu   'awáal-um   po   hunwut-i   mamayuw-qa-t-um

         "the dogs that are helping the bear"

Why otherwise would Cupeño present relativized forms have -<u>at</u> on the
surface past tense affixes -<u>qal</u> and -<u>wən</u>? Why should the Luiseño present
relatives have the same form as the recent past durative tense? Why
should the Luiseño present relatives have the same form as the recent
past durative tense? And why otherwise would all of these forms allow
past time reference—though this is far less common for Luiseño?

The Luiseño -<u>qat</u> forms, whatever their syntactic function, are
clearly nominalized forms whose ending may be broken down as qa-u-t,
exactly equivalent to *-<u>qal-ə-t</u> in Proto-Cupan and the reflexes in the
other Cupan languages. This is emphasized by the variant Luiseño form
-<u>qut</u> which has the -<u>q</u> present durative plus the -<u>u-t</u>. Although our own
consultants did not appear to use -<u>qa</u>/-<u>q</u> with any past time reference,

previous investigators have noted such a use. Kroeber and Grace, referring to -q(a) and -wun as "present-aorist" 150, claim that they "may refer to present, immediate past (today), or indefinite time."

Present relative constructions with coreferential objects have reflexes of Proto-Cupan *-və after the durative. But Luiseño retains the -qat, relying on the subject marker to indicate that the reference is different from the other relativized -qat forms:

41. Ca   -awal   pe'   mamayaw-qal-i-ve

42. Cu   'awál   pə'   pə-mamayəw-qal-və

43. Lu   'awăal   po   po-mamayuw-qa-t

The Luiseño form shows an apparent possessive co-occurring with an apparent absolutive on the same verb form. If we treat these as present relatives, then Cahuilla and Cupeño are using the [+R] *-və reflexes where this suffix does not normally occur—i.e. on non-past forms. Moreover, the Cahuilla forms and, very infrequently, the Cupeño forms are some-times used in relative constructions with coreferential subjects—a violation of the usual "switch-reference" characteristic of the *-və forms. Indeed, in Cahuilla, and less commonly in Cupeño, the durative *-və endings are used as gerundival "while V-ing" forms, requiring the subject of the main verb to be coreferential with the gerundival's implied subject. And, in Luiseño, adherence to the subject marker rule has led to a violation of the possessed nominal restriction against absolutives.

Such irregularities in just the present relatives, and the varying scope of time reference allowed, suggest that there were no Proto-Cupan present relative constructions and that Luiseño "made do" with one group of forms while PCC used somewhat different ones. And presumably, the use of the durative *-və forms in present relatives led to the use of these forms as gerundivals, while in Luiseño, the already existing -nik ~ -nuk ending was added to -qa to fill the gerundival role.

8.7 Locative Constructions

Constructions like the following in Cahuilla:

44. M. Ca   pa-hem-hici-ve

        where-they-go-[+R]

        "where they went"

45. W. Ca   tamyat   nac-qal-i-vi-yka

        sun   sit-DUR-i-[+R]-tp

        "to where the sun set"

46. D. Ca   pa-hem-cengen-va'

        where-they-dance-[+R]

        "where they danced"

are usually treated as special "local" constructions (Fuchs:39) quite
unconnected with relatives. The same constructions occur in the other
languages, although there is no pa- locative prefix. Instead an independent locative pronoun occurs:

47. Lu   'ivi   po   'ivá'   Maríya   po-pelli-vo

        this   RD   where   Maria   she-dance-[-R]

        "This is where Maria danced. "

We would prefer to consider these as special cases of relative constructions in which a locative pro-form which served as head has been deleted.
The -ve in Cahuilla, like the -vo in Luiseño, occurs because the subject
of the relative is not coreferential with the head noun phrase. The -va'
in the Desert Cahuilla form is, in a sense, a "local" element. The
Mountain Cahuilla -va variant of -ve never occurs with a final glottal
stop. In fact, 46 has another Cahuilla paraphrase identical in every
respect except that -ve-nga (or, with vowel harmony -va-nga) replaces
-va'. -nga is a postposition meaning "at, in. " Just as pa, a shortened
version of pe-nga, often has a glottal stop word-finally, so does -va',
apparently a shortened version of -ve-nga.

These location relatives are much like such English constructions as "where they danced, " which may also have deleted pro-forms as their heads.

8.8 Tense, Aspects, and Complements

We have already discussed various types of complementation both in chapter II and in our discussion of higher predicates in chapter VII. In chapter II, for example, we referred to Luiseño action nominals with -lo(w) or -la(w) suffixes. Nominals like the one in 48:

48. Lu   hunwut-m-i   wongé'-qus̸   ya'ac

      bear-PL-ACC   blame-DUR   man
                              PAST

      pom-qe'ée'o-lo-y   'atáx-m-i

      they-kill-NOM-ACC   person-PL-ACC

      "The man blamed the bears for killing the people. "

do not have obvious counterparts in the other languages, which would probably use -və or -ve for the lower verb, as in

49. Cu   mi-pəm-cix-ni-n-və-ngax

      them-they-die-CAUS-DO-[+R]-from

      "because they had killed them"

or possibly a -nuk form

50. Ca   me-m-cex-ni-nuk

      them-they-die-CAUS-after

      "for having killed them"

A full discussion of Cupan complementation is beyond the scope of this investigation and would be at least as large again as this study. We shall briefly discuss here one important type of complementation which is found in all three languages and which is relevant to our discussion of tense and aspect. In complement sentences of this kind, the verb forms are marked either with a [+R] suffix, reconstructable as *-və for

Proto-Cupan (and henceforth referred to as "*-və suffix"), or with a
[-R] *-pi suffix (after the same convention as for *-və).

The sentences below indicate not only that these constructions almost
certainly existed in Proto-Cupan but also that the underlying structure for
Proto-Cupan must have been like those for the modern languages.

51. Ca   ne'   pe-n-'e'nan-qa   pic-'e-hici-ve-y

          I   it-I-know-DUR   COMP-you-go[+R]-ACC

          "I know that you went."

52. Ca   ne'   pe-n-'e'nan-qa   pic-'e-hici-pi-y

          I   it-I-know-DUR   COMP-you-go-[-R]-ACC

          "I know that you will go."

53. Cu   nə'-nə   hiwcu-qa   (pə-ci)   'ə-haʃax-və-y

          I-I   know-DUR   (it-about)   you-go-[+R]-ACC
                                   COMP

          "I know that you went."

54. Cu   nə'-nə   hiwcu-qa   (pə-ci)   'ə-haʃax-pi-y

          I-I   know-DUR   COMP   you-go-[-R]-ACC

          "I know that you will go."

55. Lu   noo-n   'ayáli-q   'o-hati'ax-vo-y

          I-I   know-DUR   you-go-[+R]-ACC

          "I know that you went."

56. Lu   noo-n   'ayáli-q   'o-hati'ax-pi-y

          I-I   know-DUR   you-go-[-R]-ACC

          "I know that you will go."

However, there are no such "present tense" complement structures
shared by all three languages. In Luiseño, verb forms with -qa-nik, -qal
or -qal-a suffixes are used, but these simply have a variable time reference partially or fully co-extensive with that of the next higher verb. In
Cupeño, forms with -qal-i or -qal-ə-t have the same function, while in

Cahuilla, -qal-ve and -qal-i-pa are the most common suffixes. The situation thus appears similar to that for relative constructions.

But the relative constructions seem to have changed far more than these complement sentences. These constructions have obviously changed little since Proto-Cupan. Consequently they appear to have preserved most completely the Proto-Cupan [+R] and [-R] contrast and to have resisted the more general trend towards a tense system.

We conclude then that there has been a general movement towards a tense system, most of all in Luiseño, to a lesser extent in Cupeño, even less still in Mountain Cahuilla, and hardly at all in the other Cahuilla dialects. We cannot explain why. Languages constantly shift in these ways for complex internal reasons that we do not understand and also for external reasons. For example, though this is impossible to prove, the degree of change in this regard appears to correspond to the length of time speakers of these languages have been in contact with Indo-European speaking peoples. The Luiseño were the first to come into long-standing contact with the Spanish, and the Desert Cahuillas were the last. But the development of a tense system from a more general aspectual system is not unusual in human language. This is not to suggest that normally there are verb aspect stages of languages and verb tense stages. The normal situation at any given time is mixed. But here in Cupan it appears that there probably was a stage at which Proto-Cupan had a purely aspectual system, one whose primary dimensions were the contrasts realized and unrealized, durative and non-durative. The absence of any more specialized time-reference system in Proto-Cupan relatives and complements supports such a hypothesis. In one of his discussions of Hopi, Whorf (1967:114) describes his expective and reportive categories of assertion in terms not inappropriate for Proto-Cupan:

> The expective declares an expectation or anticipation of a situation. It has nothing to do with time as such.... There is no distinction in the reportive between past and present, for both are equally accomplished fact. Thus to the Hopi "he is running" need not be different from "he was running"....

Although the resemblance of Hopi to Cupan is suggestive, we should be aware that in reality there is no such phenomenon as pure tense, that there is a gradation in degree and prominence of the time reference. The so-called English "present" tense provides just such an example, with varying time reference, sometimes no absolute time reference, in some contexts. The existence of such a gradation makes some instability almost inevitable, and therefore such shifts as we have described for Cupan are likely to occur in other languages, and indeed they do.

APPENDIX A

We translated into English a Rincon Luiseño text composed by Mrs. Villiana Hyde. Then we had it translated into Mountain Cahuilla. We used Cahuilla rather than English as the eliciting language for the Cupeño passage, since our Cupeño consultant understood Cahuilla.

I. Mountain Cahuilla

'aya   tamet   nanvanek   pic-cem-ci -ĩew-ap

already   day   come   that-we-gather-go-[-R]

"The time has arrived for us to gather

kwiniĩ-i.   Pi-cem'ayaw-we   meten   pic-pi-cem-ci'-pi

acorn-ACC   it-we-want-DUR   lot   that-it-we-gather-[-R]

acorns. We would like to gather a lot

'ivi-y   tawpaxic. Supul tawpaxic metewet cem-cica-we-' ,

this-ACC year   some year   many   we-gather-DUR-PAST

this year. Some years we gathered a lot,

supul   tawpaxic   sawa-qa-'a.

other   year   lack-DUR-PAST

other years there are none.

Yéwi   tawpaxic   penícic   qamíva'-pa'

once   year   past   anyplace-at

Once, in years long past, any place

pic-pi-cem-ci'i-pi   cemi-haqwuc-we-'e.

that-it-we-gather-[-R]   us-open-DUR-PAST

was open for us to gather them.

221

'iv'ax   kiĩe   'i-yax-wa.   'iv'ax   metec-em   melkic-em

now   not   like-be-DUR   now   lot-PL   white-PL

Now it's not like that. Now lots of white people

pa-hem-qal   hem-ki-nga   he'-mexan'a

there-they-live   their-house-in   their-property

live here in <u>their</u> houses, <u>their</u> property,

hem-tema-nga   'Umu   ta'   temi-we.   Pit

their-land-on   all   indeed   close-DUR   road

on <u>their</u> land. Every place is fenced off. By the

hayva-x   ax-cem-cica-ne   miva'-pa'

edge-from   FUT-we-gather-FUT   where-at

roadsides we shall gather them where

haqwuc-wen-e-pa'.   Cemem   hec-'a'amiv-am

open-DUR-<u>e</u>-at   we   we-old-PL

it is open land. Us old Indians

hec-taxliswet-em   cem-'ayaw'a   wiwic.   Tuháyemanic

we-Indian-PL   we-like   acorn-mush   always

we like wiwish. Always we have

pi-cem-kwa-wen-i-ve   miyax-we.   'iv'ax

it-we-eat-DUR-<u>i</u>-[+R]   be-DUR   now

eaten it. Now

kikit-am   supul-em   kiĩe   hem-'ayaw'a   wiwic.

young-PL   some-PL   not   they-like   acorn-mush

some young people don't like wiwish. "

II. Kupa Cupeño

'aya   tamit nanvə-ya-qa   cəm-ci'-ləw-pi

already   day   come-be-DUR   we-gather-go-[-R]

"The time has arrived for us to gather

kwiniĩ-i.   Cəm-cəm   'ayaw-we   mat'ic   cəm-ci'-pi

acorn-ACC   we-we   want-DUR   lot   we-gather-[-R]

acorns. We want to gather a lot

'ivi-y   tawpaxic.   Supul   tawpaxic   mat'ic

this-ACC   year   some   year   lot

this year. Some years we have gathered

cəm-ci'-və   supul   tawpaxic-əp   pə-kikic-wən

we-gather-[+R]   other   year-[+R]   it-lack-DUR-PAST

a lot, other years there were none.

'aci   tawpaxic   naxcin-ax-ic   tum   miví-ta

once   year   pass-YAX-[+R]   any   where-at

Once in past years any place where

pə-ta   cəm-ci'i-pi   miyax-wa   kapəl-pə-yax-wən-i-va.

it-at   we-gather-[-R]   be-DUR   open-it-YAX-DUR-i-[+R]-at

we might gather was open to us.

'amáy   qay   hic   'i-yax-wa.   'amáy

now   not   thing   like-be-DUR   now

Now it's now like that. Now

matic-im   məmy-əm   pəm-qal   pəm-kii-nga

lot-PL   white-PL   they-live   their-house-in

lots of white people live in their houses.

pə'-mixan   pəm-təmá-ki'i-nga.   Pətá'əma

their-property   their-land-POS-on   everything

their property, on their land. Everything

təm-yax-wa.   Pit   pə-hayva-ngax   cəm-pə

close-be-DUR   road   its-edge-from   we-[-R]

is fenced off. We will gather from the

ci'   ma   mivĭ-'aw   pət-'aw   kapəl-pə-yax-wen-i.

gather   and   where-at   place-at   open-it-be-DUR-SUB

roadsides and where it is open.

Cəm   atáx-am   'a'wəl-və-m   cəm-'ayəw'a

we   Indian-PL   grow-[+R]-PL   we-like

We older Indians, we like

wiwic.   Piyáamanga   cəm-qwə'-i-və   miyax-wa.

acorn-mush   always   we-eat-i-[+R]   be-DUR

wiwish. Always we have eaten it.

'amáy   kikit-am   supul-im   qay   pəm-'ayəw'a   wiwic.

now   young-PL   some-PL   not   they-like   acorn-mush

Now some young people don't like wiwish. "

III. Rincon Luiseño

Wam-up   neckin   miy-q   kwilya

already-it   near   be-PRES   acorn

"It's already almost time for us

cam'-ci'-i-pi   Caam   heew'-a-an   muyúk-i

we-gather-do-[-R]   we   hope-be-PRES   lot-ACC

to gather acorns. We hope to gather a lot

kwilya   cam'-ci'-i-pi   'ivi-y   tawpac.

acorn   we-gather-do-[-R]   this-ACC   year

of acorns this year.

'awóy-up   tawpac   yaw-ax-ma   kwilya   pi

other-it   years   lack-be-USIT   acorns   and

Some years there were no acorns and

'awóy   tawpac   muyuk   miyx-ma.   Yamáyk

other   year   ,   lot   be-USIT   Once

other years there were many.   Once

caam   michá'   minchapan   ci'-i-k.

we   where   no matter   gather-do-PAST

we gathered anywhere.

Pi'   pitóo   qay   'ona   'aa-q.   Pitóo

and   now   not   that   be like-PRES   now

But now it's not like that.   Now

muyuk-um   moomy-um   qal-wun   pum-kii-nga

lot-PL   white-PL   live-PRES   their-house-in

lots of white people live in their

pum-ex-nga   pi'   co'on   neki-q.   Pi'

their-land-on   and   all   fence-PL   and

houses on their land and everything is fenced

caam   ci'-i-n   pet   po-hay-lu-nga   man

we   gather-do-FUT   road   its-edge-go-at   or

off.   But we will gather by the roadsides or

micá'   po-het-qal-a.   Caam   'ataax-um

where   it-open-DUR-[+R]   we   Indian-PL

wherever it is open. We older Indians,

'a'wol'-um   cam-ma'ma-q   wiiwic

grow-PL   we-like-PRES   acorn-mush

we like wiwish.

Caam   naacaxan   yamáykum-ngay   puyáamangay.

we   eat   old times-from   always

We've always eaten it from way back.

'iví-m   'amáy-um   kekut-um   'awó-m   qay

this-PL   young-PL   kid-PL   some-PL   not

Some of these younger ones don't like

pum-ma'max

they-like

it."

APPENDIX B
Some Arguments for an Underlying <u>he</u>

No linguist should feel comfortable about postulating an underlying element that apparently never surfaces on verbs. Fuchs follows Seiler (1958:69) in positing instead zero as the third person singular subject marker on verbs. There are, however, some interesting though not conclusive arguments in favor of postulating an underlying <u>he</u>- rather than a zero. The pronoun prefixes for verbs and nouns are as follows:

	Pronoun Prefixes on Verbs		Pronoun Prefixes on Nouns	
	Sg	Pl	Sg	Pl
1st	ne-	cem-	ne-	cem-
2nd	'e-	'em-	'e-	'em-
3rd	Ø	hem-	he-	hem-

The table above visually suggests the possibility of a <u>he</u>- prefix for verbs. But to establish this as a reasonable hypothesis there must be evidence for a rule deleting <u>he</u>- in environments where <u>ne</u>- and the other prefixes are not deleted.

Such evidence is available. There appears to be a rule deleting unstressed he-, but not the other unstressed pronoun prefixes. Thus, while "my bow" is ne-húyay (with the accusative form of húyal "bow"), "hiw bow" is just húyay. In certain so-called stressless roots (see Hill and Hill, 1968) which are monosyllabic with short vowels, stress is shifted to the prefix. Thus "my grandmother" is né-qa. The corresponding form for "his grandmother" is hé-qa. With perhaps one exception, Desert Cahuilla verbs are not stressless, and therefore their prefixes cannot receive the primary stress. If our hypothesis is correct, and if stress were ever shifted onto pronoun prefixes, hé- would surface as the third person singular form. Some confirmation of this is provided for another dialect by Seiler (1967), though he appears unaware of its significance.

In Wanikik Cahuilla, he claims primary stress is becoming word-initial.
Thus "I went out" is né-pisqa. And "he went out" is hé-pisqa, not
*písqa. My own Wanikik consultant preferred písqal, since in his speech
this stress shift is more restricted, but with a monosyllabic verb like qa
"lie," he gave hé-qa "he lies (on the ground)." I have found a single
counter-example. In Mountain and Desert Cahuilla, the very idiosyncratic stressless verb yax "say, do" has the first person form né-yax,
but the third person form is yax rather than *he-yax (or rather *hi-yax
after a regular phonetic change). Seiler has suggested (personal communication) that such a *hi-yax does not occur because there is already
a homophonous interrogative form where the hi- is an interrogative
prefix.

APPENDIX C

VERB FORMS IN CUPAN: CAHUILLA (MOUNTAIN DIALECT)

The Positions of Constituents of a Verb Form

I	II	III	IV	V	VI	VII	VIII
Mainly TIME and PLACE prefixes	OBJECT PREFIXES	SUBJECT PREFIXES	TIME/ PLACE ANAPHOR	VERB ROOT	DERIVATIONAL AFFIXES	ASPECT	TENSE SUFFIXES
'ax- FUTURE	SG	SG.	pe		(may co-occur with each other with mainly semantic conditions on order)	-nac FUTURE DURATIVE SG.	PRES. -qa SG.
pa- "there, where"	1. ne-	1. ne-				-wen FUTURE DURATIVE PL.	-we PL.
pax- "thence, whence"	2. 'e-	2. 'e-			-ici "V while going"	-nax INCEPT. DURATIVE SG.	PAST DURATIVE -qa'(a) SG.
piyk- "thither, whither"	3. pe-	3. Ø-			-lew, "go there -law to V"	-naxtem INCEPT. DUR. PL. (if these are used with the VIII inceptives, only the -nax form is used for the plural)	-we'(e) PL.
pic- "with it, about it"	PL.	PL.			-max BENEFACTIVE -ni CAUSATIVE		PAST PUNCTUAL -'i AFFIRMATIVE
	1. ceme-	1. cem-			-ngi "go away/ around V-ing"		-Ø NEGATIVE
	2. 'eme-	2. 'em-			-puli "come here to/and V"		
	3. me-	3. hem-			-vaneke "come V-ing" -vicu "want to V"		FUTURE
		FORMS FOR INTRANSITIVE INCEPTIVES SG.					-ne
		1. hen-					INCEPTIVE "be going to"
		2. 'et-					-ka' SG.
		3. Ø PL					-katem PL.
		1. hec-					
		2. 'em-					
		3. Ø					

VERB FORMS IN CUPAN: CUPEÑO (KUPA DIALECT)

The Positions of Constituents of a Verb Form

I	II	III	IV	V	VI	VII	VIII
OBJECT PREFIXES	SUBJECT PREFIXES	VERB ROOT	SUBJECT AFFIXES	PLURAL AFFIX	THEME	DERIVATIONAL AFFIXES	TENSE/ASPECT
SG.	These occur only on past tense forms of SIMPLE verbs (see Column VI).		Only on past tense IN or YAX theme verb forms.	Only on past tense forms of IN verbs.	a) IN /-in/ typically on transitive volitional action predicates	(more than one may occur in varying order)	PRESENT
1. ni-			SG.			-ləw- "go there to V"	SG. -qa
2. 'i-	SG.		1. -nə-	-mə-	b) YAX /-ax-/, /-yax-/ typically, intransitive and/or stative	-max- BENE-FACTIVE	PL. -wə
3. pi-	1. nə-		2. -'ə-			-mi'aw "arrive"	PAST PUNCT.
PL.	2. 'ə-		3. -pə-		c) SIMPLE predicates expressing most common notions: "see," "eat," "jump"—no thematic affix. Often have irregular paradigms, shifting stress, etc.	-nəq- "come V-ing"	Ø
1. cimi-	3. pə-		PL.			-vənəq- "come V-ing"	PAST DUR.
2. 'imi-	PL.		1. -cəm- -cə'-			-nin- CAUSA-TIVE	-qal SG.
3. mi-	1. cəm-		2. -'em- -'ə'-			-ngi- "go away/back V-ing"	-wen PL.
	2. 'əm-		3. -pəm- -pə'-			-vicu- "want to V"	FUT. PUNCT.
	3. pəm-						Ø
							FUT. DUR.
							-naʎ SG. -wənə PL.
							INCEPT.
							-qat SG. -qatim PL.

VERB FORMS IN CUPAN: LUISEÑO (RINCON DIALECT)

The Positions of Constituents of a Verb Form

I	II	III	IV
VERB ROOT	THEME	DERIVATIONAL AFFIXES	INFLECTIONAL AFFIXES
	a) -i- typically transitive	-low-, -luw-, -la- "go there and/to V" -monaa-, -ma- "come V-ing"	PRESENT SG. -q(a) PL. -wun
	b) -ax- typically intrasitive	-ni- CAUSATIVE -vicu- "want to V"	RECENT PAST DURATIVE -qat (-qut) SG. -qatum (qutum) PL. -muk (-mok) SG. and PL.
	c) SIMPLE no thematic affix	-vota-, -lota- "can V"	USITATIVE -ma(x)
	d) DERIVED position filled by no longer productive derivational affixes and rare causatives such as -xam-	-ngi-, -nge- "go away/around/ back V-ing"	PAST DURATIVE -quš
			PAST PUNCTUAL -ax, -ya, -yax, -x
			FUTURE SIMPLE -an, -n
			FUTURE DURATIVE -maan
			INCEPTIVE SG. -lowut, -lut PL. -kutum, -ktum

VERB FORMS IN CUPAN RELATIVE CONSTRUCTIONS

Basic to Cupan relative constructions is the contrast between clauses with subjects coreferential with the clause head (which is itself in a higher clause, of course) and those whose subjects are not. The analysis upon which the following table is based is, like those for the preceding tables, a very superficial one, one which is modified in the last five chapters of this study.

COREFERENTIAL LOWER SUBJECT	NON-COREFERENTIAL LOWER SUBJECT
PAST CA. verb stem - ic* CU. verb stem - ic* LU. verb stem - mokwic	**PAST** CA. subject marker - verb stem - ve CA. subject marker - verb stem - v LA. subject marker - verb stem - vo

FUTURE
 	
CA. v. stem - nax (-ka') SG.
   v. stem - { naxt - em   PL.
          { nax-kat-em
CU. v. stem - qat
LU. v. stem - { lut   SG.
         { kutum   PL.
	FUTURE
	
	CA. }
	CU. } subj. marker - verb stem - pi
	LU. }

PRESENT
 	
CA. v. stem - { qalet   SG.
         { wentem   PL.
CU. v. stem - { qalǝt   SG.
         { wǝntim   PL.
LU. v. stem - qat
	PRESENT
	
	CA. subj. marker - v. stem - { qalive SG.
	                     { wenive PL.
	CU. subj. marker - v. stem { qalivǝ SG.
	                   { wǝnivǝ PL.
	LU. subj. marker - v. stem - qat

1. All verb stems may include durative morphemes except for those asterisked, present forms, and possibly the Luiseño -lut, -kutum forms.

2. Forms for plural number are only given where they may not be easily predicted from the singular forms. Chapters II and VIII provide a fuller and more accurate account of these.

3. The use of subject markers here is related to an important property of Cupan nouns. Cupan nouns are either possessed or non-possessed. Possessed forms have a possessive prefix which is the same as the sub-markers above. Non-possessed forms have -c, -l, or -t absolutive endings (sometimes syllabified with a final a in Luiseño) and lack prefixes.

REFERENCES

Bright, W.

    1965.   "Luiseño Phonemics," IJAL 31:342-345.

    1968.   A Luiseño Dictionary. Publications in Linguistics 51.
              Berkeley and Los Angeles, University of California Press.

Bright, W., and J. Hill

    1967.   "The Linguistic History of the Cupeño." In Hymes, D., and
              W. Bittle (eds.), Studies in Southwestern Ethnolinguistics,
              pp. 351-371.

Brugmann, K., and B. Delbruck

    1893-   Grundriss der vergleichenden Grammatik der indogerman-
    1900   ischen Sprachen. Strasburg. Vols, 3, 4, and 5.

Chomsky, N.

    1965.   Aspects of the Theory of Syntax. Cambridge, Mass.,
              M. I. T. Press.

Crapo, R.

    1970.   "The Origins of the Directional Adverbs in Uto-Aztecan
              Languages," IJAL 36:181-190.

Faye, P.

    1920.   Field notes (unpublished). Lowie Museum Archive. Berkeley,
              California.

Fuchs, A.

    1970.   Morphologie des Verbs im Cahuilla. The Hague, Mouton.

Greenberg, J.

    1963.   "Some Universals of Grammar with Particular Reference to
              the Order of Meaningful Elements." In Greenberg, ed.
              Universals of Language. Cambridge, Mass., M. I. T. Press.

Hill, J.

    1966.   "A Grammar of the Cupeño Language." Unpublished doctoral
              dissertation. University of California, Los Angeles.

    1969.   "Volitional and Non-Volitional Verbs in Cupeño." In Papers
              from the Fifth Regional Meeting of the Chicago Linguistic
              Society, pp. 165-172. Chicago, Chicago Linguistic Society.

    1972.   "Cupeño Lexicalization and Language History,"
              IJAL 38:161-172.

Hill, J., and K. Hill
    1968.   "Stress in the Cupan (Uto-Aztecan) Languages,"
              IJAL 34:233-241.

Hill, K.
    1967.   "A Grammar of the Serrano Language." Unpublished doctoral
              dissertation. University of California, Los Angeles.

Hioki, K.
    1970.   "Zur Beschreibung des Systems der Klitika im Cahuilla."
              Unpublished master's dissertation. University of Cologne.
    1972.   "Die Klitika im Cahuilla." Unpublished doctoral dissertation.
              University of Cologne.

Hockett, C.
    1958.   A Course in Modern Linguistics. New York, Macmillan.

Hudson, G.
    1972.   "Is Deep Structure Linear?" In Bedell, G. (ed.), Explorations
              in Syntactic Theory. University of California, Los Angeles
              Papers in Syntax 2:51-77.

Hyde, V.
    1971.   An Introduction to the Luiseño Language. Banning, Ca. Malki
              Museum Press.

Hymes, D., and W. Bittle (eds.)
    1967.   Studies in Southwestern Ethnolinguistics. The Hague, Mouton.

Jackendoff, R.
    1969.   "Some Rules of Semantic Interpretation for English."
              Unpublished doctoral dissertation. M. I. T.

Jacobs, R. A.
    1971.   "An Introduction to the Cupeño Language." Unpublished
              manuscript. Pala Indian Culture Center.
    1973.   Studies in Language. Lexington, Mass., Xerox College
              Publishing.
    1973.   Review of Fuchs 1970. Lingua.
    Forth-   "Syntactic Reconstruction and the Compartive Method: a Uto-
    coming. Aztecan Case Study." In Studies in Honor of A. A. Hill. The
              Hague, Mouton.
    Forth-   "On Some Directions of Syntactic Change in Anglo-Saxon."
    coming. Journal of English Linguistics.

Jacobs, R. A., and P. Rosenbaum
    1968.   English Transformational Grammar. Lexington, Mass.,
              Xerox College Publishing.

Jacobsen, W.

    1967.   "Switch-Reference in Hokan-Coahuiltecan." In Hymes, D.,
              and W. Bittle (eds.), Studies in Southwestern Ethnolinguistics.

Jespersen, O.

    1969.   Analytic Syntax. New York, Holt.

    1909-   A Modern English Grammar on Historical Principles.
    1949.   Parts 1-7. London, Allen and Unwin.

King, R. D.

    1969.   Historical Linguistics and Generative Grammar. Englewood
              Cliffs, N. J., Prentice-Hall.

Klima, E.

    1965.   "Studies in Diachronic Transformational Syntax." Unpublished
              doctoral dissertation. Harvard University.

Kroeber, A. L.

    1907.   Shoshonean Dialects of California. University of California
              Publications in American Archeology and Ethnology 4:65-165.

    1909.   Notes on Shoshonean Dialects of Southern California.
              University of California Publications in American Archeology
              and Ethnology 8:235-269.

Kroeber, A., and G. Grace

    1960.   The Sparkman Grammar of Luiseño. Publications in
              Linguistics 16. Berkeley and Los Angeles, University of
              California Press.

Lakoff, R.

    1968.   Abstract Syntax and Latin Complementation. Cambridge,
              Mass., M.I.T. Press.

Lamb, S.

    1953.   "A Grammar of Mono." Doctoral dissertation. University
              of California, Berkeley.

Langacker, R.

    1969.   "The Uto-Aztecan Vowel System." Linguistic Notes from
              La Jolla I. University of California, San Diego.

    Forth-   "Predicate Raising: Some Uto-Aztecan Evidence." In
    coming. Kachru, B. et alia, Papers in Linguistics in Honor of Henry
              and Renee Kahane. Urbana, University of Illinois Press.

Lehmann, W.

    1972.   "Converging Theories in Linguistics," Language 48(2):266-275.

Malécot, A.

    1961.   "The Sparkman Grammar of Luiseño (Kroeber-Grace),"
              IJAL 27:64-71.

1963.   "Luiseño: A Structural Analysis II: Morpho-Syntax,"
         IJAL 29:196-210.

1964.   "Luiseño: A Structural Analysis III: Texts and Lexicon,"
         IJAL 30:14-31.

1964.   "Luiseño: A Structural Analysis IV: Appendices,"
         IJAL 30:243-250.

McCawley, J.

1970.   "English as a VSO Language," Language 46 (2):286-299.

1971.   "Prelexical Syntax." In O'Brien, R. (ed.), Report of the
         Twenty-Second Annual Round Table. Washington, Georgetown
         University Press, pp. 19-23.

Miller, W.

1967.   Uto-Aztecan Cognate Sets. Publications in Linguistics 48.
         Berkeley and Los Angeles, University of California Press.

Pardal, E.

1971.   "Phonologie du Portugais." Unpublished dissertation.
         University of Paris.

Peters, S., and R. Ritchie

Forth-   "On Restricting the Base Component of Transformational
coming. Grammars." Information and Control.

Seiler, H.

1958.   "Zur Aufstellung der Wortklassen des Cahuilla (Uto-Aztekisch,
         Sūd-Kalifornien)," Munchener Studien zur Sprachwissenschraft
         12:61-79.

1965.   "Accent and Morphophonemics in Cahuilla and in Uto-
         Aztecan," IJAL 31:50-59.

1967.   "Structure and Reconstruction in Some Uto-Aztecan
         Languages," IJAL 33:135-147.

1970.   Cahuilla Texts. Bloomington, Indiana University Press.

Sparkman, P.

1905.   "Sketch of the Grammar of the Luiseño Language of
         California," American Anthropologist 7:656-662.

Steele, S.

1972.   "Futurity, Intention and Possibility." Unpublished manuscript.
         University of California, San Diego.

Strong, W.

1972.   Aboriginal Society in Southern California. Banning, Ca.
         Malki Museum Press.

Tac, P. (ed. C. Tagliavini)

1926.   La Lingua delli indi Luiseños. Biblioteca de l'archiginnasio.
        Bologna (pr. Nicola Zanichelli), ser. II, no. xxxi, pp. 1-55.

Unbegaum, B.

1957.   Russian Grammar. Oxford, Clarendon Press.

Voegelin, C., F. Voegelin, and K. Hale

1962.   Typological and Comparative Grammar of Uto-Aztecan:
        I (Phonology). Supplement to IJAL 28.

Whorf, B.

1946.   "The Hopi Language, Toreva Dialect." In H. Hoijer et al.
        (eds.), Linguistic Structures of Native America. New York:
        Viking Fund Publications in Anthropology, 6.158-163.

1967.   Language, Thought, and Reality. Edited by J. Carroll.
        Cambridge, Mass., M.I.T. Press.

Winter, W.

Forth- "Switch Reference in Yuman Languages." In Langdon, M.,
coming. and S. Silver (eds.), Hokan Studies. The Hague, Mouton.